*education
and
modernization
in
asia*

To Lance and Amy

editorial foreword

Most recent writings about old and new nations have been conspicuously marked by an emphasis on change, development, and modernization. This has been especially the case with studies which approach social, political, economic, and cultural systems from a comparative, cross-cultural, or—more broadly—from an international point of view. And both modernization and comparison have been emphasized particularly in works dealing with the so-called new or developing nations that have started down the road to modernity after the Second World War.

Education has always been implied and indeed included in studies of political, social, economic, or cultural systems. And, as with the other aforementioned enterprises, comparative or cross-cultural studies of education have increasingly been using the terms development and modernization, particularly when such studies have focused on new, emerging, or developing nations.

In all these endeavors, scholars have been grappling, among other things, with problems of definition, especially with respect to the concepts "development" and "modernization." The latter concept has proved to be the more intractable and elusive. When used in conjunction with the equally befuddling term "education," modernization has been treated in different ways and has been given different meanings. "Education is the key that unlocks the door to modernization." This statement, made by Frederick Harbison and Charles A. Myers in 1964, has been widely accepted by students and other workers, e.g., policy planners, concerned with comparative and international education. It has, in the main, referred to the part played by education in economic growth and development. This instrumental role of education, approached from the vantage points of economics, sociology, and political science, has been widely discussed and has had many adherents among comparative educators. Such titles of recent books as *Education and Political Development, Post-Primary Education and Political and Economic Development, Education and the Quest for Modernity in Turkey, Education and Social Change in Ghana,* and *Education and the Development of Nations* may be cited as examples.

From this orientation, education has been examined as it bears upon the processes of economic, political, and social (in the sociological meaning of the term) development and modernization. At the same time, the educational implications for broader socioeconomic and political developments have been the subject of study by comparative educators.

Despite the various interpretations and meanings given to it, as well as the controversies still surrounding it, social analysts have found "modernization" to be a useful concept for examining social transformations in general. And in the main, comparative educators have recently attempted to reorient their approach in terms of this concept.

Previous works in comparative education were for the most part characterized by historical and/or descriptive accounts of the development and present status of educational systems. To a large extent this observation holds true for many contemporary works in the field. The reaction against this approach has taken several forms. Some writers have argued for a "science" of comparative education that would be truly explanatory and predictive; others have viewed comparative education as helping to provide guidelines for action and improvement; and still others have seen comparative education as an applied field. Hence, descriptive titles such as "Development Education," "A Science of Education and Planning," and "Toward a Science of Comparative Education" have appeared. Here the concern has been with scientific method as used in the empirical social sciences, with planning, and with a look toward the future. To some, the past is useful only if it is seen "pragmatically," i.e., only as helping to clarify present problems in order to plan and "reform" education. To others, past experiences are useful to the extent that they help in the formulation of generalizations about the relationship between education and society. Most of these writers have for all meaningful purposes rejected the "historical approach" as it has been traditionally understood, and have rallied behind the banner of the "social scientific approach."

A basic assumption underlying the present series is that history and social science can be fruitfully combined in the comparative study of educational change. This is implied by choosing to examine education within the framework of "modernization," which, in essence, denotes a historical process of long-range social and cultural change, felt also to be both beneficial and desirable.

There are several monographs, articles, and other writings in comparative and international education dealing, in one form or another, with education, modernization, and its frequent closest synonym, "development." But aside from the previously mentioned interpretations, the material available remains isolated and scattered. It has not as yet been systematized or interpreted; the isolated efforts made have not reached forms that are publicly accessible; and such enterprises have not been adequately reflected in comparative education texts or in the curriculum of colleges and universities. It is believed that the present series will contribute to filling this void in comparative and international education.

Clearly, even opting for a series rather than a single volume, the undertaking is immense. Not all countries of the world are included, nor indeed all aspects of education. In each volume countries were selected from major regions of the world (e.g., Europe, Asia, the South-Eastern Mediterranean and the Near East, Africa, the Americas, and Eastern Europe). In dealing with education and modernization, the intent has been to focus more on interpretative analyses and general principles and less on detailed accounts of educational systems, which are often found in standard texts and other sources.

The writer of each volume is a recognized expert on the regions and countries about which he has written and on the dynamics of educational change. The organization and emphasis of each volume have been left to the judgment of the individual author.

Herbert Spencer once said that "education is the never-sleeping agent of revolution." We hope that the series as a whole will inform students, scholars, and other interested persons about the multiple dimensions and ramifications of education as a social phenomenon, and whether indeed it has the power assumed by Spencer and other more recent social observers.

Andreas M. Kazamias, General Editor

preface

It has been said that the people of the world may be divided into two types, the hedgehogs and the foxes. The former, for satisfaction, must acquire a full measure of what they seek, while the latter are satisfied with partial fulfillment. The hedgehogs in comparative education worry over the purity of the word comparison and seek one grand method for cross-cultural studies. Being psychologically oriented toward the foxes, I tend to argue that considerable progress can be made in comparative studies in education by simply utilizing some of the concepts and procedures readily available in the social and behavioral sciences.

In writing this brief book I have browsed about a number of academic crevices in search of concepts and ideas which might give organization and, therefore, meaning to an analysis of education as part of the modernization process. A grossly simplified social systems model is employed in order to examine selected linkages between education and society. The concept of *societal differentiation* is exploited to assist in describing levels of modernization in the three national case studies. The derived notion of *educational differentiation* is introduced to aid in the analysis of educational systems undergoing structural or functional change. And in studying educational change, I found it convenient to borrow sparingly from the somewhat time-worn "functional imperatives" popularized by Talcott Parsons.

There is, of course, the danger of being seduced by the rhetoric of other disciplines. Perhaps it is true that those who can, do; and those who can't, worry about method. On any hand, the cursory reliance on a systems perspective does not necessitate buying all of the extravagant claims for systems analysis made by its more euphoric proponents. Nor does the assumption that the term differentiation incorporates many of the structural attributes of modernization mean that I have any illusions about the ability of this concept to fully explain social and educational change.

The constraints of space, personal shortcomings, the inadequacy and unavailability of appropriate data, and the limitations of the concepts themselves prevent a more detailed analysis and more explicit comparisons. In addition, because of the breadth of the subject, I have been forced to make frequent judgments in the selection of topics and data to be included.

I wish to thank the several graduate students at Syracuse University whose suggestions, critical comments, and snide remarks contributed to the preparation of this book. The careful library research of Patricia Snyder was particularly helpful in documenting certain aspects of social change in India and China. As with most of my efforts, the gentle but extensive influence of my wife Janet is to be found in both editorial and substantive matters. Appreciation is also extended to Andy Latchem, who with cheerful disregard for normal work loads and great forbearance with American spellings typed the manuscript with loving care. Finally, note should be taken of the crucial roles of the grandparents Cabe and of the Carringtons in making that summer in Westville, Oklahoma, remarkably productive and enjoyable.

Pittsburgh, Pennsylvania   *D. A.*
December 1969

contents

chapter one
introduction

To study a process as all-encompassing as modernization in a geocultural setting as vast as Asia requires certain arbitrary decisions as to methodological focus and substantive coverage. As for methodology, the concept of social differentiation and the perspectives of systems analysis will help in ordering data and forming a basis for analysis. With regard to scope, no attempt will be made to try to capture the full range of educational and societal variations found in this major world region. Rather, case studies of education and modernization in three major Asian nations will be undertaken. However, the final chapter, drawing both from the case studies and from data acquired through regional educational planning efforts, will offer opportunities for intraregional educational comparisons and contrasts.

In this chapter, as a preliminary to later substantive analyses, attention will be given to conceptual and methodological matters. First, the concept of modernization will be considered briefly for the purpose of developing a definitional and theoretical basis for examining specific societies. Second, the concept of differentiation, as applied to societies and to subsystems, will be explored in order to provide a framework and a perspective for understanding the educational changes taking place in Asia. Third, the term "systems analysis" will be briefly defined, and a description will be offered of the manner in which this concept provides a framework for intranational studies of education and therefore a model for cross-national comparisons.

MODERNIZATION

Modernization has been given a variety of definitions by the scholars who have used the term. As Weiner points out,

Economists see modernization primarily in terms of man's application of technologies to the control of nature's resources in order to bring about a marked increase in the growth of output per head of population. Sociologists and social anthropologists have been primarily concerned with the process of differentiation that characterizes modern societies... political scientists have focussed particularly on the problems of nation and government building as modernization occurs.[1]

Other scholars suggest that, fundamentally, modernization must be viewed in psychological or individual terms. Thus Lerner[2] argues that persons move from traditional to modern styles of life as they increase their empathic capability or, in other words, their ability to psychologically project themselves across social and occupational class lines. McClelland,[3] on the other hand, argues that the level of "achievement motivation" is the key to the level of modernization of individuals or groups. Hagen,[4] although a practicing economist, nevertheless speaks of the innovational personality and concludes that personality change is typically the first step in the modernization sequence involving urbanization, increased media participation, increased literacy, and further change in personality. In other words, urbanization and other outward signs of modernization are merely steps in the process of change, not its point of departure. Black, a historian, views modernization as a general term referring to "the process by which historically evolved institutions are adapted to the rapidly changing functions that reflect the unprecedented increase in man's knowledge, permitting control over his environment that accompanied the scientific revolution."[5]

There is still no widely accepted theory of modernization. There are theories of social change and theories of economic growth, but no adequate models exist to explain why and how individuals, institutions, and cultures prosper or decline. The confusion over the meaning of modernization is illustrated by the various uses of the term itself. Throughout the literature one can find "modernization" used with easy abandon as a synonym for such processes as industrialization, economic development, or even urbanization.

Here the term modernization will be defined as a type of social change directed by a rational belief system, whereby new social roles and new interrelationships among roles emerge. Not only are the emerging social roles and tasks increasingly specialized and complex, but recruitment to roles and evaluation of role performance are increasingly rational or achievement oriented. To contrast the ideal tradition and the ideal modern society the following dichotomies are sometimes employed: particularism-universalism; ascription-achievement; specificity-diffuseness; affective neutrality-affectivity; self-orientation-collectivity orientation.[6]

Though, technically, ideal types should not be viewed as the terminals of a continuum, the concepts mentioned do offer a perspective for examining change in social systems and even in personalities. The particularism-universalism dichotomy refers to the extent to which people are expected to act in accordance with general norms or standards rather than on the basis of particular cases. Ascription-achievement refers to the extent to which people are judged on the basis of their performance rather than in terms of characteristics of lineage, sex, etc. Specificity-diffuseness refers to the extent to which the basis for the way people act is lodged in narrowly defined categories, i.e., specialization of roles. Affectivity-affective neutrality refers to the degree to which people act to achieve immediate gratification. Collectivity orientation-self-orientation refers to the degree to which people are committed to collective or private goals. In general terms, then, modern society is oriented toward increased rationality, thus strengthening the norms of universalism, achievement, specificity, affective neutrality, and collectivity. However, even in the highly developed society particularism may still be found; witness the influence of sex and ethnic background on occupational and educational selection and promotion in the United States.[7]

There is another characteristic of the process of modernization, particularly as it appears on the contemporary scene. Although through much of history change could perhaps be described as having taken place through chance discoveries, in the contemporary world change has increasingly been the result of conscious attempts to alter techniques, norms, and institutional products. That is, change is now more closely linked to rational intention through (1) introducing appropriate innovations at crucial points and (2) anticipating the consequences of these innovations. Essentially, the conscious effort to bring about desired change may be called planning. In most Asian societies there is a high commitment to planning, as a means for attaining both sectoral (e.g., educational) and national goals.

DIFFERENTIATION[8]

The concept of differentiation relies on the basic assumption that all human societies are continuously changing, to some degree, because they must deal with basic problems for which there are no set solutions uniformly effective through time. Furthermore, it is assumed that the specific processes of change in a society are directly related to the society's institutional structure and to the means by which its institutions handle (or fail to handle) the problems resulting from change.

The basis of the principle of differentiation as defined by MacIver and Page is the correlation of the time order with the appearance of more differentiated elements. It is the thesis of MacIver and Page that differentiation of structure cannot be separated from differentiation of function. The differentiation process manifests itself as:

a) a greater division of labor, so that the energy of more individuals is concentrated on more specific tasks and so that thereby a more elaborate system of co-operation, a more intricate nexus of functional relationships is sustained within the group;
b) an increase in the number and the variety of functional associations and institutions so that each is more defined or more limited in the range of character of its service . . . ;
c) a greater diversity and refinement in the instruments of social communication, perhaps above all in the medium of language.[9]

Although it is possible to find semantic differences and real disagreement as to the meanings and limits of the concept, it is generally accepted that differentiation is a key term which, at minimum, incorporates many of the structural and functional attributes of modernization. In relatively undifferentiated societies the family or kinship group performs most of the crucial social tasks such as finding and distributing food and other goods, making decisions about crime and punishment, and educating the young. In modern industrialized societies, separate organizations and entities make and distribute goods, educate, govern, and perform other specialized functions. The process of modernization of societies is characterized, then, by the separation from the family of the economic, political, and educational institutions and the creation of a distinct place for them in the social order.

In the process of modernization drastic changes may be expected in the various sectors and subsystems of society. For example, technology will change toward the increased application of scientific knowledge; agriculture will move from subsistence farming to cash crops and commercial production; industry will exhibit a trend away from muscle power toward the use of machines which derive power from other forms of energy; religion will demonstrate an increasing secularization of belief patterns; ecological arrangements will reflect a movement toward urban concentration; familial patterns will show a reduction in size and number of functions; education will expand in terms of quantity available and variety of curricula offered.[10]

Differentiation in the form of new social structures may result from any number of antecedent changes: alterations in population structures, new moral, social, or technological inventions or innovations, changes in geographical conditions, etc. The emergence in the most advanced nations of specialized legal, economic, business, governmental, and educational institutions can be related, at least historically, to some of these changes, which may be either internal or external to the social systems in question. It is not, of course, being suggested that such differentiation always takes place in harmony or is, in every society, a matter of simple evolution. Interinstitutional and intersystem stresses and strains are all too apparent and have been well documented in both scholarly research and psychologically oriented fiction. Indeed, the increased autonomy of institutions resulting from differentiation creates "complex problems of integrating the specialized activities into one systematic framework."[11] Without the successful institutionalization of the integrative process a regression to an institutionally less differentiated society may occur.

Nor, of course, is such strain absent in advanced societies. In this regard it has been said of the American society:

In the past, heavy emphasis in American policy has been upon the goal-attainment sector, with secondary effort toward maintaining and strengthening generalized adaptive *capacities. Conspicuously neglected have been the other two main functional aspects of a social system – the integration of* components *and* pattern-maintenance. *In our national drive to "get things done" we have generated vast internal social cleavages and frictions – dislocations and disintegrations that represent enormous societal "overhead costs" of a peculiarly serious kind.*[12]

Yet, as a number of authors have pointed out, the concept of differentiation may be insufficient to characterize the conditions necessary for sustained growth. Clearly, modern economies require markets, capital, and demand for the outputs of production. These in turn would seem to require a degree of urbanization. Likewise, modern political systems apparently cannot persist without administrative centralization and specialization. However, as Eisenstadt has pointed out, the picture is more complex:

In many cases – such as several central and eastern European, Latin American and Asian countries – a negative correlation has developed at certain levels between a high degree of development of various socio-demographic indices, such as degree of literacy and the spread of mass media, of formal education or of urbanization and the institutional ability to sustain growth.[13]

Eisenstadt's basic point is that the indices of structural differentiation are more likely to describe the extent to which traditional societies or communities have been weakened than to suggest the extent to which a modern, viable society has developed or exactly what "kind" of society will develop:

The types of structural differentiation that have taken place as a result of processes of modernization certainly were not always of the type predominant in the West during its own initial stages of modernization; that is, they did not always take the form of a continuous growth of different collectivities with specialized functions in the economic, political and cultural fields, of expansion of universalistic and achievement criteria in all these institutional spheres, and concomitant receding of particularistic relations in all spheres of life. [14]

Eisenstadt goes on to argue that other variables, for example, "the modernizing orientations of different elites, the relations between these innovating groups and the broader strata and institutional settings within which they operate, the temporal sequence of modernization," [15] must be taken into consideration.

EDUCATIONAL DIFFERENTIATION

Much of the literature on education and modernization would seem to assume implicitly that education has a homogeneity which allows easy generalization and analysis. Quite to the contrary, education as an institution, process, or system has a number of features which inhibit analysis.

1. Formal education has evolved as a gradual consequence of economic, political-military, and religious needs. Thus, historically, education has been an institution operated for very limited and inherently conservative ends. By contrast, modern educational systems frequently constitute attempts to promote vast social and cultural changes beyond the purely educational innovations themselves.

2. Education is a composite of skill, techniques, and value systems, many of which have long-range rather than immediate consequences. Moreover, the likelihood of the school-learned activities being repeated in the environment depends on a number of factors, including the opportunity to engage in the new activities and the rewards for doing so.

3. Education develops a "culture" of its own which may interfere with the official educational and other objectives. This culture is the result of an emphasis on transmission of skills, community service, personality development, scholarship, the scholarly disciplines as ends in themselves, research, etc.

4. Education is marked by a complexity of levels and programs which obstruct analysis.

5. A long lag is assumed between the initiation and completion of any of the conventional stages of education.

6. Formal education systems (though not necessarily their subsystems) are multifunctional; education plays some part in a number of aspects of socialization, occupational preparation, development of self-conception, and so on.

As social differentiation proceeds, the educational system evolves with its own functional place in the society. Formal education, along with the economic and political systems in contemporary literate societies, is fully differentiated from the family. Social differentiation, by creating an ever-increasing and ever-changing number and kind of institutional needs, places new demands on the educational system. As newly formed institutions and subsystems seek to attain new goals, they develop new manpower needs. The activities of the educational system in turn become increasingly diversified and differentiated.

Development and modernization mean, then, a growing specialization of roles and organizations within the educational system. There is a growing differentiation between levels of education, creating new problems of articulation and coordination. At the same time, because of the competition between subsystems for resources and because of the increasing tendency toward planning, there is a growing unification of the system. That is, articulation and integration of the educational system and other social systems, "system strains" and to maintain internal culture. Further, some acceptable level of consistency must be developed between the educational system and other social systems, for example, the family, the polity, the economy.

The most clear and dramatic way to illustrate differentiation of the educational system is to compare primitive or traditional societies with modern societies. In a traditional society the family or kinship group typically has, along with its other functions, the prime responsibility for education. The foremost educational goal in traditional societies is the fostering of commitment of diffuse adult obligations. Structurally, then, the educational system is undifferentiated from the family; and functionally, it prepares for diffuse roles. The value orientations which structure relations within the educational system are particularistic, ascriptive, diffuse, and affective. Participation in the educational process is governed by such ascriptive criteria as sex, age, size, and lineage. Since the outcomes of education are of concern primarily to the kinship group, it may be said that the process is circumscribed by particularistic norms.

A contrast may be made with the ideal modern society. Here the educational system is recognized as an autonomous system with a large variety of subsystems. Its functions are numerous, in keeping with the specialized demands of modern society. The educational system, at the most basic level, is a source of the human productivity and creativity necessary for modernization to continue, and in addition assists in the preparation of individuals for highly specific occupational tasks. The value orientations which structure relations within the system tend to be universalistic, achievement-based, specific, and neutral. The outcomes of the system are universalistic, for they transcend the norms of particular social groups. The system seeks to promote commitments and obligations, the fulfilment of which need not be immediate. Finally, achievement criteria serve as a guide to reward and promotion within the system.

To elaborate on the simple dichotomy between traditional and modern, it is possible in a crude way to hypothesize levels of educational differentiation.[16]

1. Education at a preliterate level of society takes the form of socialization through the family and organized relations between the generations to provide economic skills and an introduction to homogeneous social life. At this level the roles of student and teacher are determined by purely ascriptive criteria. Children are "students" because of their age, and any difference in what they learn is determined by their sex. "Teachers" are teachers because they are adult members of the family, and whatever "specialization" is present is determined by sex — females may teach cooking, males hunting, and so on.

2. At a somewhat more advanced state, part of the socialization process is separated from the functions of the family, and is provided for all adolescent members of the society under the guidance of a specialized adult group. While a practical content characterizes part of the "curriculum," strong emphasis is also placed on matters relating to metaphysics and conduct.

At this stage, then, ascription in terms of age, and often sex, is the basis for determining who the students are; however, some achievement criteria are used in determining who the teachers are, since some training beyond that given to the average citizen is required. A trace of specificity is also evident, since certain adult members of the society are given more responsibility than others for training the children. These teachers are not specialized to any extent, however, for the teacher is regarded as the guide to the meaning of life, the source of all knowledge. Furthermore, some degree of universalism may be observed in that standardized tests must be passed, i.e., bravery proved, according to procedures accepted by the society.

3. As the society itself becomes more differentiated, and problems of social selection become greater, certain families or groups gain increased power or economic advantage over others and formalized education ceases to be the prerogative of all members of the society. Education can lay claim to a long history an an institution tied only to those relatively small groups who wield political, economic, or religious power. This phenomenon is in keeping with the concept of differentiation, for those groups which are the center of the societal differentiation process in the economic, political, and cultural spheres are those who would find it most necessary to build an educational institution to provide the skills, attitudes, and values through which they could maintain, adapt, and develop themselves and their other institutions.

Ascriptive norms are strong in determining who the students are in this context, particularly in terms of class lineage. Criteria for determining who the teachers are may be considered achievement oriented only to the limited extent that teachers are required to have a greater degree of knowledge. The "curriculum" exhibits differentiation in that concern is focused on language, liberal arts, and philosophy, in addition to conduct, law, and theology. Particularism is a norm in that individuals are educated according to their station.

The teacher continues to assume the role, at least at what are now termed the primary and secondary levels, of the fount of knowledge about life, rather than of a specialist in one branch of learning, and the educational institution may be described as Mark Hopkins sitting on one end of a log and the student sitting on the other. Some differentiation in terms of specificity of roles may be discernible at the level of higher education, both in administrative roles and in specialized teaching roles.

4. At a yet more advanced stage, the relation between education and social structure becomes decidedly complicated. Industrialization and

ever-increasing societal differentiation, as measured by division of labor and role specialization, become outstanding characteristics of the society. Educationists claim that education plays no small role as a cause of industrialization, since the crystallization and increasing autonomy of the institution promote a decrease of bias in communication of knowledge, skills, and ideas, both new and old, among the leadership of the society. This stage places new burdens on schooling in the form of mass instruction, occupational recruitment, and social selection.

This exercise could be continued and perhaps an even higher level of educational differentiation could be posited, in keeping with the demands of a postindustrial or technological society. At this advanced stage the educational system under various organizational arrangements might become one of the central determinants of the economic, political, and cultural character of society. However, since our focus is on Asia, where perhaps no society could plausibly be classified as "postindustrial," further conjecture about this stage is irrelevant. Indeed, most of the educational systems of Asian societies, until recent decades, fit rather nicely into stage 3. Some now appear to be rapidly in transition to stage 4. However, only Japan offers a history of at least two generations of solid entrenchment in stage 4.

Highlighting the contrasts between the educational systems of modern and traditional societies plays down their similarities. Some of the similar functions which do exist can be briefly identified. Both modern and traditional educational systems seek to transmit a body of culture valued by the superordinate system – the family or society. Both, then, contribute to the process of socialization and the certification of individuals for new roles. Further, educational systems in the full range of societies from traditional to modern frequently reflect ascriptive norms in their admission procedures, as well as in certain other internal arrangements.

Despite such similarities and continuity of educational functions, the focus here is on the nature and the extent of change. The trends in educational differentiation in modernizing societies may be summarized as follows:

1. Education becomes increasingly the channel for occupational selectivity and social mobility.

2. Education becomes more closely related to economic, occupational, and social status.

3. The increasing need for interdependence and the increasing possibilities of strain between the various educational subsystems and between the educational system and the superordinate system place new demands on educational planning.

4. The precise nature of educational differentiation depends on the peculiar characteristics of the society of which it is a part.

MEASURING EDUCATIONAL DIFFERENTIATION

Some further specification of the concept is needed if educational differentiation is to be used as a framework for the ordering of data. In contemporary Asian nations, all systems of education are graded into at least three levels: higher, middle, and primary. The higher the level, the more differentiated it becomes in terms of structure and function. Whereas primary schools may do little more than provide literacy, the secondary schools typically are expected to inculcate more specialized skills, and in higher educational institutions a great variety of professional skills and intellectual knowledge may be taught.

In the case studies that follow, no attempt will be made to quantify in any precise way the levels of educational differentiation. However, major changes which appear in the educational systems will be identified, and, when appropriate, interpreted through the concept of differentiation. Attention will be given to the appearance of significant structural alterations of emphases and the evolution of new, functionally distinct educational roles. Further, educational change will be linked to other aspects of social differentiation and social change.

In the final chapter, however, an attempt will be made to provide a regional picture of educational development through the use of scaling techniques which demonstrate the varying levels of structural differentiation in education among Asian nations. A brief explanation of the procedures and assumptions of this analysis will be given in the context of its application.

A SYSTEMS PERSPECTIVE

Students of comparative education have long argued that their field of study is interdisciplinary. The wide variety of intraeducational and educational-societal studies now being undertaken in other geocultural areas demands the tools of several disciplines. Moreover, insights into the role of education in such social processes as urbanization, industrialization, and modernization require a framework for analysis and conceptual equipment rarely found in educational literature. A "systems" approach may provide a way of transcending the limitations of a single-discipline approach yet also avoid the atheoretical (and indeed nonanalytical) descriptive studies common in comparative education.

Social systems models are not new to the academic scene; they have long been associated with analysis in both the natural and the social sciences. A system may be simply viewed as consisting of elements which have some definable relation to one another. Talcott Parsons, for example, argues that three levels of systems are relevant to the social sciences: personality, cultural systems, and social systems. Since social groupings ranging from small interest groups to whole societies are viewed as having order, they have been treated as systems.[17]

Even though one of the recent trends in systems theory is to give less attention to definitions, some further explanation of the use of the term "systems" is in order. One finds the concepts of systems and systems analysis employed in engineering, the physical sciences, communications, management studies, the new synthetic science of cybernetics, and the social sciences. It is the application and interpretation of systems in the social sciences that will be drawn upon here. Thus our concern is with social systems which are open and dynamic, not with the closed systems model common to the applied sciences.

A social system may be viewed as having four distinguishing characteristics. First, it is but one among many sets of interactions in which human beings may be engaged. Therefore, an educational system must refer not to an isolatable group of people, but to an isolatable set of interactions. Second, a social system is characterized by a particular organization of elements. Any set of elements may be organized in a variety of ways; however, such differences may have important consequences 'for the functioning of the system. For example, the articulation between identical varieties of secondary schools and universities may differ from nation to nation, depending on the organization of the educational system. In one system vocational schooling may lead to the university; in another system only the general secondary schools prepare for university entrance. Third, a social system is open;

that is, it is capable of engaging in a number of "transactions" with its environment. Unlike the closed systems of the physical world, a social system may adapt to external changes, for example, school enrollments fluctuating as a result of demographic changes. Fourth, the relations within the system and between the system and its environment involve not energy exchange, as is the case in natural or mechanical systems, but rather the exhange of ideas, information, norms, behavior, and so forth.

An educational system, then, may be viewed as a patterned array of components designed to accomplish particular objectives. Presumably the system becomes more efficient if its inputs are allocated according to a well thought-out plan and if the various interactions are accomplished harmoniously. Yet, like other social systems, the educational system is in a continual state of change or "redesign." Inputs — students, teachers, ideas, "messages" — enter the system at various points; likewise, outputs — graduates, dropouts — frequently leave the educational system, though not always at the regular portals, and cross the boundaries of other systems.

Given a systems approach, there are several additional constraints on the scope and focus of this study. First, the central focus is on that social system or subsystem called education. In general, emphasis will be placed on the formal educational system; however, systematic programs of instruction found outside the formal system will receive some treatment. In viewing the educational system, attention will be given to both the internal operations of the system and its external relationships to other social systems. The nature of the inputs to the educational system, for example, objectives, students, and teachers, will be examined in the light of the social, economic, and demographic characteristics of the societies from which the inputs are derived. Our concern here will be with the ways in which external conditions impose changes and constraints on the inputs available to the system. Detailed analysis of the internal operation of the educational system — scheduling of classes, facilities, teaching techniques, etc. — will not be undertaken. Certain general analyses will be made, however, regarding the ways in which the internal functioning of the system affects the inputs, and vice versa. The ouputs of the various levels and programs of the educational system — individuals, knowledge, skills, new roles and statuses — will be examined primarily in terms of how they relate to the demands of modernization. Thus the systems approach as utilized here will essentially consider these types of variables:

1. *Societal features such as norms and goals and the derivative educational objectives.* These inputs to the educational system are outputs of other systems, for example, the family or the superordinate social system. Answers will be sought to such questions as these: In the society in question, is there an articulated system of values influencing the direction of educational policies? What features of demography and stratification constrain the numbers and kinds of students and teachers participating in the educational system? How do ethnic, linguistic, and religious cleavages affect school participation and success?

2. *The intrasystem dynamic variables affecting the educational process.* Attention will focus on such questions as these: Do educational traditions make the existing educational system dysfunctional in terms of new economic and social goals? What techniques does the educational system employ to modify the social, economic, and political constraints on its inputs?

3. *The outputs of the educational system, which become inputs into the economic and social stratification systems.* Some attempt will also be made to examine output in terms of the commitments and predispositions of school graduates, particularly the educated elite. Here answers will be sought to questions such as the following: To what extent does the educational system meet national manpower needs? Can the economic returns to education be measured? Which social groups, classes, or castes are most rewarded by education? Does education act as a channel for social mobility? Is the educated elite committed to goals such as social equity and economic growth?

Clearly, the above discussion of inputs and outputs is an oversimplified and incomplete view of the linkages between the educational system and other major subsystems of society. For one thing, systems are not as easily separable as might initially be supposed. The economic system overlaps with the political system not only because individuals occupy multiple positions and perform multiple roles — father, banker, voter, etc. — but also some systems are of a higher order than others. Thus political motivation in a given circumstance may override religious affiliation, or family loyalty may supersede both.

The harmony between the systems theory and the concept of differentiation may be readily apparent from the previous discussion. Differentiation may be viewed as a principal process through which social systems respond or adapt to change in their environment. But it would obviously be overly ambitious to attempt any detailed historical and empirical analysis of the differentiation of educational and social systems in the modernization of Asia. The approach here is much more modest. The concept of differentiation will be emphasized, though not relied on exclusively, to help in understanding how Asian societies and their subsystems change, form new linkages, and dissolve old ones in the process of modernization. Attempts will be made to identify the emergence of new specialized institutions, new values, and altered life styles. Efforts will be made to seek an understanding of the development of education into a distinct, autonomous system and its further differentiation and diversification into hierarchical levels and programmatic variations. Finally, an examination will be made of the extent of national and regional attempts to rationally alter the inputs and the process of formal education in keeping with the goals of modernization.

An understanding of educational change within the process of modernization is clearly enhanced by the perspective of history. While perhaps inadequate with respect to detail, the subsequent chapters, in addition to examining the current scene, will attempt to portray the historical roots of the functioning of contemporary educational systems. In order to avoid the superficiality which might result from any attempt to treat the vast Asian continent as a whole, three nations representing various cultural heritages and different stages of modernization — Japan, India, and China — have been selected as case studies. In the final chapter some tentative generalizations will be offered regarding the regional educational planning efforts.

NOTES

1. Myron Weiner (ed.), *Modernization*. New York: Basic Books, 1966, p. 3.

2. Daniel Lerner, *The Passing of the Traditional Society*. Glencoe, Ill.: The Free Press, 1958.

3. David McClelland, *The Achieving Society*. Princeton, N.J.: Van Nostrand, 1961.

4. Everett E. Hagen, *On the Theory of Social Change: How Economic Growth Begins,* Part II. Homewood, Ill.: Dorsey Press, 1962.

5. C. E. Black, *The Dynamics of Modernization.* New York: Harper and Row, 1967, p. 7.

6. For elaboration of these dichotomies and for further background to the subsequent discussion see, for example, Talcott Parsons, *The Social System*, New York: The Free Press, 1951.

7. Inkeles has suggested that modernization implies "external" and "internal" changes for man. The external changes – the ways of dealing with environment – include urbanization, industrialization, mass communication, mass education, etc. The internal changes – attitudes, values, and feelings – have been commented on above. See Alex Inkeles, "The Modernization of Man," in Weiner, *op. cit.*, p. 139.

8. The concept of differentiation has been somewhat refined and given many new applications since the days when evolutionary theory was popular in the social sciences. Yet the distinguishing features of differentiation are apparent whether the concept appears under the name evolution, division of labor, neo-evolution, societal complexity, social development, or the concept of levels. The term social differentiation in contemporary times is frequently associated with studies of social mobility. Here, as the context makes clear, differentiation refers to certain structural and functional changes in societies or their subsystems.

9. R. M. MacIver and Charles H. Page, *Society: An Introductory Analysis.* New York: Holt, Rinehart and Winston, 1962, p. 527.

10. Neil S. Smelser, "The Modernization of Social Relations," in Weiner, *op. cit.*, pp. 110-111.

11. S. N. Eisenstadt, *Modernization: Protest and Change.* Englewood Cliffs, N. J.: Prentice-Hall, 1966, p. 51.

12. Robin M. Williams, Jr., "Industrial and Group Values," *The Annals,* Vol. I (May 1967), p. 22. The terms "goal-attainment," "integration," and "pattern-maintenance" have been described by Talcott Parsons as the functional imperatives of all societies. "Pattern-maintenance" refers to maintaining the stability of the value system and its institutionalization. "Goal-attainment" refers to a "relation between the system of reference and one or more situational objects which . . . maximizes the stability of the system." In more complex societies the polity is the major subsystem providing this function. The adaptive imperative "deals with the problem of controlling the environment for purposes of attaining goal states in a more developed society." The adaptive function relates largely to the economy and to technology, although some educational institutions may be seen as performing a primarily adaptive role. The integrative imperative is to "maintain solidarity" in relations between the various interacting social units in the interest of the effective functioning of society. See also Talcott Parsons and Neil J. Smelser, *Economy and Society,* Glencoe, Ill.: The Free Press, 1956, pp. 15-18.

13. Eisenstadt, *op. cit.,* p. 146.

14. *Ibid.,* p. 146.

15. *Ibid.,* p. 147.

16. These levels were originally suggested by Janet C. Adams, a sometime graduate student in sociology.

17. The following are among the many advantages attributed to the systems approach by its advocates: "1. A common vocabulary unifying the several 'behavioral' disciplines. 2. A technique for treating large, complex organizations. 3. A synthetic approach where piecemeal analysis is not possible due to the intricate

inter-relationships of parts that cannot be treated out of context to the whole. 4. A veiwpoint that gets at the heart of sociology because it sees the socio-cultural system in terms of information and communication nets. 5. The study of *relations* rather than 'entities' with an emphasis on process and transitions, probabilities as the basis of a flexible structure with many degrees of freedom. 6. An operationally definable, objective, non-anthropomorphic study of purposive, goal-seeking system behavior, symbolic cognitive processes, consciousness and self-awareness, and so socio-cultural emergence and dynamics in general." Walter Buckly, *Sociology and Modern Systems Theory.* Englewood Cliffs, N.J.: Prentice-Hall, 1967, p. 39.

SELECTED READINGS

Adams, Don, and Farrell, Joseph P. (eds.), *Education and Social Development.* Syracuse, N. Y.: Center for Development Education, Syracuse University, 1967.

Buckly, Walter, *Sociology and Modern Systems Theory.* Englewood Cliffs, N. J.: Prentice-Hall, 1967.

Eisenstadt, S. N., *Modernization: Protest and Change.* Englewood Cliffs, N. J.: Prentice-Hall, 1966.

Levy, J. Marion, *Modernization and the Structure of Societies: A Setting for International Affairs.* Princeton, N. J.: Princeton University Press, 1966.

chapter two

japan

Japan is the only Asian nation, with the exception of such European-settled areas as Australia and New Zealand, that does not readily fit into the class of underdeveloped nations. Although the per capita income of Japan in 1967 fell well below that of the most advanced European and North American nations, it was exceeded by no Asian or middle-African nation and by only six countries of Latin America. Other indices of modernization — technological development, societal differentiation, diffusion of social services, and the like — suggest approximately the same conclusion. Thus an intriguing question is raised. Why should Japan almost alone among the non-Western nations be able to break out of traditional ways and turn to new modes of living? Why did the Japanese leaders reach out to pluck the fruits of Western technology, military science, and education at the same time that Japan's neighbors, China and Korea, were attempting to shore up their nations against subversive modern influences? And how was it possible for the Japanese people to accept so readily the personal and social consequences of new modes of production, new occupations, and a new education?

THE ROOTS OF JAPANESE TRADITION

Japan learned much from its early contacts with other East Asian nations. Prior to the mid-nineteenth century it was from China and Korea that social, political, and religious ideas were imported and then adopted to provide direction for Japanese leaders and citizens. Among the early Chinese cultural exports that were carried over the Korean bridge to Japan were Chinese writing, literature, arithmetic, and the Chinese calendar. By the sixth century, through the medium of the Chinese language, and frequently via the exchange of scholars, both Confucian classics and Buddhist writings were known in the Japanese court.

Confucian rationalism and humanism met little opposition among the primitive cults of Japan, and except during certain periods of reaction were the accepted basis for social thought until the later decades of the nineteenth century. Japanese chronicles depict an unbroken line of imperial descent from 660 B.C.; however, Japanese traditions prohibited the Emperor from being merely a Confucian sage-king. Although the Japanese emperors were, in colloquial phrasing, Sons of Heaven, they usually ruled in the paternalistic Confucian manner, even to the extent of making wide use of learned court advisers. Yet, in the final analysis, the judgment of the Japanese Emperor in carrying out his divine mission was infallible; he was, indeed, a God-Emperor and his position was inviolable.

Since their nation had been created by divine will and their ruler was not only divine but also a descendant of the gods who created the world, the Japanese considered themselves divine children. They were, so to speak, a "chosen people." The element of divinity contributed to a sense of national superiority which was used by various Japanese leaders to emphasize, alternatively, isolationism or imperialism. The former was promoted for centuries as the Japanese scorned foreign ideas and attempted to retain a "pure" national life. At other times efforts to establish an empire through military and economic means were justified because of Japan's divine mission of leadership. This basis for the establishment of national policy was undermined in 1946 when Emperor Hirohito under the insistence of Allied military forces shed his cloak of divinity.

Any discussion of the historical and religious traditions of Japan must give attention to Shintoism (The Way of the Gods) and Bushido (The Way of the Warrior). Ancestor worship, nature worship, animism, fertility cults, and shamanism are all identified with early Shinto, while Modern or State Shinto was essentially an instrument of the state designed to strengthen national unity, loyalty, and obedience. Even the spread of Buddhism and the faith in Confucian teachings, rather than producing extended conflict with Shinto, merely added to the Japanese family of beliefs. Japanese scholars rationalized a metaphor to show the interrelation of the existing faiths. It was said that there was really only one tree of life, of which Shinto was the root, Confucianism the flower, and Buddhism the stem. Indeed, the combination of the more joyous rituals attached to Shintoism with the somber Buddhist rites seems to serve the needs of the Japanese. A popular anecdote tells that at birth it is common for the baby to be taken to a Shinto shrine for blessing, but at death the funeral is presided over by a Buddhist priest.

The twelfth through the sixteenth centuries constitute what is often called the medieval period of Japan. Strong clans carved out huge estates and engaged in open conflict with one another and with the Imperial court. Even the great Buddhist temples formed their own armies for protection, or – in some cases – for aggression. During this turbulent period there developed a warrior class representing an adjustment through specialization to new social needs. For the fighting man, a special education in both the home and the school and a special code of conduct gradually took form. The term now used to describe the chivalric code of the Japanese fighting men which developed during this period is Bushido (literally, military-knight-ways). The sources of Bushido were to be found in Shintoism, Confucianism, and Buddhism. From Shintoism came a sense of loyalty to the sovereign and reverence for ancestors. Confucianism, in addition to lending weight to the contributions of Shintoism, made its peculiar and important contribution by furnishing the warrior with disciplined social ways and a sophisticated ethical system. Buddhism, more particularly the Zen sect, contributed "a sense of calm trust to Fate, a quiet submission to the inevitable, that stoic composure in sight of dangers, or calamity, that disdain of life and friendliness with death."[1]

The development of character, achievement of fighting skill, and acquisition of knowledge, in that order, were the educational goals of the bushi (or samurai as they are known in recent literature). The virtues needed in molding character were courage, benevolence, politeness, truthfulness, honor, loyalty, and self-control. The curriculum deemed appropriate for training the samurai consisted of fencing, archery, jujitsu, horsemanship, the use of the spear, tactics, calligraphy, ethics, literature, and history. The samurai obviously was a man of action; he did, however, study the Confucian classics, largely for moral purposes rather than for their profundity of scholarship or fine literary style.

The lasting imprint of Bushido on the character of the Japanese people has been emphasized by many students of Japan. One avowed apologist for Bushido wrote at the turn of the twentieth century: "Bushido, the maker and product of Old Japan, is still the guiding principle of the transition and will prove the formative force of the new era. . . . The great statesmen who steered the ship of our state through the hurricane of the Restoration and the whirlpool of national rejuvenation, were men who knew no other moral teaching than the Precepts of Knighthood."[2]

THE GROWTH AND DECLINE OF TRADITIONAL SOCIETY: THE TOKUGAWA SHOGUNATE (1603-1868)

Under the military leaders of the Tokugawa clan, unification and some 250 relatively peaceful years were brought to a people who had been besieged by feudal strife for several centuries. The early part of this period not only reflected tranquillity but orthodoxy as well, for the Tokugawa vigorously sought to spread an acceptable ideology, namely that of Neo-Confucianism, while prohibiting the entrance of Western ideas and peoples. Under the highly centralized Tokugawa rule the emperor was allowed to keep his court but lived in splendid isolation, performing little more than ceremonial functions. That part of Japan not under the direct control of the Tokugawa was ruled by feudal lords known as daimyos, who were allowed considerable autonomy in matters of primary concern to their fiefs but who owed ultimate allegiance to the Shogunate. Indeed, each daimyo was required to spend part of his time in the capital city and upon departure for his estate to leave some of his family behind, presumably as hostages. Yet, so long as the actions of the daimyo did not threaten the Tokugawa Shogunate, he could expect a free rein.

The Tokugawa society was highly stratified, and during the early part of Tokugawa rule four separate social orders could be found within the population. In descending order of prestige these were: the warrior, the artisan, the peasant, and the merchant. The daimyo and the upper-class samurai (knight-in-arms) lived apart from the others and, for all practicable purposes, were inaccessible to the lower classes. The feudal lords and their retainers depended on the crops grown by the peasants for their income, and in turn the artisans and the merchants sold their wares to the lords. National unity was promoted by direct or indirect obligations to the ruling clan, and by a common racial and cultural heritage communicated to the people through familial education, religious ritual, drama, and edict. The unity of the "extended family" was enhanced by a strong binding force of filial piety which dictated the responsibilities and authority of each family member.

Social status in the early Tokugawa period was ascribed largely on the basis of heredity. Social, as well as economic, behavior was tied to kinship or to social class and the family was the primary unit of social organization, although it was not always the recipient of the first obligation of loyalty. In Japan, unlike China, obligation to one's code or lord might well supersede familial loyalties.

But Tokugawa social structure was not quite so rigid as it might seem at first glance. Although the Shogunate gave detailed orders encompassing the behavior, dress, rituals, courtesies, and obligations of all people, on occasion allowances were made for excellence, and some mobility took place within the several classes. Ideally, one was expected to be born into and die in the same social position held by one's parents; yet exceptions to the ideal are important. A competent young samurai might be adopted by a daimyo and even replace the daimyo's eldest son in the line of succession and inheritance. Once elevated to that position, however, the adopted son was cut off entirely from his former family and friends.

Nor did the relative lack of mobility between social classes entirely thwart development. The merchants, who found higher status closed to them, were forced to concentrate their efforts on improving their wealth and security within their own class. The growth in power of the merchants, who became not only traders but all types of entrepreneurs, coincided with the disintegration of the old regime.

Educational Activities

Education received varying emphases and was given different directions under the first several Tokugawa Shoguns. Iyeyasu, the first Shogun, was a scholar, and took a keen interest in the status of culture and learning in Japan. He urged his descendants to follow the golden rule: "Human happiness may naturally be found in learning, and should be sought therein."[3] There were four specific measures undertaken by Iyeyasu to foster learning: "(1) investigation of old books and documents, (2) employment of learned men, (3) establishment of schools and (4) publication of books."[4] The ban on the importation of foreign books was temporarily lifted under the eighth Shogun, Yoshimune (1684-1751). Although this breach in the seclusion of Japan was later filled by the isolationist policies of the ninth Shogun, Western learning continued to seep into Japan through the small port and trading facilities the Dutch were allowed to maintain at Nagasaki. The modernizing implications of the continued infiltration of "Dutch learning" will be considered later.

Yet the formal learning, promoted during the first half of the Tokugawa period, can be related roughly to stage 3 as identified in Chapter One, and can hardly be said to have been oriented toward the fostering of economic and social change. The educational institutions which were controlled directly by the Shogunate existed largely for advanced classical studies of Chinese learning or, more rarely, Japanese learning. The han or clan schools were established by the daimyo for the samurai, and their curriculum consisted of the Chinese classics and military arts. These schools were not numerous, however, in the early Tokugawa period, and not until the latter part of the period was a sizable portion of the formal educational facilities extended to families other than the ruling clan. Reflecting particularistic norms apparent in the larger society, those who acquired education did so according to their station in life.

For the younger children, aged seven to thirteen, of lower-class Bushi, merchants, and peasants, there existed the *terakoya* schools. The curricula of these schools typically included calligraphy, reading, letterwriting, arithmetic, and etiquette. Usually the content of the texts and copybooks were of archaic origin, far removed from the children's experience. The lessons varied somewhat according to the future calling of the children, as determined by the parents' occupation, and occasionally an attempt was made to provide practical studies. The relationship between teacher and student frequently resembled that between father and son, and stories of the warm and lasting friendships which developed in these schools are legion. Accurate statistics on the enrollments of the *terakoya* are not available. It is unlikely, however, that in the first half of the Tokugawa period more than a small percentage of school-age children received any formal schooling.

Indeed, it may be considered that until the later decades of the Tokugawa period limited differentiation and specialization had taken place in education. The curriculum was still largely directed toward ends of morality and conduct. Teaching was yet to be recognized as a highly specialized role; rather, teachers were still viewed as general moral guides for privileged youth. Attempts to build an articulated educational system with ramified social and economic functions were still somewhere in the future.

Ingredients for Change

One of the most unique hypotheses concerning the ingredients fostering development in Japan has been proposed by Levy in a comparison of the conditions of modernization in China and Japan.[5] To Levy one of the keys to fostering social change lies in individualism, "the manner and basis on which a person makes and/or is expected to make decisions affecting his future and the future of others with whom he interacts."[6] There are, however, two types of individualism according to Levy — "individualism by ideal" and "individualism by default." The former implies that individualism is at least somewhat institutionalized for various activities and for persons in various social categories. Rarely is individualism by ideal widespread through a society; however, in certain of the highly developed societies (according to Max Weber, those imbued with the Protestant ethic) such a quality of independence may be expected. Individualism by default implies that the individual must make choices on the basis of his own criteria because of the absence of generalized criteria for judgment. Both types of individualism tend "to increase if not maximize the probability and/or the possibility of heterodox decisions." However, only those societies where individualism by ideal is widespread "have made social change a central virtue...."[7]

In contrasting the conditions in nineteenth century China with those of Japan during the same period, Levy notes the prevalence in the former of individualism by default. The Chinese merchants in particular, because of the social stigma attached to their occupation, were forced to accept a degree of self-reliance — at least within the moral limitations of family codes and the technical limitations of bureaucratic laws. When, under the impact of new occupations and new individual freedoms, the traditional family structure began to break down, a new impetus to individualism by default was forthcoming. Without the security or stability of family values and standards, fleeting public support was given first to one radical cause, and then to another.

According to Levy, the keys to change in the early stages of Japan's modernization were the merchants and samurai. Although the merchants ideally occupied a socially marginal role, as they did in China, the presence of individualism by default was less apparent in Japan. Merchants in Japan, for example, could not hope for quick profit through land speculation, since the Shogunate prohibited the sale of lands. Furthermore, in contrast to the situation in China, the Japanese merchants in actuality had important ties with other elements of the national power structure. To the daimyo, who controlled the fief where he lived, the Japanese merchant owed certain allegiance and thus indirectly had responsibilities to the people as a whole. Also, the samurai and merchants found a mutual need for each other's strengths in fulfillment of their respective goals of efficiency and profit. Moreover, the merchant, because of his financial role, probably was at times used by the Shogunate as a buffer to the ambitions of the daimyo.

It may seem somewhat unusual to stress any kind of individualism in a discussion of Japan's development, or in China's development either; however, Levy's argument has merit. To the extent that individualism by ideal is related to the individual internalization of achievement goals, then such an ingredient was amply visible in Tokugawa Japan. Yet individualism presumably implies that an individual might readily follow his own goals even if these were in conflict with family or class goals. Such was not the typical case in Japan. While class and national goals could, and often did, supersede family goals, the type of rugged individualism associated with the American frontier, or even the politically organized and ideologically cohesive dissenter groups of eighteenth century England, were not characteristic of Tokugawa Japan.

What is frequently overlooked or played down in generalized statements regarding Tokugawa Japan is that several distinct traditions existed throughout the entire period. Each class in the hierarchical society had its own well-defined and religiously prescribed tastes and customs;

however, since cultural preferences varied not only on the basis of class origin, but also were related to the degree of urbanism of the family, it has been suggested that three separate traditions pertinent to the modernization of Japan can be identified. These are (1) the village tradition, (2) the elite tradition, and (3) the townsman tradition.[8]

It was in the village tradition that conservatism and traditionalism were most pronounced. The patriarchal family system, the paternalistic nature of the village power structure, and the deepseated superstitions were all characteristic of this tradition. The elite urban tradition is identified mainly by its contributions to the classic Japanese arts – the Noh, tea ceremony, and certain cultured literary forms. It has been argued, however, that contemporary industrialized Japan owes little to either of these traditions, but rather, to a substantial degree, is the product of the townsman's culture.[9]

The townsman tradition was born among the commoners of the great cities of Yedo (Tokyo), Osaka, and Kyoto, but later gathered followers in all classes.[10] The townsman rejected the simple ways of the village folk and parodied the classical arts of the urban elites. The term bourgeois has even been used in the description of this way of life, for unlike the samurai who practiced rigorous "unostentatiousness," the townsman loved to make and spend money. The flamboyance, luxury, and even dissoluteness of new urban living patterns contrasted sharply with the frugality, restraint, and discipline practiced by the samurai. Consider, for example, the difference between the spartan heroes in traditional Tokugawa literature and the hero of the very popular Genroku novel, *The Man Who Spent His Life in Love-Making*. By the turn of the eighteenth century, literacy among the urban population was fairly widespread, and knowledge of the new culture penetrated Tokugawan society to a considerable extent, even converting some of the samurai. The materialistic tastes and entrepreneurial spirit incorporated in the townsman tradition spurred rapid economic advancement under Meiji rule. But whether these characteristics played an important role in the downfall of the Shogunate and led to the establishment of the Meiji government is highly controversial. As Bellah successfully argues,[11] the revolution of 1868 was not entirely or even primarily a bourgeois revolution.

Not only was the townsman tradition an exception to the static image usually painted of the Tokugawan culture, but other exceptions may also be discovered. New religious and social thinkers were appearing on the scene, and their views were being heard. One such thinker, Ishida Gaigan (1685-1744), founded a movement called the Shingaku, which propounded, among other things, a defence of the merchant class and justified the accumulation of wealth. Moreover, and of fundamental importance, the displacement under the Tokugawa of Buddhism by Confucianism was the triumph of the practical ethic over abstract speculation, or even over the kind of resignation implicit in Buddhism.[12] The Confucian canon of traditional knowledge had thwarted social change in the Chinese society and produced a highly conservative class of scholar-officials; however, the doctrines of Confucius played a somewhat different role in Japan. Neo-Confucianism placed emphases on the legitimacy of the Emperor and thus cast the Tokugawa in the role of usurpers. This interpretation was made most apparent upon the appearance of *The History of Great Japan* produced by the Mito branch of the Tokugawa family; and though this history was the product of Neo-Confucian scholars, it stressed patriotism, nationalism, and Japanese literature.

Historical scholars appear to be in agreement concerning the influence of the Mito school on generations of teachers, and in turn upon those who became the leaders of the Meiji Restoration and later industrialization. The teachings of the Mito school seemed to combine Confucian philosophy, the historic findings of its research scholars, and Shinto beliefs. So important a figure as, for example, Yoshida Shoin was influenced by the Mito school, and spread its ideas widely among the young samurai. The particularly strong hold which these ideas had taken in western Japan by the 1850's has been interpreted as one cause for the country's early industrial development.

The work of one Japanese, Kaibara Ekken (1630-1714), illustrates the consequences of following the nationalistic tendencies of the Neo-Confucian movement to their ultimate limit. Kaibara, through his popular writings, perhaps more than any other Japanese, brought Confucian ethics into the homes of the average Japanese. He did not limit himself to humanistic studies, but also carried out extensive biological research. While not a modern scientific thinker like the "Dutch" scholars of the following century, Kaibara's belief that one cannot understand man without understanding his environment was a significant step toward differentiating Confucian studies beyond the literary classics.

The latter part of the Tokugawa period saw the fruition of the several earlier diverse traditions and social theories in many significant economic, social, and ideological changes. The top-heavy social structure with an increasing number of families in the leisure, or semileisured, classes put inordinate pressures on the farmer. Taxes increased to the level where the farmer was unable to profit even from a good harvest. Merchants, through manipulation of rice prices, increased the likelihood of the farmer starting down the one-way path of indebtedness. The daimyo, for his part, contracted further financial obligations to the merchants and in turn sought to wring an even greater output from the farmers. The inevitable result of this continued pressure was several bloody peasant uprisings in the late eighteenth century. The government's reaction to the worsening economic situation was essentially to urge thrift and frugality on all classes, although the opening of new rice fields and the cultivation of new crops were also encouraged. The samurai and daimyo, though generally respecting the call to frugality, at times had to move outside the exclusive agricultural economy to support themselves. Some fiefs began to establish small textile and wine industries.

Even after their real power began to weaken, prestige continued to reside with the daimyo and their samurai; but, with the purse strings held by the merchants, and human nature being what it is, certain compromises were made. Envious of the townsman, some samurai forgot their knightly oaths and emulated entrepreneurial pursuits and the carefree ways of the merchant class. The commoners, for their part, aspired to samurai titles and privileges, and were not above paying for them. Further, the habit, so popular in much of Western history, of exchanging the daughter of a wealthy family for a titled but penniless son-in-law became common.

The situation in the later Tokugawa period thus became right for what E. E. Hagen has called the five operative laws in the process of social change: (1) the law of group subordination, (2) the law of rejection of values, (3) the law of social blockage, (4) the law of group protection, and (5) the law of nonalien leadership. All of these laws are found operative in late Tokugawa Japan. The groups subordinated were Tozama hans (politically), samurai (economically), wealthy peasants (locally in social and political power), and merchants (socially). These groups rejected the status quo values of the Shogunate by seeking education — even "Dutch studies" — or, in the case of the merchants, by seeking to rise above their assigned class. As an example of the third "law," merchants were prevented, by statutory law, from owning land, and persons were not allowed to change occupations. In Japan the subordinated groups sought to protect their own members through loyalty codes and other mutual aid arrangements. Hagen's fifth law suggests that the whole society will follow the deviant group only if this group's values and practices are not too alien. In Japan the deviant groups were Japanese racially and culturally and, while rejecting certain Tokugawa policies, they were supportive of much in Japanese tradition.[13]

It may be argued that, once the process of change toward a radically different society was under way, some of the traditional aspects of Japanese culture served to bulwark this process. Certainly the ideals of the samurai (ideals frequently emulated by other social strata) were not necessarily antithetical to economic progress. The emphasis on hard work, the purifying nature of frugality, and the sense of duty to parents, emperor and nation bear resemblance to the "Protestant ethic" frequently discussed as a significant motivating force for industrial development in the West.

Reaching even deeper into Japanese tradition, one finds the means for fostering integration and unity even during the trauma of change. The relationship between family (through ancestor worship), village (through local deities), and the whole nation (through the Emperor) to imperial ancestors is a matter of history. Individual existence resulted from the blessings of spirits and ancestors. To repay these blessings the individual had an obligation to work, and, if necessary, to sacrifice himself for the group. The submergence of the individual to the group did not necessarily obstruct the diffusion of modern ideas:

First of all, because of its stress (stress of value patterns) on group coherence and group discipline it provided a relatively well organized, disciplined social structure on which a modern state could be erected rather rapidly and that modern state then was able to direct and control the energy of the society in the direction of, at least in some spheres, very rapid modernization. And, secondly, I think the structure of values provided the energy for work necessary in a modern economy by gearing the obligation of individuals to work for the group into the structure of economic life.[14]

Moreover, even the hierarchical nature of society aided development by making it possible to "exercise intense discipline and motivate a high labor output".[15] Perhaps the elements of transcendence also had historical importance in providing a backdrop for modernization. The presence of such elements "often ended up not in breaking through the traditional pattern of values but in rationalizing it, codifying it, and creating the ideological basis for the famous Meiji absolutism."[16]

EDUCATION AT THE BEGINNING OF THE MODERN ERA

Before examining the linkages between education and other social systems during Japan's modern period, it is well to summarize briefly the educational situation at the close of the Tokugawa period. In doing so, attention will be focused on the goals of Tokugawan education and on the content as differentiated for the several groups of recipients.

There were at least three purposes of formal education in the Tokugawa period. One was moral – to learn the wisdom of the Sages concerning the proper ordering of human relations. The second was to gain useful skills such as medicine, military strategy, administration, and Chinese prose writing. The third was to gain knowledge of men and affairs which would enable rulers to govern wisely. Because working for the government was a duty under the Tokugawan Confucian ethic and since the government required knowledge, "men of talent" came to be sought. Because of the stress on talent in the late Tokugawa period, it became possible for men of modest hereditary rank, through acquisition of military skills or by mastery of Chinese or Western learning, to emerge as national leaders. Moreover, as has been pointed out, this aspect of the late Tokugawa period encouraged young samurai to have more of an individual self-assertiveness than self-identification with his group, while at the same time maintaining a desire to obtain recognition and admiration from the group and power within it. Therefore, prestige and power were the chief objects of self-assertive ambition. However, men of talent, such as Confucian teachers and Government advisers, were still specialists; and specialists, whether of swordsmanship or of letters, were traditionally ranked well below the "all-round men" who were expected to exercise leadership at the highest level. As one example of the persistence of the suspicion of specialists even after 1868, the scholars who studied Western culture, like Fukuzawa Yukichi, were sometimes considered mere "geisha-specialists" in intellectual life. Social classes and education were closely related during the Tokugawa period. Education for the nobility, in the form of Confucian studies, was given through tutorials or at Gakushuin, established in the 1840's in Kyoto. For the samurai there were a number of institutions offering instruction at various levels. Shogunal schools and fief-endowed schools offered the sons of samurai studies in Confucianism, history, calligraphy, composition, and etiquette. Those who wanted to enter into scholarly professions went to private schools, some of which offered the languages and sciences comprising "Western learning." Even among the samurai schools there were class divisions. There were differences in dress, number of attendants, and seating position, and even the classrooms were carefully specified. To some extent there were separate curricula for the different ranks of the samurai. For example, the higher samurai tended to look down on arithmetic, and valued swordsmanship, riding, or archery as spiritual training. The lower samurai studied arithmetic as well as military tactics.

Although studies in Japanese educational history frequently indicate that no institutions of higher education had been established prior to the Meiji period, the functional equivalent to such institutions did exist. That is, although universities did not exist as such, administrative and intellectual leaders were being prepared. Since the turn of the eighteenth century there had been in operation the *Shōheiko* (School of Prosperous Peace), a center of orthodox Confucian scholarship, located in Tokyo, controlled completely by the Tokugawa clan and limited to members of the clan. This institution was run in such a way that no true dissatisfaction with social system goals were communicated to the participants.

To satisfy their own needs, and in reaction to the monopoly of the Shoheiko, a number of feudal clans began their own higher schools. By 1850 there were 250 clan schools dedicated to what can be loosely called higher learning. These schools competed with the Shōheiko for the services of the most distinguished scholars, and some of these schools, such as the Mito and Satsuma, emphasized Japanese history and literature much more strongly than did the Shōheiko. The approach to these topics stressed the role of the Emperor and of national destiny in opposition to the Shoheiko, which, as was indicated, remained a center for the study of Confucian classics and was uninterested in national movements which threatened Tokugawa rule. People who attended these clan schools became progressively more discontent with the political posture of Japanese society and at the same time became more sensitive to the military and material advantages of the West. Lombard points out:

That there were men ready to lead in the restoration was due in large measure to the influence of certain schools, notably that of Mito; and that there were men ready to welcome foreign association was also due to the work of certain independent teachers whose efforts kindled the foregleams of the second great awakening.[17]

For the commoners there were *terakoya* and possibly other local schools for the learning of the "three R's." During the earlier period the *terakoya* school was organized and run by Buddhist priests, but under the Tokugawa, *terakoya* became a secular institution for commoners. The social and occupational backgrounds of *terakoya* teachers in the later Tokugawa have been estimated as follows: commoners, 38 percent; samurai, 23 percent; Buddhist priests, 20 percent; doctors, 9 percent, Shinto priests, 7 percent; and unclassified, 3 percent.[18] These schools were coeducational and served children between ages 6 to 8 and 11 to 13. Understandably, the number of girls in attendance was far fewer than the number of boys. *Terakoya* schools were usually supported by patronage of wealthy people and by contributions. Concerning the general value of these schools it has been said:

If many of the terakoya did little more than provide the basic rudiments of literacy, others, particularly in the cities, attained rather high standards of primary education. . . . It is also quite clear that toward the end of the Tokugawa Era some of these schools were sufficiently effective to awaken in their pupils a high degree of awareness of the political problems of their time.[19]

The later part of the Tokugawa period saw a considerable extension of literacy and schooling throughout Japan. At the beginning of the seventeenth century, illiteracy was the norm; but by the middle of the nineteenth century nearly every fief had its fief-endowed school and there were hundreds of private schools for samurai. By 1868, 40 to 50 percent of all Japanese boys and 15 percent of the girls were getting some formal schooling outside their homes. The spread of literacy (see Table 1) was greater than in most contemporary underdeveloped countries and in any European country at a comparable stage of economic development except Prussia, Holland, and Scotland.[20]

TABLE 1   Literacy in the 1870's

Social group	Literacy (%)	Proportion in total population (%)
Samurai	Men 100 ⎫ Women 50 ⎬	7
Merchants	Large cities 70-80 ⎫ Small cities 50-60 ⎬	3
Artisan classes	Large cities 50-60 ⎫ Small cities 40-50 ⎬	2
Village notables	100 ⎫	
Village middle layers	50-60 ⎬	87
Lower peasant levels	30-40	
Peasants in isolated areas	20 ⎭	

Source: Irene Taueber, *The Population in Japan,* Princeton, N. J.: Princeton University Press, 1958, pp. 26-28; quoted in Herbert Passin, *Society and Education in Japan,* New York: Teachers College, Columbia University, 1965, p. 27.

EDUCATIONAL INPUTS DURING JAPAN'S MODERN CENTURY

The Meiji Restoration in 1868 symbolized the transition from traditional to modern society. The Shogun and feudal lords in a remarkably peaceful manner abdicated their power to a centralized administration which ruled in the name of the Emperor. The country was opened to foreign trade and commerce, and "self-cultivation" and "merit" became the watchwords of the day, since the new Meiji leaders considered the men of talent, even if of common origin, to be more valuable to the new state than the less qualified samurai. Japan moved haltingly to stage 4 in the process of educational differentiation.

Changing Educational Goals

If educational changes are viewed in the systems perspective being employed throughout this work, the new national goals and the social, demographic, and economic conditions of the early Meiji era may be considered as the sources of inputs to Japan's first comprehensive and unified educational system. More particularly, attention here will be given to the evolving educational objectives, the major economic and social constraints on education, and the character of the teaching and student population.

The overriding national goal influencing the nature of the educational system was utilitarianism. It has been argued that by the beginning of the Meiji Restoration "the ideological transition to an ambitious knowledge-seeking and qualification-seeking society had not only begun; it was well under way."[21] Yet it was left to the Meiji era to articulate and fully implement this transition. The Emperor's Charter Oath in 1868 stated that knowledge was to be sought throughout the world. The progressive or "Western" scholars, who had been increasingly asserting themselves for more than a generation, achieved complete victory with the Government Order of Education in 1872. In the preamble, education was identified as "the key to success, and no man can afford to neglect it. . . . Learning having been viewed as the exclusive privilege of the samurai and his superiors, farmers, artisans, merchants and women have neglected it." The Code aimed for the goal that "there shall, in the future, be no community with an illiterate family, or a family with an illiterate person."

The intent of the aggressive policy of expanding education was, like that of other national policies at this time, to contribute to a "prosperous country and a strong military." Japan in the 1860's lacked modern communication and transportation systems as well as an industrial and commercial class who were familiar with Western production techniques and trading methods. Moreover, Japanese society was predominantly agrarian, with some 80 percent of the 20 million gainfully employed persons engaged in agriculture. It was consequently the instrumental value of education which Japanese leaders sought to exploit as Japan strove to develop a position of strength comparable with that of the Western world powers.[22]

But the goals of economic prosperity and military power were not the only goals affecting the inputs of the new educational system. In the Meiji era education was early seen as a means for unifying a people and directing them toward new national symbols and a common national purpose.

Although the Western-oriented scholars had generally won the day and Western educational models were very much in vogue, the conflict between foreign ideas and national traditions continued to be a matter of debate. "National" scholars argued that education should be centered on Chinese learning, deemphasizing Western learning.

But by the early 1880's, a sort of rapprochement had been established between the liberal and conservative forces in education. The views of the more ardent advocates of Westernization were rejected and the wholesale imitation of Western education, use of Western textbooks, advisers, and the like had given way to a more independent educational approach. On the other hand, little serious discussion remained concerning the utility of or the need to acquire technical knowledge from the West. Such learning, however, had to be acquired within a context of socialization emphasizing national loyalty and filial piety. Thus popular education, in addition to being a means of mobilizing talent, became viewed above all as an instrument of nationalism. This reconciliation of the indigenous with the cosmopolitan was reflected in the establishment of a highly significant general educational policy. Arinori Mori, while Minister of Education, established a dual educational system — compulsory education to indoctrinate the spirit of morality and nationalism, and university education for the education of the elite "in an atmosphere of the greatest possible academic freedom and critical rationalism."[23]

Student Input

The two major inputs to the educational system, students and teachers, need now to be considered. These inputs will be examined primarily in quantitative terms but, when data permit, attention will also be given to the social origin of students and teachers. Moreover, these inputs will be viewed dynamically as their size or character changed throughout Japan's modern century.

The first major attempt at the establishment of a national primary school system came with the promulgation of the Government Order of Education of 1872. At this time, sending children to school was made a parental obligation. School attendance requirements, which varied over the subsequent decades, were extended to 6 years in 1907 and reached the present period of 9 years in 1947. Attendance rates grew rapidly from somewhat less than 30 percent in 1873 to over 90 percent in 1907.

A further examination of the expansion of primary education shows that the school attendance rate did not, however, exhibit regular growth. Moreover, the rate of classroom attendance did not always parallel the school attendance rate.[24] Both the school attendance and classroom attendance rates peaked first at about 1883 and failed to show significant growth for the following nine years. Indeed, during this period the rate of class attendance fell to a level below that at the time of the Government

Order of 1872. After the turn of the century, when modern industrial development was well under way, attendance again rose rapidly, and by the last year of the Meiji period (1911) the rate of school attendance exceeded 98 percent and the rate of classroom attendance was approximately 90 percent.[25]

Sex differences in attendance were great during the opening decades of the Meiji period. For example, the rate of attendance for boys in 1877 was 56 percent, as compared to 22 percent for girls. However, by the end of the Meiji period, the institution of compulsory education was nearly completed; regional, cultural, and sex disparities in school attendance were largely eliminated; and illiteracy was reduced to a rate comparable to contemporary modern nations. On the one hand, this rapid growth of a broad foundation of education, in addition to supporting modernization through an extension of literacy and an introduction to secular knowledge, also made possible rapid growth at the higher levels of education. Viewed differently, the promotion of compulsory education represents in itself an early modernization policy.

As was the case with primary education, the beginnings of a national system of secondary education were laid by the Government Order of Education of 1872. At this time the term secondary education was defined as "an institution for teaching general subjects to primary school graduates" and served students 14 to 19 years of age. Although secondary education underwent several reorganizations, until 1945 this level of schooling typically included secondary schools for boys, high schools for girls, and vocational schools.

Table 2 indicates the rapid expansion of all types of secondary education during the Meiji and post-Meiji periods. In terms of percentages of the total population of corresponding age groups, the total secondary school enrollment during this period ranged from approximately 1 percent to 65 percent.

By 1960 the enrollment in the common middle or lower secondary schools had risen to nearly 6 million students, while the total enrollment (both regular and technical) in higher secondary schools exceeded 3.2 million students. The total enrollment comprised over 80 percent of the appropriate age grouping. In terms of percentage of elementary school graduates advancing to secondary school, the growth for males was from 5.1 percent (1895) to 63.6 percent (1961).

In addition to the overall growth pattern, of particular interest are the extremely rapid growth rates of enrollment in girls' high schools and vocational secondary schools. These enrollments appear to have been stimulated particularly by the development of modern industry. Between 1895 and 1915, for example, the enrollment in girls' high schools increased more than 50 times, while enrollments in vocational courses increased approximately 15 times. During the same period, enrollments in the general course increased less than 5 times.

TABLE 2 The Number of Secondary School Students, 1885 to 1945

Year	Secondary schools	Girls' high schools	Vocational schools
1885	14,084	616	990
1900	78,315	11,984	16,981
1915	141,954	95,949	102,593
1930	345,691	368,999	318,681
1945	639,756	875,814	845,497

Source: Japanese National Commission for UNESCO (ed.), *The Role of Education in the Social and Economic Development of Japan.* Tokyo: Ministry of Education, 1966, pp. 74-75.

The expansion of higher education from the Meiji period to the 1960's shows dramatic but irregular growth. In the 1880's higher education in Japan was relatively more popular than secondary education. However, between 1900 and 1910 enrollment in secondary education increased 6 times while higher education enrollments only doubled. Growth at these two levels was roughly parallel between 1910 and 1940, while the postwar period showed a greater proportional increase in students pursuing higher education.[26] Table 3 shows the expansion in higher education prior to World War II.

In terms of diffusion of higher education within the appropriate age group (about 17 to 21), rapid growth did not begin until the turn of the century. The percentage of university age students enrolled in higher education was approximately 0.4 between 1875 and 1900. This rose to 1.0 in 1910, 3.7 in 1940, and 10.2 in 1960. At this latter date the percentage of males (18 to 21 years of age) enrolled was 16.4, while that of females was 4.1. With regard to female enrollments, it should be repeated that junior colleges (esentially a postwar creation) were absorbing much of the demand for postsecondary education. These institutions had grown in number from 149 in 1950 to 339 in 1964. At the latter date they were enrolling over 90,000 females.[27]

TABLE 3   Number of Schools and Students in Higher Education, 1890 to 1940

Year	Universities Schools	Students	Higher schools Schools	Students
1890	1	1,312	7	4,356
1900	2	3,240	7	5,684
1910	3	7,239	8	6,341
1920	16	21,915	15	8,839
1930	46	69,605	32	25,551
1940	47	81,999	32	29,283

Year	Colleges Schools	Students	Vocational colleges Schools	Students
1890	–	–	–	–
1900	–	–	–	–
1910	60	26,244	17	6,725
1920	74	39,835	27	9,172
1930	111	70,010	51	20,033
1940	121	98,967	72	42,511

Source: Japanese National Commission for UNESCO (ed.), *The Role of Education in the Social and Economic Development of Japan.* Tokyo: Ministry of Education, 1966, p. 86.

An important stimulus to the development of the needed high-level manpower for economic development during the Meiji period came from government programs to send students abroad for advanced study. The regulations established in 1874 said that such a person must show excellent academic achievement and be a man of good conduct. The government paid the student's school expenses on a loan basis, and the period of overseas study was set at five years. In the early part of the 1870's, there were about 400 such students. In the later part of the 1880's, about 1900 students were studying in England, the United States, France, Germany, Russia, and China.[28]

The Government Order of Education in 1872 gave all Japanese people equal opportunity for education and officially abolished the class divisions of samurai, farmers, artisans, and tradesmen. Moreover, the opportunity for advanced education for those who completed primary education was open to all on the basis of academic qualifications. Table 4 shows the rapidity of the "democratizing" of the student body at the University of Tokyo.

TABLE 4   Distribution of Tokyo University Students by Social Status in Meiji Era

Year	Peers (%)	Ex-Warriors (%)	Commoners (%)
1878	0.6	73.9	25.5
1880	0.9	73.6	25.5
1882	0.1	49.1	50.8
1884	0.2	50.2	49.6

Adapted from Japan, Ministry of Education, *Japan's Growth and Education*, Tokyo: Ministry of Education, 1962, Table 3, p. 34.

Quite obviously the ex-samurai class at the University of Tokyo was represented out of proportion to its size. One reason for this situation appears to be the greater desire for education on the part of samurai families. It is important to note, however, that by 1882 approximately one-half of the enrollment at the most prestigious educational institution in Japan came from the class of commoners.

Further reliable data on the social origin of students during more recent decades are difficult to locate; however, it is known that a disproportionately high enrollment of sons from the ex-samurai class persisted for several decades in secondary as well as higher education. One source has estimated that 73 percent of the contemporary students in Japanese higher institutions are from the white-collar (independent, professional, clerical workers, etc.) class and 27 percent from the "laborer" class (farmers, industrial, transportation, and communication workers). This crude classification suggests that opportunities for higher education among the children of the laborer class are better in Japan than in most European and other Asian nations, but not as extensive as in the U.S.S.R., the United Kingdom, or the United States.

Teacher Inputs

Primary school teachers were provided for the expanding educational system through national and prefectural normal schools. The expansion of normal school enrollments rose from approximately 5000 in 1880 to nearly 63,000 in 1943. In general, the rate of increase in the number of normal school graduates exceeded the rate of increase in the numbers of primary school pupils, and the percentage of teachers qualified grew from 55 percent in 1895 to 89 percent in 1935. After World War II, teacher training was shifted from normal schools to universities and the percentage of qualified primary school teachers reached 96 percent in 1960. Teachers for secondary schools historically have been graduates of secondary normal schools and universities. However, the number of graduates from both of these sources has never been adequate to meet the demand created by increased secondary school enrollments, and a significant proportion of secondary teachers prior to World War II qualified by examination.

During the last quarter of the nineteenth century foreign teachers (mostly from Great Britain, the United States, Germany, France, and the Netherlands) provided certain essential skills at the secondary and higher education levels. The numbers of Western teachers ranged from 362 in 1872 to 841 in 1897.[29] A glance at student enrollments during this period (pages 38-39) will suggest the extent of dependence on foreigners for advanced instruction. Indicating the posture of the Meiji leaders, most foreign teachers were employed in the natural sciences, humanities, and social sciences, in that descending order.

The proportion of women in the teaching force increased steadily from 1880 until 1945, and dramatically since the latter date. At the primary school level the percentage of women teachers grew from 3.1 percent in 1880 to nearly 40 percent in 1940. By the mid-1960's approximately half of the primary school teachers were women. At the secondary level, by this latter date, women comprised roughly one-fifth of the teachers.[30]

Educational Expenditures

The fiscal constraints on educational development in the early stages of modernization are usually severe. This condition could be found in Meiji Japan, requiring the national government at various times to insist on extensive local educational support and to urge the private sector to become involved in educational activites. Nevertheless, educational expenditures, except during periods of war, have been in line with the increased national attention given to education. The percentage of national income spent for public education rose from slightly under 2 percent in 1885 to over 5 percent in 1960.[31] During this same period, the percentage of total public expenditures spent for public education rose from approximately 12 percent to over 20 percent. The cumulative increase in educational expenditures from 1905 through 1960 represents an increase of over 2400 percent.

An index of educational effort may be created by relating national income spent on public education to national income per capita. On this index, Japan's educational effort compared with that of other nations has consistently been high. Except during wartime, Japan has, since 1900, expended proportionately more income for education than any European or other Asian nation. In 1960 Japan was the only nation (at least for which data were available) whose national income per capita was less than $500 which spent over 5 percent of its national income on education. Moreover, rather consistently since the late nineteenth century, the percentage of national income that Japan has spent on public education has compared favorably with that of the United States and Western European countries.

THE STRUCTURAL AND FUNCTIONAL DEVELOPMENT OF JAPAN'S CONTEMPORARY EDUCATIONAL SYSTEM

Without attempting a detailed historical analysis of the internal characteristics of the Japanese educational system — or, in other words, of the manner in which the inputs are processed — attention will now be given to the major organizational, structural, and curricular changes which have marked the development of contemporary Japanese education.

When the Meiji government established a nationally unified administration, the Ministry of Education was established as part of it. In the early attempts to develop a unified educational system, Japan showed a preference for a high degree of centralization. With the French pattern as a model, Japan was divided into eight university districts, each of which was to have one university. Each university district was to have 32 middle school districts and each middle school district was to have 210 primary school districts. Through this arrangement, each unit of 600 people was to have one primary school, and each unit of 130,000 people was to have one middle school. Although this system was not realized, administrative offices were created in the districts to encourage the development of new schools and, through the initiative of local governmental and educational officials, a fairly rapid diffusion of education did result.

After an extended period of experimentation with decentralization of educational control and financing, a fairly centralized pattern of control, with a strong Ministry of Education, became established and persisted until 1945. In good American tradition the principle of decentralization of educational control was promoted by Allied officials during the occupation period. The following comment by the United States Education Mission (a consultative group of experts) is indicative:

The principle is accepted that, for the purpose of democratic education, control of the schools should be widely dispersed rather than highly centralized at present. . . . The Ministry of Education, under the proposals of the Mission, would have important duties to perform in providing technical and professional counsel to the schools, but its direct control over local schools would be greatly curtailed. [32]

The new role of the Ministry of Education (not unlike the traditional role of the U. S. Office of Education) did not survive the occupation period. From the mid-1950's until the early 1960's, there was a steady movement by the Ministry of Education to regain its prewar power. These efforts were most clearly successful with regard to fiscal control, but even in matters of curriculum the Ministry also significantly tightened its grasp.

Structural Changes in Secondary and Higher Education

Structurally, the Japanese educational system has gone through four basic reforms. The first three structures offered primary education of varying length; in these, the students followed either of two routes — one leading to general secondary and higher education, the other providing terminal training. The last structure, established after World War II, provided essentially a single-track 6-3-3-4 pattern, with the first nine years constituting compulsory education.

The structural response to Japan's modernization may be discerned at the level of secondary and higher education. In 1880 secondary education consisted of middle schools (junior and senior divisions) and normal schools. In subsequent reorganizations secondary schools were redivided into two stages: ordinary secondary schools (five years) and higher secondary schools (two years). In 1891 girls' high schools became part of ordinary secondary education. In 1894 higher secondary schools were separated from secondary education, and later, in 1899, girls' high schools were likewise separated from the definition of secondary education. Thus, at the turn of the century secondary education included only general education for boys.

The Vocational School Order of 1899 unified various vocational school regulations and defined secondary vocational education as being "education for those who wish to be engaged in vocations such as industry and agriculture."[33] With the Vocational School Order the modern secondary school system may be said to have been completed. Three distinct categories were provided: secondary schools for the general education of boys, high schools for girls, and vocational schools.

Not until 1943 was secondary education redefined to include, on an equal footing, girls' high schools and vocational schools. In 1947 the school system was reorganized into a linear or single-track 6-3-3-4 system. The new arrangement provided for common and compulsory middle schooling as well as primary schooling. High schools, frequently coeducational, offered either general or technical courses.

The differentiation and elaboration of secondary education may be seen in the movement from a single course of general education for boys to a continually increasing number of specialized programs for both sexes. Moreover, vocational education through part-time schooling, industry-related programs, and correspondence courses likewise showed rapid growth. Until well into the 1880's industrial and vocational education existed largely outside the control of the Ministry of Education. After this time the various schools and training arrangements gradually became classified as higher or secondary education.[34]

The types and lengths of vocational programs offered in higher primary and secondary schools (institutions at both levels are typically classified as secondary education) varied considerably. For example, technical, agricultural, and commercial schools demanded a higher primary school diploma for entrance and required attendance for three years. Merchant marine and fishery schools offered more flexible programs varying in length from one to eight years. And the apprentice schools, which for entrance required only graduation from an ordinary primary school, conducted courses ranging in length from six months to four years.

It is not possible to go into detail regarding the changing nature of the vocational specializations for which training programs were available. It is significant to note, however, that between 1890 and 1954 specialization of courses within the major occupational sectors increased manyfold. During this period courses related to agriculture increased from five to more than eleven. In technology education the differentiation and specialization was even greater, with the number of courses growing from 10 to more than 26.

The new Meiji government — whose slogan was "the rapid promotion of industry, civilization and enlightenment" — was very conscious of the need to develop modern institutions of higher education. In 1869 the government combined the Shōheiko, the Kaiseijo (Institute of Western Learning), and the Igakusho (Institute of Western Medicine). In 1877 this became the Tokyo Imperial University, which remained the only full-fledged university in Japan until 1897.

Yet at the secondary and higher educational levels it was not only Western science and medicine that attracted students. Interest extended to Western literature and philosophy, Western novels, Spencerian philosophy, and later Hegelian philosophy. These interests were fanned by foreign instructors, students returning from abroad, and student discussion clubs.

A rather remarkable amount of attention was given to the sciences and mathematics in the new university. The study of Western medicine being well entrenched, courses in physiology, biology, and chemistry found a natural place in the curriculum. Other natural sciences and mathematics also came to form a significant part of the curriculum at the University of Tokyo. As a further indication of the scholarly interest in mathematics and the sciences, academic societies were formed to promote their study.

Nor were the applied sciences overlooked. Courses in civil and mechanical engineering, veterinary science, mining, metallurgy, forestry, and "practical astronomy" were offered. Scientific agriculture became so respected that in 1890 a college of agriculture was added to the University of Tokyo.

Specialized preparatory study for the universities evolved within the higher schools created by the Secondary School Order of 1886. In 1894 these institutions became independent from secondary schools, a move which eventuated in the higher schools being equated to university preparatory schools. Moreover, in addition to differentiation in terms of courses of study within the universities, a clear functional distinction developed between the graduate school, whose purpose was "investigation," and the college, whose purpose was "education."

Two further structural changes in higher education should be noted. The College Order of 1903 approved a number of national, prefectural, and private colleges, many of which had evolved from higher schools. The colleges tended to specialize in one of a variety of fields such as medicine, technology, agriculture, fine arts, music, literature, or foreign languages. Some colleges were developed only for girls and it was at this time that higher education for girls was begun.

Postwar higher education strongly reflected the vocational and social demands of a modern highly differentiated society. New departments in the applied, natural, and social sciences and newer professional fields were created. Examples of these were education, homemaking, social welfare, communication, and physical education. This period also brought a new institution of higher learning – the junior college. In 1950, influenced by American models, two- and three-year junior colleges were created as the result of a demand for less difficult and more applied higher education. These were at first viewed as a "provisional measure" and did not affect the principle of four-year university education. For a number of reasons, including the increasing affluence of the population which increased the demand for higher education, coupled with a disinclination for postponing marriage for four years, these frequently became institutions for women.

Changing Functions of the Educational System

To understand the functioning of an educational system, it is necessary, in addition to examining organizational, administrative, and structural changes, to get even closer to the procedures for transmitting new information and conveying ideas, values, and skills. It is usually not possible to determine the degree of causal relationship between the behavior of graduates and the curriculum, teaching techniques, etc., to which they were exposed while in school. That is, because of the absence of good measures, it is extremely difficult to determine what any particular type or period of schooling has contributed to a person's general or specialized knowledge. The approach typically taken, and the one taken here, is to assume certain contributions from formal educational institutions as perceived from the nature and intent of school programs, institutional objectives, etc. The discussion of the internal operation of the Japanese educational system will be limited here largely to a study of the changing curriculum at various educational levels and, to the extent feasible, to an examination of student and teacher roles.

As has already been suggested by the nature of changing educational policy, the Meiji leaders came to view the functions of lower and higher levels of education as distinctly different. While universities and other higher education institutions were expected to develop specialized leadership and were given the necessary freedom to exploit novel ideas, primary schooling, in addition to laying the foundation for further study, was expected to reinforce traditional norms and values.

The early function of the primary school system in reinforcing those trends which made for further change and societal differentiation became very important. Note, for example, the following facts about Japanese primary education during the decades following the beginnings of basic social change in Japan:

1. Even the fief schools which were still in existence in the 1860's had by this time begun to offer instruction in Western scholarship for the young. (Instructors were frequently Western missionaries.)

2. During the fifth year of Meiji (1872), a proclamation was issued dividing schooling into three levels (primary, middle, and higher), and defining a scheme for compulsory education. By 1875, 35 percent of primary-age children were in school.

3. By the early Meiji period the Western approach to arithmetic, hygiene, and science was becoming entrenched in the primary school curriculum.

4. Particularly in the early Meiji period, Japan copied the American approach to the training of teachers, emphasizing techniques common to the American normal school (Pestalozzian progressive methods, object lessons, etc.).

Yet it would be wrong to view the primary schools as that subsystem of the educational system which acted as the vanguard in the process of modernization. After the first few years of imitation of foreign practices, use of translated Western texts, and the like, new regulations dictated a more conservative role for the primary schools. From the 1880's until 1945 a major function of primary education was one of pattern maintenance — the safeguarding of certain traditional values of the people. This new function did not mean a rejection of Western science or other of the newer subjects, except where ideological conflict was assumed to be present.

It was through special courses in "morals" and by creating a school atmosphere supportive of the concepts of loyalty and filial piety that the primary schools were expected to make their contribution to national unity. The tightening of government control over teacher training and textbooks facilitated the exposure of pupils to approved moral and ethical experiences. From the time of its promulgation in 1890 until 1945, all schoolchildren memorized the Imperial Rescript on Education, which subsumed all private virtues under the general virtue of loyalty to the Emperor. During wartime periods the concepts of dignity and obedience (including the willingness to die for the Emperor) took on new intensity. But while emphases might change slightly from "love of country" to "love of Emperor" or vice versa, the goals of unity and spiritual solidarity through the idea of a nation-family remained paramount. One Japanese scholar says of the family-state ideology:

Our country is based on the family system, and indeed our whole country is one vast family; the Imperial Family our founding family, the stem family from which we are all descended. With the same sense of loving respect as the child bears toward its parents, we Japanese revere the Imperial Throne, descended in direct line through ages eternal. It is in this sense that loyalty and filial piety are one and indivisible.[35]

World War II, defeat, and the Allied occupation marked an end to the heavy emphasis in the primary schools on the training of loyal and obedient patriots. While prewar primary education was always considered in social terms — that is, in terms of the common social role expected of all citizens — the rights and needs of the individual also received attention under the radical changes brought about by the occupation. The Allies dismissed many Japanese teachers, banned State Shinto from the schools, suspended the formal morals course (shushin) from the curriculum, and supervised the rewriting of social studies texts which replaced the history and geography courses. The new social studies course was designed to promote the objective and critical study of Japanese institutions. "History was written to make students mindful not of the glorious reign of former Emperors, but of class divisions, of economic exploitation, and of struggles for freedom and equality in the face of opposition and despotism."[36]

Since the end of the occupation, some retrenchment in primary education has taken place. In 1958, for example, the Ministry of Education, which had been consistently promoting a program of recentralization of authority, reinstituted formal moral instruction. This move was apparently taken with considerable governmental and popular support, although opposed by a large proportion of teachers.[37] While this and other moves were taken to "correct the excesses" of the occupation, the extent of reaction was not such as to restore the thought-control measures of prewar days. No serious attempt was being made to resurrect a national policy, with its imperial rescript and sacred rituals.[38]

It would be more accurate to say that the new morals courses and other postoccupation changes, such as the reinstitution of history as a separate subject, reflect dissatisfaction with the highly visible restlessness and even delinquency among postwar Japanese youth. The rather modest goals of the conservative leaders, Dore suggests, are "for a world in which children will once again sing the national anthem with enthusiasm, show a proper respect for their elders, and cease to imagine that the critical application of ideas from books can compete with the accumulated wisdom of men of character."[39]

While Japanese primary education is best seen in its "pattern-maintaining" function, a much more dynamic role has historically been expected from advanced education. From the beginning of the Meiji era until 1945, the universities in particular were expected to produce a small governmental, administrative, and technical elite. The prestige given to the universities may be seen in the prefix "Imperial" attached to a selected number of national universities.

The acquaintance of the new generations of intellectuals and specialists with Western studies is well documented. Much of what passed for advanced learning at the beginning of the Meiji period took place in "institutes" and "colleges" for Western studies. Moreover, as was pointed out earlier, a significant fraction of the students in higher education during the last quarter of the nineteenth century studied in the United States or Europe. Finally, an examination of the curriculum at the University of Tokyo – the only major Japanese university until nearly the turn of the twentieth century – reveals a heavy Western orientation. By 1873, for example, a student entering this institution was required to demonstrate some competence in a modern language (typically English) and some knowledge about the modern (Western) world. During his studies at the university the student was expected to extend his learning in both of these areas.[40]

By a glance at the several school ordinances promulgated by the government in prewar days, one can easily recognize what outputs the Japanese government expected of the various types of higher schools. The imperial universities and high schools were expected to produce national and municipal officials; the higher normal schools were expected to produce leaders in the field of education; the technical and professional schools to produce business leaders and professionals in various fields; and private universities to provide leaders for private enterprises. These hierarchical distinctions among the Japanese higher schools were first promoted, and even encouraged, by the government at the time of their foundation.

An important continuing function of Japanese higher education – one frequently decried and obstructed by the government – has been the politicization of student bodies. For a time, university political activity and criticism centered on the implications of certain general policies being fostered by the ruling oligarchy. In the twentieth century, however, the universities were penetrated by waves of ideologies which totally rejected the existing social order. Socialism, democracy, fascism, and Marxism at one time or another found significant holds in the universities. From the 1920's onward, except for a hiatus during World War II, the Japanese academic world could be described politically as distinctly to the left of center. Marxism, which in prewar decades had struggled to gain influence in the face of intensive governmental countermeasures, after World War II captured most of the social sciences departments. The departments of economics and politics of nearly all major Japanese universities became heavily Marxist in orientation. The situation in the 1960's indicated that there was less ideological solidarity among scholars and students, although the center of gravity was still well to the left.

Dore offers a succinct description of the interaction of Japanese higher education and politics:

In the latter half of the Meiji period the political conflict was between the samurai oligarchy and its favored industrialists on the one hand and the rising individualistic middle class on the other. The state universities were identified with the former, the private universities with the latter. Today, the industrial middle class, grown corporate and bureaucratic rather than individualistic, has achieved political dominance, and the private universities, supported by it and retaining their allegiance to it, are well satisfied with the status quo. The state universities, on the other hand, have preserved the "devotion-to-high-principle" strain in the Confucian scholar-ruler tradition of the oligarchy and remain the home of the politically minded intellectual – now typically "alienated" and forming the nucleus of political opposition.[41]

Although the decades prior to World War II saw continued expansion and structural differentiation of Japanese higher education, a basic shift in general function had to await the sweeping postwar educational changes. Reflecting the popular demand for increased educational opportunities and a more open educational system, postwar colleges and universities lost much of their elitist character. The social composition of their student bodies became more varied, a curriculum in general education was provided, and the preparation for a number of vocational pursuits became elevated to the university level. The School Education Law as revised in

1964, indicates the dimensions of the changes; for, while higher education under the Meiji was intended to prepare a few leaders for institutions in the polity and the economy, the 1964 School Law comments: "A university may . . . aim at teaching and studying specialized academic work and training abilities that are necessary for vocations or practical life."[42]

EDUCATIONAL OUTPUT DURING JAPAN'S MODERN PERIOD

Since Japan has had a longer period of modernization than India or China, linkages between a modern educational system and other social systems may be examined in more dynamic terms. For this reason, it is felt that the space available here should be devoted to examining explicit educational-societal linkages rather than reviewing gross output (graduates or dropouts) of the system. We have selected for scrutiny here (1) educational output as it has related to economic development and (2) educational output in the structuring of social elites.

Education, Manpower, and the Economic System

The modern Japanese educational system was not developed in the light of manpower requirements formulated from explicit national educational planning. Indeed, the first manpower development policy was incorporated into the long-range economic development plans prepared by the Economic Deliberation Council in 1960. The lack of formal attempts at the national level to adjust educational inputs in terms of forecasted occupational demands does not mean, of course, that the educational system was necessarily unresponsive to changes in occupational and technological structure.

To focus for the moment only on high-level manpower, a general summary of the fit between supply and demand throughout Japan's modern period would run as follows: During the first few decades of the Meiji period, higher education expanded fairly slowly and the demand by the economy for high-level talent outran the output of the universities. However, by the end of the nineteenth century, with industrial expansion well under way, competition for "good" jobs had increased, particularly in the sciences and technology. After the first decade of the twentieth century, government manpower needs began to account for a decreasing percentage of university graduates. In 1900, for example, of 2247 graduates of Tokyo and Kyoto Imperial Universities, 68 percent had gone into government positions and 32 percent into private industry; by 1918 only 48 percent went into government and 52 percent went into private industry. This trend continued and in 1959 only 10 percent of the graduating class at Tokyo University entered government work.[43]

Shortages in technical and scientific areas persisted, and Hall reports that in 1936 "the technical schools were able to supply only 16.4 percent of the 17,630 technicians needed in industry."[44] A survey of employment rates for the years 1913 to 1956 concluded that "the curve for engineering graduates is seen to have been a relatively stable 70 to 90 per cent. . . ." The range for technical school graduates was approximately the same. Yet, in spite of the rather elitist nature of Japanese higher education, in gross terms the output of universities and colleges at times exceeded manpower needs. By the 1920's the unemployment of certain groups of intellectuals became a serious problem. This was particularly true in law, literature, and economics, where the employment rates for graduates from 1913 to 1956 ranged between 50 and 80 percent.[45]

While temporarily ameliorated by the military conscription and industrial expansion of World War II, unemployment of intellectuals again threatened in the postwar period. Passin notes:

> . . . the end of the war brought it [unemployment] back with even greater severity, and it was further exacerbated by the enormous increase in the university population resulting from the American educational reforms. The threat of unemployment and the difficulty of finding satisfactory work, in spite of years of sacrifice and effort, provided an enormous reservoir of support for socialist and anti-conservative movements.[46]

The situation has improved considerably in the 1960's. Indeed, generally, there has continued to be a shortage in the scientific, technical, and social scientific fields. An oversupply remains, however, in the humanities and, to some extent, in education. Moreover, the employment possibilities for graduates from the prestige universities still far surpass those for graduates from the lower-ranking ones.

The relation of educational output to middle- and low-level manpower demands also needs to be considered. In the early stages of economic development, production is in the primary stages of technological development and requires large masses of manual labor. The extent to which a fairly widespread base of literacy during the early decades of the Meiji period contributed to the productivity of labor is not known. Presumably literacy allowed some laborers an opportunity to become foremen in factories. Possibly some improvement in agricultural technology was transmitted to the farmer through written words. But this is largely conjecture. What literacy did as a minimum was to prepare young workers academically, and to some extent psychologically, for the training programs being established by many industrial and commercial concerns.

In the period 1860 to 1890, government factories and shipyards built their own schools, or at least installed classrooms. Persons were recruited to be trained for specific skills needed to run the existing factory or commercial establishment. Thus in the early states of modernization in Japan, in contrast to most contemporary underdeveloped nations of Asia, the training agency for middle-level skills was not within the regular school system. In this manner the painful process of adjusting academic training to the practical situation was eliminated; moreover, this policy represented an economical way to develop manpower resources. No mass technical program was provided in anticipation of future development and, as a result, little training was wasted on persons whose talents remained unutilized.

In addition to considering the manpower contributions of education, a more direct exploration of the economic value of education might be attempted. For example, Japanese scholars have formulated an estimate of the rate of return on education for the period between 1930 and 1955. In the methodology described by the Ministry of Education, the reasoning goes as follows. National income may be increased by (a) increases in physical capital, (b) increases in the size of the labor force, and (c) increases in human capabilities. Presumably the level and quality of education comprise a major component in (c) above. The question becomes how to determine which portion of the national income is attributable to increases in human capabilities and, further, how to identify and measure the educational factor.

During the period 1930 to 1955, the Japanese labor force earned 1154 billion yen more than was estimated by assuming the quality of labor to be constant. The increase of 1154 billion yen may thus be attributed to education "and other factors." Based partly on international comparisons and partly on historical judgment, the rates of return to each level of education were estimated as follows: 30 percent to primary education, 20 percent to secondary education, and 10 percent to higher education. By taking into consideration the percentage distribution of employed workers by level of school completed, it was then estimated that the average rate of return to all levels of education was 23 percent. Applying this rate to the increase in the total stock of educational capital (accumulated cost of education) invested in the labor force between 1930 and 1955 (3515 billion yen), the return on the educational investment was calculated as 808.4 billion yen. This latter figure is approximately 70 percent of the 1154 billion yen, the increase in national income not explained by the increase in physical capital and size of labor force. That is, 70 percent of the unexplained increase in the national income may be attributed to the increase in educational investment. Since the unexplained increase in national income is 37 percent of the total increase in national income, the amount of return on the educational investment represents approximately 25 percent of the total increase in national income.[47]

Comparable data on returns on educational investment are not available for India or China. However, studies in the United States and the U.S.S.R. regarding the contribution of education to the increase in national income give some credence to the figure for Japan. For the United States and the U.S.S.R. the rates of return during approximately the same time period have been estimated at 33 percent and 30 percent, respectively.[48]

Education, Social Stratification, and Elite Formation

By the latter half of the nineteenth century the transition to an occupationally based stratification system had taken place. In viewing the social background of the elites of this period, Dore distilled certain characteristics:

First, that a high proportion of the governmental, professional, and even business elites were drawn from that 6 percent of the population which was of samurai ancestry; second, that, nevertheless, within this group there was considerable mobility – a good many of those in positions of the greatest power, prestige and wealth came from the humbler ranks of the samurai class; third, that this proportion of ex-samurai in the elite was steadily declining; and fourth, that insofar as it did not decline more quickly, this was less and less because of advantages attaching to samurai ancestry as such.[49]

This new elite, which was frequently drawn from the lower samurai group, was distinguished by the possession of two nontraditional characteristics: Western education and contact with nontraditional political behavior.[50] It is the former characteristic which is of concern to us here, for our interest is focused on the social and occupational destination of the output of various kinds and levels of education and on the strength of education as a vehicle for social mobility.

A number of empirical and historical studies describe the occupational and social advantages of those who acquired schooling through Japan's modern educational system. The new industrial and commercial enterprises required technical knowledge and a pragmatic and optimistic view toward change. Dore, for example, points out that during Japan's modern century education "especially in the modernized sectors of industry" has been a chief instrument of upward mobility.[51] As the "modernized sectors" (manufacturing, transportation, etc.) attained higher priority and expanded, the demand for educated persons likewise grew.

Thus an expanding educational system, responding both to external demand and to internal pressures for growth, increasingly became the "skeletal core of the social achievement ladder. Those with elementary education went into agricultural or manual labor jobs, middle school graduates into lower-ranking white-collar positions, and university graduates into the higher administrative and executive positions."[52]

Historical data on the educational background of various elites show that higher education, especially in particular universities, is very much associated with occupational status. Asō conducted a study of elites in Japan for the years 1903, 1915, 1928, 1939, 1955, and 1964.[53] Drawing a sample from the Japanese Who's Who of these particular years, he was able to identify some significant changes in the occupational composition of the elite over this period of time. The percentage of business leaders and government officials remained relatively constant: usually over 60 percent for the former and 10 to 15 percent for the latter. Landowners, military leaders, and nobles dropped out of the sample after 1939. The postwar period was marked by a gradual advance of cultural leaders in education, art opinion, and the professions. The percentage of this elite who had graduated from universites rose from 25.5 percent in 1915 to 83 percent in 1964 passing the 50 percent mark in the early 1940's. The changing opportunities for persons achieving elite status with and without higher education are shown in Table 5.

TABLE 5   Opportunities for Entrance into the Elite Class

	1915	1928	1939	1955
Person with higher education	1 to 12	1 to 15.9	1 to 13.8	1 to 25.3
Person with less than college education	1 to 1035	1 to 1394	1 to 1420	1 to 2392

Source: Aso Makoto, *Eliito to Kyoiku* [*Elites and Education*], Tokyo: Fukumura Shuppan, 1967, Table 27, p. 235. Reported in Tsuyoshi Yoshizawa, "Higher Education and Elites in Japan," unpublished paper, Syracuse University, 1968.

Another study of Japanese elites was conducted by drawing a sample of 915 subjects from the *Asahi Yearbook* (a directory of Japanese leaders prepared by a prominent Japanese newspaper) of 1965. The great majority, 85 percent, of this sample were graduates of colleges or universities. The percentages of this elite with reference to the university they attended were as follows: Tokyo University, 38.4 percent; imperial and national universities other than Tokyo University, 26.8 percent;

private universities 17 percent; foreign schools in other countries 2 percent; and less than college education, 15 percent. Of those who had not attended a college or university, most had distinguished themselves in the arts.[54]

Analyses of specialized elite groups tend to yield the same results as investigations of general national elites. The governmental elite was examined by Passin when he calculated from a survey in 1958[55] the educational background of Class I, II, and III government officials. The percentage of Tokyo University graduates and the percentage of total national university graduates declined from Class I to Class III. The percentage of all other sources (which included private universities, senmongakko, middle schools, and other) increased from Class I to Class III. Tokyo University graduates claimed 80.5 percent of the Class I jobs and 39.9 percent of the Class III jobs. National universities almost blitzed Class I with their graduates, 97.6 percent, and they even dominated Class III, with 57.1 percent. The only other substantial source in any class was the senmongakko, which contributed 23.6 percent of the workers in Class III.

One analysis of political elites (Diet and Cabinet members)[56] reported that almost 62 percent of the 1962 House of Representatives of the Diet had completed university education. About 37 percent of this specialized elite group graduated from one of the government universities, around 23 percent from private universities, and about 2 percent from other institutions. Tokyo University graduates totaled approximately 26 percent of this Diet. The educational backgrounds of the ruling and the opposition party members of the Diet may be compared. The Liberal-Democratic Party appeared more academically oriented, with 74 percent of its members having received university education – 46 percent of whom attended government universities. Sixty-two percent of the members of the Japan Socialist Party had a university education, 21 percent of whom attended government universities.

In all studies of the educational background of Japanese elites, the graduates of national universities have an exceedingly high proportional representation.[57] Among the national universities, Tokyo University continues to hold preeminence, as shown in Table 6, which summarizes the findings of pertinent studies of elites.

By way of conclusion, during Japan's modern century, (1) higher education has become a basic requirement for entrance into the elite class,

TABLE 6 Educational Background of Japanese Elites

	Tokyo University	Other universities and colleges (excluding Tokyo)	Less than complete university or college education	Other (foreign schools, unknown, language university)
Asō study of general elite[1] 1915	14.3%	11.7%	74.5%	
1964	17.2%	65.1%	17%	
Governmental elite, 1959[2] Class I	80.5%	19.5%	0	0
Class II	67.2%	31.6%	0.9%	0.4%
Class III	39.9%	49.7%	7.0%	3.4%
Diet, 1962, House of Representatives[3]	26.4%	33.4%	38.2%	1.9%
Business elite, 1961[4]	26.2%	60.7%	9%	4.1%
Cabinet, 1962[5]	35%	55%	10%	
Yoshizawa's national elite, 1965[6]	38.4%	44.5%	14.8%	2.4%

1. For source of calculations see note 53 at end of chapter.
2. For source of calculations see note 55 at end of chapter.
3. For source of calculations see note 56 at end of chapter.
4. Calculated from Dayamonda-sha as reported in Herbert Passin, *Society and Education in Japan*, New York: Teachers College, Columbia University, 1965, p. 145.
5. Calculated from Asahi (July 18, 1962) as reported in Passin, *op. cit.*, p. 146.
6. Calculated from Tsuyoshi Yoshizawa, "Higher Education and Elites in Japan," unpublished paper, Syracuse University, 1968.

although there is still some room left for those who have acquired high competence in their vocation, (2) the elite positions in Japanese society have been largely dominated by the graduates of prestige universities, and (3) the hierarchical distinctions between prestige and non-prestige universities in both national and private schools are quite clear. As a result of these distinctions, a rigid system of university-based cliques from the more prestigious institutions has developed.[58]

SUMMARY

Using the Rostow metaphor of stages of economic growth, Japan's "take-off" stage is usually viewed as occurring in the first few decades after the Meiji Restoration (in contrast with China and India, where the "take-off" stage is viewed as beginning about 1950). Significantly, then, in Japan at least, modernization of the economy had begun before the development of an extensive system of modern education. However, by 1868 literacy and basic schooling were fairly widespread, even though an articulated school system had not yet been established.

During Japan's modern century the initial emphasis was on mass literacy. With the development of industrialization and urbanization, a more differentiated educational system evolved with a variety of levels, courses, and academic and professional roles associated with it. The development of modern Japanese education did not result, however, from explicit attempts to relate educational output to the needs of other social systems. Indeed, until the 1890's the demands for most technical manpower were met from training programs outside the formal educational system. Yet the schools and universities have increasingly performed both selection and certification functions in Japanese society. In the process of modernization, leadership in all fields except possibly the arts has been strongly associated with higher education. A university degree may never confer guaranteed elite status, but the prospects of attaining such status without an advanced education have always been slim and are growing less likely with the passage of time.

NOTES

1. Inazo Nitobe, *Bushido: The Soul of Japan.* Tokyo: Shokwdso, 1901, p. 7.

2. *Ibid.,* pp. 115-116.

3. Count Shigenobu Ōkuma, *Fifty Years of New Japan,* Vol. II. New York: Dutton, 1909, p. 125.

4. *Ibid.,* p. 126.

5. Marion J. Levy, "Some Aspects of Individualism and the Problem of Modernization in China and Japan," *Economic Development and Cultural Change,* Vol. X (April 1962), pp. 226-240.

6. *Ibid.,* p. 226.

7. *Ibid.,* p. 227.

8. Robert J. Smith, "Pre-Industrial Urbanism in Japan: A Consideration of Multiple Traditions in a Feudal Society," *Economic Development and Cultural Change,* Vol. IX (October 1960), p. 242.

9. *Ibid.,* p. 242.

10. Lerner has demonstrated that a certain level of urbanization fosters the interrelation between literacy, urbanization, mass media, and modern styles of living. Modern society is "participant" – hence the need for literacy programs and the use of mass media. However, Lerner hypothesizes that these ingredients go hand in hand with urbanization, and argues that only when 7 to 17 percent of the population resides in cities of over 50,000 inhabitants can literacy rates begin to rise significantly. Detailed data on the Japanese population and the degree of urbanization are not available. No census was taken between the beginning of the Tokugawa era and 1721. Although demographers estimate that the population growth under the Tokugawas was slight (from approximately 18 million to 25 million), there is evidence that the seventeenth century and the first part of the eighteenth century saw considerable population shift from rural to urban areas. At least by the early Meiji period Japanese urbanization had reached the 7 percent level. See Daniel Lerner, *The Passing of Traditional Society,* Glencoe, Ill.: The Free Press, 1962. See also Irene B. Taeuber, "Urbanization and Population Change in the Development of Japan," *Economic Development and Cultural Change,* Vol. IX (October, 1960), pp. 1-28.

11. Robert N. Bellah, "Values of Social Change in Modern Japan," *Asian Cultural Studies,* Vol. III (October 1962), p. 33.

12. George B. Sansom, *Japan: A Short Cultural History.* New York; Appleton-Century, 1943.

13. E. E. Hagen, "How Economic Growth Begins: A General Theory Applied to Japan," *Public Opinion Quarterly,* Vol. XXII (Fall 1958), pp. 373-390.

14. Bellah, *op. cit.,* p. 33.

15. *Ibid.,* p. 41.

16. *Ibid.,* p. 40.

17. Frank H. Lombard, *Pre-Meiji Education in Japan.* Tokyo: Kyo Bankwan, 1913, p. 90.

18. Herbert Passin, *Society and Education in Japan.* New York: Teachers College, Columbia University, 1965, p. 27.

19. *Ibid.,* p. 36. See also Chapters 8, 9, and 10 in R. P. Dore, *Education in Tokugawa Japan.* London: Routledge and Kegan Paul, 1965.

20. Marius B. Jansen (ed.), *Changing Japanese Attitudes Toward Modernization.* Princeton, N. J.: Princeton University Press, 1965, p. 101. These estimates of school attendance agree roughly with those of R. P. Dore. See Appendix I of *Education in Tokugawa Japan.*

21. Jansen, *op. cit.,* p. 102.

22. An episode which illustrates the practical ends being sought through education involved Arinori Mori, the first Japanese diplomatic representative to the United States. In 1871, Mori sent a letter to prominent Americans, asking their advice on the possible effects of Japanese education on the material prosperity of the country, its commerce, agricultural and industrial interests, etc. David Murray, of Rutgers University, one of the 13 Americans who answered Mori's letter, accepted an invitation to serve as special adviser to the Japanese Ministry of Education from 1873 to 1879.

23. The concern for unity of national thought and for moral education supportive of such unity has been pervasive in the history of Japanese education down to the present day. See Don Adams, "Rebirth of Moral Education in Japan," *Comparative Education Review,* Vol. IV (June 1960), pp. 61-64; Mamoru Oshiba, "Moral Education in Japan," *The School Review* (Summer 1961), pp. 227-244; Michiya Shimbori, "A Historical and Social Note on Moral Education in Japan," *Comparative Education Review,* Vol. IV (October 1960), pp. 97-101. Attention will be given later to the changing content of explicit moral instruction, but to some extent the dualistic view of the teaching of morality and national unity established under Mori persisted until World War II, and, some would say, has had a rebirth through new morals courses introduced after the Allied occupation.

24. The school attendance rate is the ratio of the number of children attending school to the total number of school-age children. The rate of classroom attendance is the ratio of average daily attendance to the total number of school age children.

25. Japanese National Commission for UNESCO (ed.), *The Role of Education in the Social and Economic Development of Japan.* Tokyo: Ministry of Education, 1966, pp. 48-66.

26. *Ibid.,* p. 93.

27. *Ibid.,* pp. 91-92.

28. *Ibid.,* p. 19.

29. *Ibid.,* p. 114.

30. *Ibid.,* pp. 101-103.

31. Japan, Ministry of Education, *Japan's Growth and Education.* Tokyo: Ministry of Education, 1962, p. 113.

32. *Report of the United States Education Mission to Japan.* Washington, D. C.: U. S. Government Printing Office, 1946, p. 59.

33. Japanese National Commission for UNESCO, *op. cit.,* p. 73.

34. Under the leadership of the Ministry of Industry a technical school was established in 1871 which consisted of six divisions: civil engineering, mechanical

engineering, electrical communications, architecture, applied chemistry and metallurgy, and mining engineering. When this school started, the staff was almost entirely foreign, including 41 British, 7 Italians, and 1 French. By 1885, when this technical school was closed, it had produced more than 200 engineers who became the pioneers in the nation's industrialization.

35. Ishida Takeshi, *Kindai Nihon Seiji Kōzō no KenKyū,* 1956, p. 23. Quoted in R. P. Dore, "Education: Japan," in Robert E. Ward and Dankwart A. Rustow (eds.), *Political Modernization in Japan and Turkey,* Princeton, N. J.: Princeton University Press, 1964, p. 193.

36. *Ibid.,* p. 196. For detailed descriptions of the functioning of schools in contemporary Japanese communities, see John Calhoun Singleton, *Nichu, A Japanese School,* New York: Holt, Rinehart and Winston, 1967; and Theodore Brameld, *Japan: Culture, Education and Change in Two Communities,* New York: Holt, Rinehart and Winston, 1968.

37. The teachers, who had since 1945 become organized into a powerful trade union, tended to resist all moves to centralize more authority in the Ministry of Education. One study concludes that primary school teachers at least satisfactorily verbalized "reform-consistent" attitudes such as "valuing pupil interests and purposes, emphasis upon inquiry, 'permissiveness' in pupil-control, willingness to encourage pupil participation in education, viewing subject as having instrumental value (rather than disciplinary), willingness to recognize and provide for individual differences in ability, and optimism about pupil capactiy for self-responsibility." Arthur P. Coledarci, "The Professional Attitudes of Japanese Teachers," *Journal of Educational Research,* Vol. LII (May 1959), pp. 323-324.

38. For a comparison of the Imperial Rescript of 1890 and post-World War II reforms, see Ronald S. Anderson, *Japan: Three Epochs of Modern Education,* Washington, D. C.: U. S. Office of Education, 1959.

39. Dore, in Ward and Rustow, *op. cit.,* p. 197.

40. Western influence came about not only through curriculum changes and because of the presence of Western instructors, but also as a result of a large advisory cadre of Europeans and Americans attached directly to the national government. For example, the Ministry of Industry employed 749 foreigners as technical advisers during the period between 1871 and 1885. These advisers offered specialized assistance in such fields as railway transportation, engineering, shipbuilding and operation, mining, lighthouse construction and operation, and telegraph services. Between 1872 and 1880, about 42 percent of the total expenditures of the Ministry of Industry was devoted to the salaries of these foreign advisers.

41. Dore, in Ward and Rustow, *op. cit.,* pp. 186-187.

42. Japanese Commission for UNESCO, *op. cit.,* p. 91.

43. Passin, *op. cit.,* p. 137.

44. Robert K. Hall, *Education in the New Japan.* New Haven: Yale University Press, 1949, p. 228.

45. Japan, Ministry of Education, *Demand and Supply for University Graduates.* Tokyo: Ministry of Education, 1958, p. 18.

46. Passin, *op. cit.,* p. 139.

47. Japan, Ministry of Education, *Japan's Growth and Education,* pp. 146-148.

48. Seeing its economic gains threatened by a high rate of population growth, Japan

after World War II embarked on a vigorous and successful program of family planning and fertility control. Since most of the educational efforts in this regard took place outside the formal system of education, they will not be examined here. It should be noted, however, that the attitudes toward family size and toward the practice of birth control shifted significantly, and by 1960 Japan's birthrate (17.2 per 1000) was lower than that of any other Asian nation and well below the median rate among European nations.

49. R. P. Dore, "Mobility, Equality and Individuation in Modern Japan," in R. P. Dore (ed.), *Aspects of Social Change in Modern Japan,* Princeton, N. J.: Princeton University Press, 1967, p. 114.

50. Bernard Silberman, *Ministers of Modernization: Elite Mobility in the Meiji Restoration, 1868-1873.* Tucson: University of Arizona Press, 1964.

51. Dore, *op. cit.,* pp. 202-203. Original source: *Nihon Sha Kai Gakkai Chōsa Iinkai, Nihon Shakkai no Kaiso-Teki Kōzō,* 1958, p. 152.

52. Passin, *op. cit.,* p. 122.

53. Asō Makoto, *Eliito to Kyoiku [Elites and Education].* Tokyo: Fukumara Shuppan, 1967. Reported in Tsuyoshi Yoshizawa, "Higher Education and Elites in Japan," unpublished paper, Syracuse University, 1968.

54. Yoshizawa, *op. cit.*

55. Calculated from *Kakushochō Kachō-kyu Ijō no Gakureki, Shikaku, oyobi Keireki [The Education, Qualifications, and Records of Branch Chiefs and Above in All Departments and Bureaus],* mimeographed report of survey by the Japanese Government, June 1959. Reported in Passin, *op. cit.,* p. 129.

56. Nihon Seikei Shimbunsha, *Koklai Binran 37 [Register of the National Diet, 1962].* Tokyo, 1962, pp. 99-130. Reported in Passin, *op. cit.,* p. 145.

57. One way in which the prestige of a university is translated into employment advantage to its graduates is through the institution of *batsu.* Passin defined *batsu* as "intimate, informal groups based on personal loyalties that span many fields from the university into business, the professional world, government, and politics. A person without a batsu faces Japanese society unsupported, with no one to sponsor him or to help him in times of crisis. It is one's batsu that opens the closed doors. Characteristically, each batsu has its own sphere of influence, which it guards jealously against outsiders and opens only to its intimates. Universities form their own batsu, and even individual departments within the university may have batsu on their own." Passin, *op. cit.,* p. 125.

58. If one were to extend the examination of the educational backgrounds of elites to schooling at the secondary level, he would find (1) that national and municipal high schools are more successful in getting students into national and graduate universities than are private schools, (2) that the size of the communities in which the schools are located is important, with the graduates of schools in larger cities having better opportunities to enter prestigious universities, and (3) that the more successful high schools tend to draw students from the high socioeconomic groups.

SELECTED READINGS

Anderson, Ronald S., *Japan: Three Epochs of Modern Education.* Washington, D. C.: U. S. Office of Education, 1959.

Brameld, Theodore, *Focus on Japan: Culture and Education of Two*

Communities in Flux. San Francisco, Toronto, and London: Holt, Rinehart and Winston, 1968.

Dore, R. P., *Education in Tokugawa Japan.* London: Routledge and Kegan Paul, 1965.

Hall, Robert K., *Education for the New Japan.* New Haven: Yale University Press, 1949.

Kato, M., "Organization of Education in Japan," *International Review of Education,* Vol. XIV (1968), No. 1, pp. 85-91.

Ministry of Education, *Japan's Growth and Education.* Tokyo: Ministry of Education, 1962.

Passin, Herbert, *Society and Education in Japan.* New York: Teachers College, Columbia University, 1965.

Singleton, John, "Urban-Rural Comparisons in Japanese Education," *International Review of Education,* Vol. XIII (1967), No. 4, pp. 470-482.

UNESCO, Japanese National Commission for (ed.), *The Role of Education in the Social and Economic Development of Japan.* Tokyo: Ministry of Education, 1966.

chapter three
india

India boasts one of the oldest cultures of the world, at one time rivaling China as the most advanced of all Asian nations in literature and the arts. Indian civilization is usually traced to 4000 B.C. India, the Fertile Crescent area, and China formed the three great cultural hubs from which radiated many of the dominating patterns of Asian ideological and social traditions. It was during the two millenia B.C. that the great philosophic-religious Vedic literature and the speculative and interpretive treatises it inspired were born. The Vedas, Upanishads, and the great epic poems *Mahabharata* and *Ramayana* not only reflected the sophisticated taste of a few Indians with the advantages of wealth and birth, but also embodied a philosophy and religious ethos which were widely accepted among the Indian people. Found in the Vedas, for example, is the belief that beyond the experiential world and beyond the pantheon of naturalistic gods lies a unifying principle or spirit, Brahma. The individual self, the Atman, is related to the Brahma, for the "Universe is Brahma, but the Brahma is the Atman." There is thus a unity among all living things – a view reminiscent of certain other Asian philosophies but sharply in contrast with the dualistic views common in Western tradition. Shils has noted that the need to experience this identity, this quest for a unity of the individual and the universal, remains a significant force among Indian intellectuals today.[1]

The religio-social system called Hinduism is usually associated with the Vedas, thus making these writings a body of revealed and absolute truths the authority of which is still recognized in contemporary India. More than a religious dogma, Hinduism has been a way of life with social, economic, and political implications for the majority of the Indian population:

Hinduism has viewed the worldly existence and its entrappings as unimportant in the soul's journey to its ultimate goal of nirvana (a term originating with Buddha) in which individuality is lost in a mystical union with Brahma. A Hindu, to achieve nirvana, or nonbeing, must perform the secular duties and religious rituals appropriate to him in his station of life, but even more important must engage in meditation so that his thought may be purified of worldly rewards through successive reincarnation in the bodies of persons in higher social positions as it progresses toward its ultimate goal. Thus Hinduism has tended to produce a society tinged with fatalism in which the status of the individual is considered the result of his behavior in previous lives.[2]

The Hindu ideal may be found in the scriptual concept of *dharma,* or sacred duty. According to this concept each person should faithfully attempt to fulfill the obligation of his position in life. He should not attempt to improve his station, since it is the result of merit or demerit accumulated by his soul in previous existences and is meant to persist for a lifetime.

Associated with Hinduism, but also reflecting a desire to maintain cultural stability in the face of successive invasions by different peoples, is the caste system. The origins of caste appear to be related both to occupations and to color. Within the Indo-Aryan tribes, caste cleavages were defined occupationally, while color prejudice was practiced between the Indo-Aryan and other peoples. Wallbank suggests that in modern times all castes may be placed in three broad categories. The first group includes the Brahmans; the Rajput clans (the declared representatives of the ancient

Kshatriyas), and the traders, who claim descent from the Vaisyas; all of these constitute the twice-born. In the second group are the traditional Sudra castes that are now all lumped together as not twice-born. At the bottom are the untouchables, also known as the "depressed classes" or "scheduled castes."[3]

Each social category is fixed in its respective rank, and presumably those in one do not compete with those in others. Thus the Brahmans traditionally were the scholars and priests; the Kshatriyas were the warriors and rulers; the Vaisyas were the tradesmen; and the Sudras (or Shudras) were the laborers and cultivators. Within village society, the jatis (a subcaste representing the family and status grouping a villager inherits) rather than the broad caste became the main social unit.

Buddhism, India's second religio-social system, which arose during the sixth century B.C., had for a time a democratizing influence on Indian society. Guatama Sakyamuni, later known as the Buddha, taught that man's troubles stem from his inability to discipline himself against desire for material advantages. He could point to the ostentation of the aristocratic Hindus and the opulence of Indian merchants to demonstrate that wealth did not necessarily bring happiness and peace in its wake. Rather, the route to nirvana was to be found by following a course of carefully disciplined moral conduct, culminating in the life of concentration and meditation led by a Buddhist monk. Buddhism as exported to East and Southeast Asia has remained a potent force to this day. However, in India, by the twelfth century Buddhism was absorbed into the mainstream of Hinduism. It has contributed a number of concepts such as *ahimsa,* or love and nonviolence toward all living things, yet the absorption of Buddhism by Hinduism cannot be viewed as the wedding of two distinctly different religions. As has been noted:

It cannot be said that the most notable features of the Buddhist speculation – its "rationalism" (. . . antipathy to every kind of ritualism and superstition), its atheism (that is, its negation of a God creator and providence), its high morality, its pessimism, its anti-caste tendency, its mildness and humanity, and so on – are specifically Buddhist. . . . In short Buddhism is only the "buddhised" aspect of contemporaneous Hinduism.[4]

In spite of successful ideological penetration by Buddhism and of military conquests by a number of alien armies, the Indian subcontinent did not achieve unification until its domination by the Moslems in the eleventh century A.D. In contrast to previous invaders of India, and largely because of the influence of Islam, which was as much an all-encompassing way of life as was Hinduism, the Moslems refused to be absorbed by the Hindu-dominated society. Although these communities remained separate, they exerted a great deal of influence on each other. During the succeeding seven centuries, Islamic culture and institutions became infused into every major part of society. At times there were group conversions to Islam, frequently by those who sought political favor or who were disenchanted with the restrictions under Brahmanism. In contrast, for example, with the caste system sanctified by Hinduism, Islam expounded the principle of equality for all (that is, all males). Yet in spite of occasional conversions and some intellectual rapprochement among Hindu and Muslim scholars, there was no fusion or synthesis between the two groups. And while in the matters of everyday living they became accommodated to each other, a deep tension persisted between the two ways of life.

HINDU AND MUSLIM LEGACIES IN EDUCATION[5]

Under Hinduism, a formal education evolved for upper-caste boys which was designed to develop moral character through the study of Vedic literature and other religious writings. The common pattern of education, which might be viewed as representing a later phase of the second stage of educational differentiation (see Chapter One), was a private tutorial arrangement under the direction of gurus or masters — a class of men who originally had performed prescribed religious rites and who were frequently of the Brahman caste. A guru would accept a certain number of students into his household where they would serve him, beg alms (as a form of moral training), and engage in academic studies in which great emphasis was put on oral work and memorization. The close bond between student and teacher was the key to successful education.

The educational function, although separated from the family, was not differentiated from religious instruction. The acceptance of a boy by a guru took place only after religious training, and the primary objective of the teachings was the development of self-discipline and the acquisition of religious knowledge. Indeed, the educational process was envisioned as a spiritual birth. Yet at an early date another type of educational institution arose to satisfy the needs of advanced students. Bands of students in ancient India, much like those of medieval Europe, wandered through the countryside to study, listen, and debate at the feet of learned scholars. Such arrangements, as they became more institutionalized, were called academies, debating circles, or sometimes "universities." The large universities were open to all scholars, and studies were not assigned according to caste. By the fourth century B.C. these universities, particularly at Taxila and Benares, had gained distinction as great centers of learning and were attended by students from all over Asia. For the vast majority of the population, of course, there was no formal instruction.

Yet some education developed outside the main Hindu tradition. At times, particularly during the first few centuries A.D., princes, noblemen, and merchants acquired sufficient power and wealth to develop an education for their young which in content and purpose was different from the traditional pattern. The education provided was a more practical, worldly type and included such areas as administration, warfare, trading, construction, and medicine. Since these specializations required teachers outside the Brahmanic tradition, the monopoly of the Brahmans over all education was fractured, if not broken, and a new educated upper stratum began to emerge.[6]

The Muslim legacy to Indian education was considerable in terms of both the development of new educational institutions and the provision of an ethos supportive of planning. Among the precepts from the Holy Koran are: "Acquisition of knowledge is incumbent upon all the faithful, men as well as women"; and "knowledge should be sought from the cradle to the grave." The Muslim contributions to the world's knowledge in mathematics, science, and medicine are well known and need not be described here. What is most important in the context of Indian modernization was the impetus for new educational activities generated under Muslim rule.

Islamic education and religion, which entered India as early as the tenth century A.D. with the Muslim invasions, were closely related, and formal schooling took place largely in or near the mosques. Although Islam, unlike the Brahmanic and Buddhist religious systems, recognizes no priestly class, the individual in charge of the mosque also controlled the schools, and religious endowments provided financial support. Schools at the lower level were known as *maktabs,* while those of the more advanced stages were called *madrasas.* The curriculum at the "elementary" level consisted of religious instruction and the "three R's." At the "secondary" level, in addition to further religious studies, arithmetic, algebra, economics, administration, physics, and history were also taught. Yet, basically, the Muslim culture was an elite culture and accounts of accomplishments in the field of popular education believed by many contemporary scholars to be exaggerations.[7]

At the higher educational level, there developed a literary tradition for elite groups; however, at the lower levels those Muslim children who did attend school concentrated mainly on learning to recite the Koran. At all levels formal educational activities were limited largely to males. Thus education, while further institutionalized and possibly expanded under Muslim rule, never developed into a system separate from the religious system, for three reasons: (1) the control and support of educational endeavors were linked to the mosque; (2) education and learning were encouraged, indeed in theory were obligatory, for religious ends; and (3) as was the case with Buddhist and Hindu educational efforts, the teachers were religious leaders. It could be said that at the beginning of the period of extensive cultural contact with the West, India was still struggling to enter the third stage of educational differentiation.

THE IMPACT OF BRITISH COLONIALISM

Although India had been subject to several invasions throughout its history, none had effects as pervasive as those resulting from its cultural exchanges with European nations. During the sixteenth and seventeenth centuries a number of European trading companies began negotiating with Indian princes and merchants and eventually, after "an amazing story of courage, audacity, and often downright chicanery," the British East India Company emerged not only as the major trading company, but also as political sovereign of India.

The Company, however, was slow to concern itself seriously in educational matters. Moreover, since both of the great traditions of scholarship, Hindu and Muslim, had by the eighteenth century lost their vitality, the initial involvement in education by the East India Company, as Ashby points out, was merely to "fan the embers of these indigenous systems."[8] Thus under Company leadership a new madrasa was formed in 1781, and ten years later a comparable institution was created to further the study of the culture of the Hindus.

It was the Western missionaries, not the secular authorities, who made the only serious attempts to promote education in India prior to the nineteenth century. At times this effort was obstructed by the East India Company. However, the missionaries succeeded, supported occasionally by princely rulers, in establishing schools, spreading literacy, and generally improving popular education.[9] Myrdal points out that the Protestant missionaries were from lower social strata while the British colonial officials were largely from the upper class, and suggests that such class differences might have affected their relationships. He further comments.: "It is interesting to speculate on how the history of Indian education might have turned out if India had been colonized and ruled by a Catholic country – or, in more recent times, if the British had been a nation early committed to the ideals of popular government and popular education at home, as were the Americans."[10]

By the early nineteenth century interest in education had grown considerably among both the British officials and the Indian upper strata. With the need to develop explicit policy regarding the kind of education to be supported, an important controversy emerged. While broad in scope and subtle in detail, the controversy usually has been simplified and described in terms of "Orientalist" versus "Western" learning. Missionaries, scholars, government officials, and literary figures all became involved and stood up to be counted on one or the other side of the issue. From England came pressure from the utilitarians and from the evangelical movements in support of an education drawing from European accomplishments. Within India, European missionaries and a few cosmopolitan Brahmans also argued against the exclusive emphasis on traditional learning. As early as 1792 attempts were made by a Member of Parliament to introduce into the charter of the East India Company specific provisions for the encouragement of the work of missionaries and schoolmasters in India. In opposition to this proposal, the directors of the Company argued for a hands-off policy and suggested that the Hindus "... had as good a system of faith and of morals as most people. ... " Moreover, one Member of Parliament is said to have remarked, "we. . . lost our colonies in America by importing our education there; we need not do so in India, too."[11]

While an entrepreneurial desire not to rock the boat and therefore risk spoiling a good thing may be read into the position of the British East India Company, a more academic issue was also involved. Competing claims as to the advantages of Oriental literature and language as compared with the European heritage taught through the medium of English were widely discussed. Several scholars and officials (mostly Englishmen) insisted that "a policy of making 'a whole people dependent upon a remote and unknown country for all their ideas and for the very words in which to clothe them' must 'degrade their character, depress their energies, and render them incapable of aspiring to any intellectual distinction.' "[12]

Slowly, however, the proponents of Western learning won the day. The *coup de grace* to the Orientalists was delivered by Macaulay who, in a famous Minute, argued that on the basis of utility and providing access to a culture he deemed superior, Engligh language and literature had to form the core of instruction in higher education. Macaulay further recommended that no support be given to indigenous studies and that the printing of Sanskrit and Arabic books cease. Nor was this policy in conflict with the views of most Indian intellectuals. As one Indian writer observes, "The curious fact is that the Orientalists were almost all Englishmen in the service of the Company, whereas all Indians of repute were Anglicists."[13] And, as Ashby notes, to many Indian scholars, "English was deemed more significant than Sanskrit; Skakespeare more relevant than the Mahabharata, the teaching of Milton and Burke more appropriate than the teaching of Buddha."[14]

The policy of anglicization in Indian education has been criticized from many quarters. Rather naturally anthropologists and social historians have found Macaulay's argument for "a class of persons, Indian in blood and color, but English in taste, in opinions, in morals and in intellect" lacking in cultural sensitivity and humanistically distasteful. Yet many of these criticisms fail to recognize the positive contributions of the English system of education as an agent of modernization. As Macaulay had wished, institutions patterned after the English did indeed help create a new class "Indian in blood and color but English in taste." And, to be sure, this class was, as all privileged classes before them, separated from the masses. Yet this new class was distinct in many ways. First, it was unified by a common language which allowed communication between educated men from all parts of India. Second, this class has at least partial access to information concerning the industrializing nations of Western Europe, particularly the nature of European governments and the social thought supportive of social change. Third, from the group of Indians educated in the English traditions came the most ardent nationalists, persons concerned not with the maintenance of privilege but with the welfare of a nation and all of its peoples. But the English educational system did even more. In the relatively undifferentiated social structure of early India, education was thoroughly embedded in the familial-religious systems. With the introduction of, and reward for, new secular activities and with recruitment into civil roles becoming increasingly achievement oriented, the allocation and certification functions of education became more pronounced. This was particularly true with regard to government service. Literacy had traditionally had status, for it was the key to sacred Hindu scriptures and to the classic literature. Under the British East India Trading Company and later under the British Government, the civil service, long prestigious in India, gradually opened its doors to those Indians who were educationally and intellectually qualified.

The first systematic and comprehensive statement of English educational policy in India is found in the Educational Despatch of 1854. The Despatch, which signified, among other things, a long leap into the third stage of educational differentiation, called for the establishment of a degree-granting university. Modeled after the University of London, the first universities were essentially examining institutions for affiliated colleges rather than teaching intitutions. The new universities were particularly well received by Indian middle classes (especially by Hindus, for the Muslim educational system was still well entrenched), who were lured by the prospects of administrative positions. In 1857 the Indian universities enrolled 200 students; however, by 1882 the enrollment had grown to approximately 4000. The main functions of the universities may be identified as (1) the transmission of European culture and (2) selection for government employment. Reflecting these functions and also following what has been called the concept of "lagging emulation," Indian students flocked to the faculties of arts and law; the resulting popularity of these areas persists and causes much concern to the present day.[15]

Both the Educational Despatch of 1854 and the Hunter Commission of 1882 recommended the promotion of literacy and primary education. Yet because of fiscal constraints on government action and a lack of popular demand, such proposals were not implemented and the spread of popular education had to await the pressure of the nationalist movement of the twentieth century.

The last century of the colonial period saw a rapid expansion of facilities for secondary education. At the secondary level English was appropriately the language of instruction, since the function of the secondary schools was to prepare students for government employ or for further education. The colonial government, again in good English tradition, subsidized private secondary education instead of founding a system of public schools. With the growing strength and prestige of universities during the later half of the nineteenth century, secondary schools came to be dominated, in curriculum, teaching methods, and standards, by university entrance examinations.

There were, however, several qualitative and quantitative limitations in education under the British rule. First, for a variety of reasons, education exported to a colony tends to be of a lower quality and less flexible than that found in the home nation – a generalization supported by the case of India. Second, because of the limitations of curricula and the lack of experience on the part of the British instructors, little intellectual effort was exerted on local (in contrast to British or European) problems. Third, English higher education in the nineteenth and early twentieth centuries was neither fully responsive to, nor supportive of, the modernizing (and particularly industrializing) forces at home. For example, following the International Exhibition of 1867 at which British products received few rewards, a government committee found education defective at all levels in Britain in that it failed to train adequately scientists, technologists, and industrial managers. Finally, because of the priority given to the creation of an educated class of Indians, English effort in education in India was limited almost exclusively to higher education. Furthering the cause of popular education was left to the missionaries, whose resources were far from equal to the magnitude of the task. The result of this policy may be seen in the fact that at the end of the colonial period the literacy rate in India was the lowest in South Asia.

British rule, in a variety of ways, contributed much of the impetus for contemporary India's drive toward modernization. A new administrative and judicial system reduced the importance of law by custom. The introduction of the British concept of civil liberty stimulated new political aims. As has been commented, "John Locke and John Stuart Mill provided more effective standards of government for educated South Asians than did the Vedas, the Koran, or the Tripitaka."[16] New modes of education,

trade, and production accompanied the new style of government. Thu.
structural changes in society, with foreigners of secular taste at the top,
the spread of universalistic norms in educational and occupational
selection, a limited expression of the spirit of industrialism and some
tentative applications of technology in commerce and manufacturing, all
become superimposed on the traditional Indian cultural pattern.

THE BEGINNINGS OF NATIONAL EDUCATION

The British Government had limited aims for the educational system it
provided India. The system was designed to teach the English language and
to familiarize selected Indian students with certain aspects of Western
learning. In general, the preservation and cultivation of Indian culture was
not promoted, although some attention was given to classical languages.
Education was not viewed as instrument for social reform or for the
deepening of national consciousness.

Until British rule the ascriptive ranking of social groups and the
reinforcing social organization were highly visible. However, the processes
of secularization and differentiation fostered throughout the colonial
period somewhat weakened existing stratification patterns and provided
the beginnings of an organizational arrangement designed to accomplish
the functions of society on a secular rather than a religious basis. The
Indian elite transformed themselves in terms of British values of humanity
and rationality by attending the new educational institutions, entering
professional and bureaucratic jobs, and engaging in commerce in the towns
and cities.

It was a segment of this Westernized, secularized, Indian elite, in
combination with more traditional Indian scholars, that provided
leadership for an abortive nationalist movement in education early in the
twentieth century. The gap has so widened between the achievements of
education under the British and the aspirations of the nationalists as to
stimulate demand for a truly "national" education. The new educational
system was to be Indian in every respect. The ancient culture, traditions,
ideals, and religions would find a place in the curriculum, and modern
Indian languages would replace English as the language of instruction. But
this was not merely a movement to herald and romanticize Indian
accomplishments, for one of the first aims of national education was to

productive capacities of its citizens."[17] And to all of these
tually were added suggestions for compulsory education and
ne for "basic education."

Although a number of "national" schools were actually created in the
second and third decades of the twentieth century, the movement
foundered on financial and administrative obstacles. In a revised order of
priorities the nationalists called for political freedom as the first step
toward the achievement of their other targets. Regarding education, they
concluded: "A national system of education . . . must be provided for,
financed and controlled by the nation, and in performing that function,
the nation must be represented by the 'state.' "[18]

The educational system visualized by the nationalists, albeit in rather
vague form, was perhaps the first proposal for a modern educational
system for India. At least the educational aspirations articulated by the
nationalists were much in keeping with what has been described as the
fourth level of educational differentiation (see Chapter One). The
proposed educational system would not be tied to a small power-wielding
group but, reflecting universalistic norms, would serve the entire society.
The implication follows that the national curriculum would encompass a
wide variety of modern learnings.[19]

INPUTS TO THE CONTEMPORARY EDUCATIONAL SYSTEM

Within the context of a systems approach the social and cultural milieus
are viewed as the sources of major inputs for the educational system. From
the cultural heritage of a people and the fabric of their society are derived
the objectives, norms, and roles which give form and direction to the
educational system. This section, then, will focus on contemporary India,
on the articulated national aspirations and goals, the nature of social and
cultural change, the magnitude of teacher and student inputs, and the
contemporary national problems which particularly affect and constrain
the educational system.

Since independence in 1947, the government of India has assumed
wide economic and social responsibilities in attempting to provide the
security of an adequate standard of living for its people. The
acknowledgment of these responsibilities was embodied in the Indian
Constitution in the form of goals of justice, liberty, equality, and

fraternity for all, and in the priority role given to national economic development viewed as a means toward social well-being.

There is, of course, always some distance between the general, frequently politically inspired, national goals and the effective subsystem or institutional objectives. Social justice, economic growth, and national integration articulated at a societal level may not offer explicit guidelines for educational policy. Or to place the focus differently, the explicit educational policy necessary to support such general goals may be a matter of considerable controversy. Thus educators may wholeheartedly endorse the recognized national goals while disagreeing vehemently on the appropriate educational changes. For example, should social justice mean equal opportunity for education for all Indian children and youth? And what should be the nature of the educational opportunities for adults? Should equal opportunity mean simply free education? Or should there be compensatory education for the children of such "culturally deprived" groups as the Scheduled Castes? Should social justice imply the same education for all, or, for example, should rural children receive an education substantively different from that received by urban children?

Controversies over explicit educational policies are to be expected, and in a democratic society such as India, where the locus of educational policy rests extensively with the states, clear and unequivocal answers to such questions are not to be expected. Nevertheless, consensus among national leaders and policymakers regarding certain major directions for education does exist. First, the goal of economic growth and full employment is overriding. Both the level of national income and the rate of growth are seen as most unsatisfactory, and improvement in these areas is considered fundamental to other social ends.

India is classified as an economically underdeveloped nation. Using the common indicator of economic development, gross national product per capita, India ranks in the lower fifth of the Asian nations and in the lower sixth of the nations of the world. During the first two Five Year Plans, India achieved considerable economic growth. However, since the beginning of the Third Five Year Plan, the rate of economic growth has slowed down. The target for annual growth in national income was five percent under the Third Five Year Plan; the actual growth, however, was only two to three percent per year — barely sufficient to keep up with the rate of population growth.[20]

Several questions need to be raised in view of the decelarated rate of economic growth. Can the blame be placed mainly with the industrial or the agricultural sector? What has been the extent of population growth as an inhibiting factor? And, most significantly for our purposes, to what extent were human resources generally, and the educational system specifically, inhibiting factors? What are the prospects of injecting new vigor into the Fourth Five Year Plan, which aims at an ultimate target of a minimum per capita income of 100 rupees per month per family by 1975-1976? This level of income is seen as "sufficient to meet the essential food, clothing, housing, education, and health requirements of *every* person in India by that date."[21]

The prime means to the end of economic growth has been identified in the Five Year Plans as the development of India's human resources, and through such development the educational system becomes a major link with the economy. This line of reasoning has led to the belief that the educational system, at least at the postprimary level, in general should be related to manpower needs, and each of the series of national Five Year Plans produced by the Planning Commission has devoted a chapter to education. While each Plan purports to give attention to the ultimate goals of a "better intellectual and cultural life" and "deeper social values," the emphasis in both analysis of needs and expenditure of funds is on economic productivity. Curiously, the Five Year Plans have been imprecise if not ambivalent in their recommendations for adjustments in educational input to meet manpower needs. The First Plan (1950-1955) recommended maintaining the existing ratio of students enrolled in secondary education to the number enrolled at the primary level (about 22/100). The Second Plan (1956-1961) called for further expansion of secondary education in both academic and vocational courses but established no targets for university education. The Third Plan (1962-1967) called for the extension and improvement of the teaching of science but offered no specific suggestions as to how enrollments might be adjusted in keeping with anticipated manpower needs. The Fourth Plan has been somewhat more explicit, as exemplified by its recommendations designed to foster terminal vocational courses at both the secondary and university levels.[22]

Table 7 suggests something of the magnitude of educational growth during the first two decades after independence. The discrepancies between the goals articulated and the resources allocated, e.g., the inputs in terms of expenditures and enrollments, need to be accounted for. First, it appears that in spite of the national interest in relating educational inputs to manpower priorities, the administrative mechanism needed at the center and at the state levels to assist in this direction has not been present. For example, most of the institutions of higher education are not fully under public control. Second, the pressures of social demand in the uncontrolled expansion at the secondary and higher education levels are exceedingly great and must be reckoned with in a democratic society such as India. Finally, not until the early 1960's were extensive manpower surveys undertaken which identified the educational attainment of workers in the various sectors. Until this time there was little in the way of available data from which projections in needed educational manpower could be made.[23]

TABLE 7   Enrollment Ratio Targets of India's Five Year Plans

| | | Grades | |
Year	I-V	VI-VIII	IX-XI
		Enrollment ratio	
1951 base[1]	40.0	10.0[2]	10.0[2]
1956 target[1]	60.0	15.0[2]	15.0[2]
1956 base[3]	51.0	19.2	9.4
1961 target[3]	62.7	22.5	11.7
1961 base[4]	61.1	22.8	11.5
1966 target[4]	76.4	28.6	15.6
		Percentage increase	
1951-56[1]	50.0	50.0	50.0
1956-61[3]	22.9	17.2	24.5
1961-66[4]	25.0	25.4	35.7

Adapted from John A. Laska, *Planning and Educational Development in India,* New York: Teachers College Press, 1968, p. 701.

1. First Five Year Plan.
2. Combined figure for both middle and high school levels.
3. Second Five Year Plan.
4. Third Five Year Plan.

In the final analysis, the increasing interest on the part of the Indian government and Indian educators in better adapting the educational system to economic goals has served not so much to adjust specifically the course of study and the number of entrants to the various levels as to bring under criticism certain existing educational conditions. The educational tradition which in the past had been articulated by poets, philosophers, and priests and which in more contemporary times even at best has meant broad liberal learning of questionable quality is being rejected by a growing body of Indian leaders. Clearly the denigration of manual labor and technical pursuits and aspirations for white-collar work persist among Indian students. Nevertheless, the monetary, and, to a degree, the social, rewards for vocational and technical employment have become increasingly visible. Indeed, as studies by Blaug and associates have indicated, engineering and science courses are popular among students aspiring to higher education.[24] Such courses, however, are more expensive and typically have much more restrictive admission policies than do courses in commerce and the arts.

The perceived value of education for the achievement of national economic goals perhaps to some extent may be judged by the amount of educational expenditures. The financial input to the Indian educational system has steadily increased over the last two decades. In 1946-1947 in British India the total expenditure per capita was 1.8 rupees. By 1965-1966 the expenditure was 12 rupees per capita.[25] As a percentage of national income, the total educational expenditure represented 1.2 percent in 1951 and increased to 2.9 percent in 1966.[26] Thus the rate of growth of educational expenditure was more rapid than the growth in national income.

Some comparisons may help place the financial input in perspecitve. In absolute amounts per capita, educational expenditure in India is about one-hundred of that of the United States. As a percentage of gross national product, the United States, the U.S.S.R., and Japan spend about twice as much on education as India. Such disparities between expenditures in the underdeveloped and in the highly industrialized nations are to be expected. More valuable would be comparisons with the industrial nations during their earlier stages of development comparisons with other contemporary underdeveloped nations. For example, Japan in 1935 was already spending a slightly larger proportion of its gross national product on education than was India in the mid-1960's. In comparison with neighboring Asian nations, India's total expenditure on education is proportionately less than that of Ceylon but roughly similar to that of Pakistan, a nation more comparable in terms of educational development.

Furthermore, in an examination of the breakdown of governmental educational expenditures, one striking characteristic may be observed. In terms of recurrent expenditures, India spends a disproportionately high amount on secondary and higher education in comparison with other South Asian nations. Or, to place the emphasis differently, India's expenditures on primary education — at least for the decade 1955-1965 — have been proportionately less than those of neighboring governments.

In addition to economic development, a second major national aim which influences educational inputs is the achievement of social and national integration. Indian society is too hierarchical and presents too many social cleavages to satisfy contemporary democratic and socialist goals. Economic, ethnic, linguistic, and social class differences divide the nation. Power and prestige are concentrated in a few families; it has been estimated, for example, that two percent of the population commands one-third of the wealth.[27] Regardless of the accuracy of this particular statistic, the great range in wealth and concomitant educational opportunities is apparent. The level of poverty of the great masses of the Indian population makes even "free" education a luxury for many.

The diversity of languages in India is an important impediment to the unification and integration of the nation and a constraint on educational development. When independence was attained, the government was faced with the fact that English was the major language of the educated elite, while 1652 dialects and 14 major languages were spoken with varying frequency among the people. The national government has acted to adopt Hindi (the most widely spoken language in India) as the official language (English as an associate official language) with the expectation that in the course of time it will become the *lingua franca* of the nation.

With certain exceptions for linguistic minorities, the regional languages are the media of instruction in the lower schools. The study of Hindi becomes compulsory beginning at the upper primary stage. Other regional languages, Hindi, and English are offered at the secondary stage. The medium of instruction at the university level, which in the past has been English, is increasingly becoming the regional language.

In addition to linguistic diversity, the variety of existing religious and social groups also contributes to the divisive force of communalism. The predominant Hindu religion is itself linked to deep social class, caste, and occupational cleavages. The actual functioning of caste as a social force in contemporary India is a subject of considerable controversy. Some writers argue that caste severely constrains mobility and innovation, thus acting as a brake to economic development. Shils finds that the caste system leads to profound alienation:

It inhibits the growth of those sensibilities which are required for the perception of the moral quality of other human beings. It is the caste system which cuts human beings off from each other by denying to them the possibilities of connubial and commensal intimacy and a more basic affinity as moral entities. It is the caste system which helps deaden the imagination to the state of mind of other human beings. [28]

Other viewers perceive a weakening of the caste system in that it no longer has such a limiting effect on vocational and educational roles. They cite evidence, dating back for decades or even centuries, which suggests that a sizable percentage of sons do not engage in the same occupation as the father.[29] A partial survey conducted by the Census Commission of India, for example, found that only half of the male workers in 1931 were engaged in occupations traditionally associated with their castes.[30]

Evidence from these and other studies, however, describes mobility primarily between occupations of comparable rank and thus does not disturb the correspondence between caste and occupational hierarchies. A contemporary study in central India, drawing data from interviews,[31] reinforces the conclusion that, while the caste system is not particularly obstructive to occupational change, such mobility is generally confined to occupations of similar rank. In this study, 30.1 percent of the rural workers and 59.9 percent of the urban workers deviated occupationally from their fathers. In examining the association between position in caste and occupation, this research indicates that, in the rural sample, most of the Brahmans and High Caste members are professionals or cultivators while over half of the persons in the "Backward" and "Scheduled" castes are semi-skilled and unskilled workers. The association between occupational and caste positions is even closer in the urban sample. (See Table 8.)

TABLE 8 Percentage Distribution of the Employed in Occupational Classes, by Caste and Residence

	Brahmans	High castes	Trading castes	Low castes	Backward castes	Scheduled Castes	Total
Rural							
Total employed	50	41	32	704	256	161	1244
Percent:							
Cultivators	36.6	45.7	18.8	38.4	20.0	18.5	33.4
Professionals	19.5	6.5	9.4	3.4	2.2	2.4	4.4
Managerial	7.3	2.2	6.3	2.2	3.3	9.7	3.5
Commercial	17.1	28.3	31.2	3.8	4.4	9.7	6.3
Semi-skilled	2.4	4.3	9.4	27.2	44.4	17.8	25.9
Unskilled	17.1	13.0	24.9	25.0	25.7	41.9	26.5
Total	100.0	100.0	100.0	100.0	100.0	100.0	100.0
Urban							
Total employed	165	59	50	221	97	87	679
Percent:							
Cultivators	3.6	0.0	0.0	1.8	1.8	2.7	1.9
Professionals	26.1	11.5	4.0	1.8	5.5	1.4	8.1
Managerial	13.3	9.8	10.0	10.0	1.8	2.7	7.8
Commercial	43.7	44.3	68.0	44.3	10.9	14.9	27.2
Semi-skilled	3.0	16.4	2.0	19.0	54.5	48.6	29.3
Unskilled	10.3	18.0	16.0	23.1	25.5	29.7	25.7
Total	100.0	100.0	100.0	100.0	100.0	100.0	100.0

Source: Edwin D. Driver, "Caste and Occupational Structure in Central India," *Social Forces*, Vol. XLI (1962), No. 1, p. 28.

The social stratification system interacts with the educational system at many points. Social class and caste determine who goes to school, affect the dynamics of promotion, reward, and learning within the system, and may constrain the roles to be played by graduates. The educational process, in turn, as will be seen in the later discussion of educational output, may soften or harden social cleavages, that is, act to certify ascribed status or to promote interclass mobility.

Analyses of the educational attainments of caste groups reveal that Brahmans typically have the highest education; they are followed by the middle-group castes and the agricultural castes. Scheduled castes have the lowest level of education. As would be expected, within the same caste urban residents have higher levels of education than their counterparts in rural areas. In the Driver study of employed persons, for example, 68.3 percent of the rural and 87.2 percent of the urban Brahmans had received more than a primary education, while only 5.7 percent of the rural and 17.5 percent of the urban Scheduled Castes had obtained that level.[32] From this and other evidence, the conclusion is inevitable that the advanced levels of education in India represent a socially select segment of the population.

In an examination of educational opportunity, the focus could be placed at the family level instead of at the level of broad categories of social classes. Differences in home environment appear to exert the prime influence on the stock and flow of students through the various levels of the educational system. Parents who are illiterate or who suffer economic and social deprivation are not as likely to seek enrollment for their children in the school system as are those parents who have benefited from the system.

At the primary school level, for example, home influence has been described as exerting pressures on attendance, which in turn affects performance. Myrdal discussed this effect in terms of the discrepancy between enrollment and attendance. Enrollment rate was taken to be the reported number of enrolled children as a percentage of the total number of children in the modal age range for the particular level of education. Attendance was defined as an estimate of "regular participation in school work, uninterrupted by repeated or prolonged absences...."[33] Attendance rate then became the number of students who regularly participated in schoolwork as a precentage of the total number of children in the appropriate cohort. In 1960 the enrollment rate in primary education was 49 percent, while the estimated attendance rate was only 30 percent.[34]

The demographic features of contemporary India also represent an important source of educational inputs. The population of India in 1961 was tabulated to be 439 million, and projections estimate 555 million people in 1971. The rate of annual population growth has been increasing since 1921, and in 1961 had reached approximately two percent. Population growth in India can be generally explained in terms of a fairly stable birthrate and a declining death rate. Recognizing that direct attention must be given to reducing the birthrate, the Indian government instituted a planning commission to sponsor research on attitudes toward family planning and on effective educational techniques for reducing family size. Moreover, government clinics have been opened and information and contraceptives made available to the population. As a further indication of the extent of government concern, sterilization facilities are also becoming more accessible.

Like most developing nations, India has a youthful population structure. In 1961 the median age of the total population was 20.4 as compared to 34.0 for Germany and 29.5 for the United States.[35] Moreover, the school-age population in India is growing at a much more rapid rate than the total population. It is estimated that the total student population by 1985 will reach 170 million, requiring by that date the services of more than 2 million teachers.

Table 9 suggests the extent to which the educational system is affected by the impact of rising population rates and social demand ratios. During the period 1950 to 1965 school enrollments expanded at a greater rate than the school-age population. Table 9 indicates that the gap between these two statistics will be dramatically larger in the years to come, suggesting something of the magnitude of the anticipated demand for schooling. Inasmuch as this condition reflects the usual desire of a nation which is becoming better educated to seek still more education, it may, of course, be thought of as a happy situation. Yet, clearly in the case of India, the anticipated increases in enrollment will make tremendous demands on the facilities and teaching staffs of the educational system.

Even if the number of available teachers is, say, doubled during the next 20 years (an increase possible given the accuracy of the estimates in

TABLE 9   The Impact of Increasing Population and Participation on Enrollment: India

Educational level	1965	(1950 = 100) 1975	1980	1985
Lower primary				
Population of the age group	148		199	
Enrollment ratio	183		293	
Enrollment	272		584	
Higher primary				
Population of the age group	151		220	
Enrollment ratio	258		596	
Enrollment	389		1311	
Secondary				
Population of the age group	137		207	
Enrollment ratio	309		594	
Enrollment	420		1232	
Higher				
Population of the age group	138			
Enrollment ratio	300			
Enrollment	416	837		1582

Source: Data taken from India, Ministry of Education, *Report of the Education Commission (1964-66)*. Delhi: Manager of Publications, 1966, Chapter V. Data for 1950 are taken to represent the index of 100. Figures in the table indicate growth in the respective categories beyond the index.

Table 9), what would be the level of qualifications of the new teachers? Nearly all Indian educators decry the present low standards among the teaching profession, arguing for higher pay, more extended training, lower pupil-teacher ratios, and the like. Thus the unenviable task before the Indian nation appears to be that of improving the quality while doubling the size of the teaching force.[36]

In the face of these challenges, education in contemporary India is being called on to assist in a social revolution of a magnitude which would have mystified or even horrified leaders of the earlier colonial period. A harsh summary of the constraints on the contemporary educational system is offered by Naik:

Educationally, the country has only a small class of indifferently educated persons while the masses are still illiterate and ignorant. The prevailing technology is largely primitive and we still live in, what Pandit Nehru called, the "cow-dung era." The very unity of the nation ... is now threatened with several fissiparous tendencies. Social cohesion, never very strong, is now probably at its lowest ebb due to an upsurge of parochial or casteist considerations and the still unresolved problems of Hindu-Muslim unity. In the political field, the only organized party which won the freedom is now beset with factions, groupism, and internal squabbles of an unprecedented character and there is no other well-organized nation-wide political party to take its place. The great creative impulse which the country revealed in throwing up a galaxy of great men to fight with British imperialism now appears to be on the wane and we do not seem to have any giants in our midst comparable to those who lived and fought for us between 1860 and 1960. The old faith and values in life are slipping fast under our feet and their place has not yet been taken up by new ones with the result that there is an immense crisis of character which manifests itself in reprehensible and disorderly behavior among students and in corruption and inefficiency in official and public life.[37]

As the educational system is adjusted to meet the new tasks, all inputs must be justified and evaluated in terms of their anticipated congruence with democratic and socialist principles. A democratic and socialist pattern of society suggests such goals as (1) an end to socially or linguistically based inequalities in educational participation, (2) free compulsory education, and (3) school programs which seek to develop a broad concept of participant citizenship. The inputs described in the above paragraphs (and others) thus may reinforce or contradict, but on any hand must be rationalized with, national ends. Questions of appropriate organization and control, curriculum, and teaching roles must – at least by those who would seek for India a coherent educational system – be seen in this context. So, too, must questions of educational strategy, e.g., selectivity in higher education, vocationalization of secondary education, and the like, which affect the character of the entire system.

THE STRUCTURE AND FUNCTIONS OF
THE CONTEMPORARY EDUCATIONAL SYSTEM

With the coming of independence and the articulation of new national goals and aspirations, new demands were made upon the educational system. Some of the more important of the new social ends and constraints which can be identified as inputs to the educational system have been described in the previous section. The changing nature of these inputs and the changing social context impinging on the educational system have also been reflected in structural and functional changes within the system itself. Some of the more important changes include those in organizational arrangements, in teacher, administrator, and student roles, and in curriculum.

Educational Organization and Control

The role of the Government of India in education has gone through a number of stages. Prior to 1833 it played virtually no role; between 1833 and 1870 the situation was almost completely reversed. Between 1870 and 1921 five major functions were reserved for the Government: general policymaking, information collecting and dissemination, research and publications, and coordination and financial assistance. From 1921 until 1935 educational policy was again largely divorced from the Government. Since 1935 the involvement of the Central Government in educational matters has once again been on the increase.[38]

The Indian Constitution, formally adopted in 1949, gives the state governments almost complete control over education; that is, "education including universities" became a "state subject." The more important rights reserved by the Central Government include the right of religious and linguistic minorities to administer their own schools and the right of the Central Government to pass legislation involving vocational and technical training. Moreover, the Central Government is responsible for certain universities and institutions of national importance (as so declared by Parliament) and has the right to establish standards for institutions of higher education (it exercised this right through the creation of the University Grants Commission). Finally, since the Government shares with the states the responsibility for economic and social planning, it exercises considerable influence over the nature, and particularly over the magnitude, of the educational enterprise.

The Central Government carries out its educational responsibilities through the Union Ministry of Education and a number of advisory bodies. Of the latter, the University Grants Commission and the Central Advisory Board of Education are perhaps the most significant. Thus while the Consititution of India provides for a decentralized pattern of educational control, with basic educational responsibilities reserved for the states (see Table 10), the Central Government is much more than a disinterested spectator.

TABLE 10   Proportion of Educational Institutions Managed by Different Agencies, 1958

| Management | *Percentage of total number of institutions managed* | | | |
	Primary level	*Middle level*	*High school level*	*Arts and science colleges*
Government[1]	26.1	25.2	19.0	23.6
District boards	46.7	37.4	7.3	0.3[2]
Municipal boards	3.0	3.1	2.8	0.0
Private bodies	24.7	34.3	70.9	76.1

Source: India, Ministry of Education, *Education in India: 1957-58.* Delhi: Manager of Publications, 1962, Vol. I, Tables XVIII, XXXIX, LI, and LXII.

1. Includes state and central governments.
2. Includes municipal boards.

The National Ministry of Education is the official national body responsible for planning, guiding, and coordinating educational development. Its functions include the following:

1.   Providing exclusive educational direction in the centrally administered areas (the new Indian Union formed in 1956 includes fourteen states and six centrally administered territories).

2.   Directly administering to the eighteen public schools, four central universities, and a variety of research and training centers.

3.   Granting scholarships for scheduled castes and backward tribes.

4.   Giving grants-in-aid to the states and, under certain conditions, directly to institutions of higher education.[39]

Nevertheless, there appears to be some confusion, if not ambiguity, in the provisions of the Constitution regarding the control of education. Like the Constitution of the United States, the Indian Constitution makes education a responsibility of the various states, except for certain aspects explicitly specified. Yet the exceptions involving the Central Government are subject to various interpretations. For example, the responsibilities of the Government in such activities as compulsory education, equalization of opportunities, and educational planning would imply that involvement by the Central Government could legitimately be extensive indeed. Thus, rather than being a state preserve, education is actually very much of a joint effort between administrations at the federal and state levels.

Types of Educational Institutions

The structure of the educational system varies somewhat from state to state throughout India. The variations usually represent differences in the length of the course at one or more of the educational levels; however, the total length of time required to obtain the B. A. degree (or its equivalent) typically does not differ by more that one year (15 or 16 years).

Primary education in India usually covers seven or eight grades and is divided into two levels: lower primary and upper primary. Article 45 of the Constitution established the goal of free and compulsory education up to the age of 14 years. As a result of population increases, inadequate financial resources, and apathy among certain elements of the population, this remains an unfulfilled goal. Estimates now place the realization of universal primary education in the 1980's.

The primary schools are expected to offer an undifferentiated curriculum designed to prepare for effective citizenship. In addition to the usual subjects — native language, arithmetic, general science, social studies, art, music, and physical education — Hindi is required where it is not the native tongue of the area. Finally, reflecting an educational view promoted by Gandhi and a number of his followers, all primary schools have become "junior basic schools" and offer several periods of arts and crafts.

Dissatisfaction with the pattern of secondary education under the British has led to considerable debate about, and some experimentation with, contemporary secondary schools. Particularly, there has been a movement toward the introduction of vocational courses, "enrichment" of the curricula with "practical" subjects (e.g., crafts and agriculture), and greater emphasis on Hindi and the regional languages. Rather clearly the secondary school, whose curriculum had been restricted to those subjects traditionally regarded as the best preparation for the university, did not articulate well with a primary school which stressed socially useful labor. Therefore, the concept of basic education was extended to include lower secondary schools.

Contemporary secondary education may be viewed structurally at two levels. The lower secondary schools typically include grades eight, nine, and ten. The explicit objectives articulated by the government and perhaps by most leading educators call eventually for multipurpose schools at this level and, hence, separation of students according to anticipated career patterns. The curriculum at present, however, continues the courses initiated in the primary grades and also includes study in classical European and Asian languages. The language of instruction is the regional language and Hindi is taught as a separate subject (except where it is the regional language). In 1965, only 9 per cent of the lower-secondary school students were enrolled in vocational courses of study.

At the second or higher level of secondary education, the revised course of study extends for two or three years, leading to the Secondary School Certificate or the Secondary School Leaving Certificate. Considerable variation in structure and function exists at grades eleven and twelve, reflecting a partial transition from the British system, which had placed matriculation examinations at the tenth grade level to determine entrance to the Intermediate Colleges (grades eleven and twelve). The movement toward three-year Higher Secondary Schools has caused alterations in examination arrangements, the creation of a new terminal certificate, and a reorganization of university structure. At the end of grade eleven, the Higher Secondary School Certificate is offered, indicating graduation from the grade and also permitting matriculation to the university (or, where the older system persists, to grades eleven and twelve of the Intermediate College).

Although the curriculum is in considerable flux, the higher secondary schools offer substantial diversification. By the mid-1960's, the proportion of enrollment at this level in vocational courses had reached 40 percent and Government plans were calling for increased vocationalization. In addition to full-time study in a choice of several programs in general and vocational education, a variety of short-term, part-time, and industry-related vocational courses were becoming available.

The heavy language burden for the student persists at the higher secondary level. Although one of the reasons for the shift in structure was to modify the British system, which required what many Indian educators thought to be an excessive emphasis on examinations given in the English language, the present curriculum of the higher secondary schools is still highly oriented toward language skills. Admission to study for the Bachelor of Arts degree requires a secondary school background in English, Hindi, a modern Indian language, and an "Ancient Indian," "Ancient European," or a modern European language.

Higher education in India has probably been subject to even more debate and controversy than education at the lower levels. Universities have a history of approximately one century and, as noted earlier, began as purely examining bodies patterned after the University of London. In the twentieth century a new type of institution, the teaching and residential university, has gained popularity while the examining or "affiliating" university has come under increasing criticism.

In viewing the contemporary universities, the Education Commission (1964-1966) comments:

Perhaps the most onerous responsibility which the Indian universities now have is to shake off the heavy load of their early tradition which gives a dominant place to examinations, to improve standards all-round, and, by a symbiotic development of teaching and research, to create at least a few centers which would be comparable to those of their type in any other part of the world.[40]

Eric Ashby adds his evaluation:

Looking at Indian Universities a century after their foundation, one cannot help but feel that they have failed to adapt themselves sufficiently to the vast and unique opportunities which surround them; they seem to have lost enthusiasm and initiative under the crushing problems which have beset them. Despite three major commissions, they have not been able to extricate themselves from their own brief history. With a few notable exceptions they remain examining bodies and their students naturally regard success in examinations as the sole end of an undergraduate career.[41]

The traditional university functions of teaching and advancement of knowledge, at least as these functions were defined in colonial India, are much too limited to describe the scope of the task of the contemporary Indian university. The fixation on degrees and the certification function provides an inadequate response to the national need for intelligent and creative leadership. In addition to the preparation of a wide variety of specialists and professionals, Indian universities are expected to assume a social responsibility for serving, if not as the conscience of the nation, at least as critics of both the ends and means of societal change.

By 1966 there were 64 universities and 2565 affiliated colleges in India.[42] The latter were of two types: colleges of arts and sciences, and professional and technical colleges. It was particularly the professional and technical colleges that reflected the newer social demands and industrial pressures for high-level manpower. In these institutions increasingly diversified curricula made possible specialization in such fields as commerce, agriculture, teacher training, engineering, forestry, medicine, and law. The rapid expansion of enrollments and differentiation of courses of study in higher education since independence still could not keep up with the bewildering growth of specializations demanded in an industrializing society. Supply noticeably lagged behind demand in such fields as electronics, chemical technology, nuclear power generation, and aeronautics.

But it was the general quality of instruction and research, rather than the restricted number of courses of study, which caused Indian leaders the most concern. The professional programs in engineering and agriculture, so vital in meeting high-level manpower needs, were poorly articulated with the requisites of production. Agricultural programs in universities gave little attention to extension work, and frequently the fruits of agricultural technology failed to reach the farmer. In engineering, cooperation between universities and industries in professional training was still in the exploratory stage; moreover, academic study in engineering appeared to be weakened by poor preparation in the basic sciences. The social sciences, which, with the exception of economics, tended to be associated organizationally with humanities departments remained underdeveloped. Even the humanities, which have occupied a central place in the universities since their development, have been criticized for their lack of vitality and lack of relevance.[43]

The struggle to adjust Indian higher education structurally and functionally has been obstructed, not only by the unaccommodating historical traditions and the human and financial shortages common in the less developed nations, but also by the language problem, which continues at the university level to act as a qualitative constraint on learning. In a sense, the language situation is but a manifestation of the more general problem of synthesizing India's cultural traditions with the demands of a changing economy. The combined effects of poor preparation of students, questionable selection procedures, large classes, low-quality instruction, and a language burden result in a high rate of wastage and low level of achievement among students in higher education. These characteristics, in turn, increase the student unrest and unruliness so characteristic of contemporary Indian universities.

Teacher Roles

Comments have been made earlier concerning the role of the guru as a moral and intellectual leader in ancient India. In idealized form the teachers' traditional aspirations are expressed in the teacher's prayer found in Upanishads:

May that Indra who is the greatest in the Vedic hymns. . . may he cheer me with intelligence, O God, may I be the possessor of immortality. . . Bringing to me and increasing always clothes and cattle, food and drink, doing this long, do thou, then, bring me prosperity in wool along with cattle. . .
May I become famous among men.[44]

The principles guiding teacher-student interaction have been described as the doctrine of combination. The teacher is the prior form, the pupil is the latter form, knowledge their junction, and instruction their connection. The "organic" relationship between teacher and pupil is this: the pupil is the observer and the emulator of the teacher, while the teacher observes the pupil without imposing on him and provides guidance and direction when needed.

The purpose of teaching is the inculcation of moral or self-realized conduct by overcoming the empirical self with all its dross, weakness, vulgarity, lusts, passions, desires, and ambitions, and nurturing the growth of the soul. The moral life is not only a life of sense and instinct, but also one of understanding and reason.[45]

In more recent times, the teacher's roles, in keeping with the level of differentiation of the educational system, have become more specialized. Although teachers are still viewed as moral guides for children and youth, they are no longer expected to be the fount of all knowledge. However, within the context of the changing prestige and economic patterns in Indian society, the teacher has found it difficult to maintain status and security.

The village schoolmaster of the mid-nineteenth century, although bound by rigid village custom and tradition, had full autonomy over the content and method of teaching. In this regard he was subject to no external authority. In terms of economic status, the village teacher appears to have been comfortable and rewarded according to his accepted station in life. His social status was likewise assured. Typically he was honored and respected and was identified with one of the higher castes.

The contemporary Indian teacher is a member of a giant bureaucracy in which he is neither so secure nor so autonomous as the teacher of old. His roles link to a variety of professional and lay groups which, in turn, at the higher levels, act as interpreters of national policy. He no longer directly accepts student fees, even when they are given — a further loss of autonomy and economic independence.[46]

Much of this change is to be expected as a natural concomitant of increasing social complexity and greater division of labor. Yet, in the case of India, there is much ambivalence regarding the contemporary roles of teachers. Many leaders still exhort present-day teachers to play the diffuse roles of the teacher of old. Clearly, however, exhortations and campaign slogans which designate teachers as "builders of a nation" are not substitutes for increased salaries and improved status. On the other hand, teachers, while aware of their changing roles, have been unable to clearly define the bounds of their professional purview and to organize in such a way that their professional rights are protected.

The gravity of the contemporary situation and the difference between the desired and actual roles of teachers may be seen in the following quotations:

At present, the bringing up of the next generation is being left more and more to the lesser representatives of the present generation. . . .

Our expansion has far outrun our capacity to produce good teachers and this is the main reason for the dilution of quality. It would, therefore, be worthwhile to concentrate, for a few years, on all such measures which improve teachers at all stages, elementary, secondary, and university.[47]

Regardless of difficulties, a higher social, economic and professional status for teachers in primary schools is an absolute pre-condition for raising the levels of teaching.[48]

Indian political leaders, planners, and educators expect the quality of the educational system to relate closely to the quality of teaching. Teachers must introduce and reinforce the difficult and novel ideas undergirding modernization. And this must be accomplished where the surplus of educated graduates (largely arts graduates) decreases the scarcity value of education and threatens to drive teachers' salaries even lower.

An Educational Experiment

With the shift in educational policy from that of limited toward that of extensive (and ultimately universal) educational opportunities for young Indians, the need was felt by some Indian leaders for a different focus, a new unifying theme. Perhaps the most fundamental shift in the orientation of lower schools in keeping with their contemporary functions was the introduction of *basic education.* The concept of basic education was enunciated by Gandhi and spread by his followers, who saw the Indian village as the center of Indian life and the key to national progress. Its goals were to build on the villagers' sense of solidarity, improve their capacity for self-government, and develop their skills for increasing their economic potential. In Gandhi's words:

The principal idea is to impart the whole education of the body and the mind and the soul through the handicraft that is taught to the children. You have to draw out all that is in the child through teaching all the processes of the handicraft, and all your lessons in history, geography, and arithmetic will be related to the craft.[49]

There were pedagogical, economic, and social reasons for the movements in basic education and community development. Pedagogically, basic education was viewed by its proponents as a progressive movement which replaced memorization and drill with "purposeful" and "creative activity." Deriving content from the immediate community was seen as a way of stimulating pupil interest, and cooperative activites in socially useful endeavors were to replace harsh competition. Indeed, the arguments used by Indian educators in condemning the traditional educational pattern and in supporting basic education are remarkably like those used by the advocates of progressive education in the United States in the 1930's.

The Gandhian rejection of the large-scale and the centralized in favor of the simplicity and decentralization of the village community was not entirely without economic foundation. It was argued, for example, that a focus at the village level would maximize employment opportunities:

In Europe and America mechanization was a necessity because those countries had adundant capital and suffered from the scarcity of labor. To exploit and develop their natural resources fully, they were compelled to invoke the asistance of machinery, but in India, conditions are just the reverse of those obtaining in the Western countries; there is paucity of capital and abundance of labor.[50]

Moreover, some Indian planners pointed to the Japanese example, where small-scale enterprises continue to enjoy prosperity even in the face of competition from large-scale industries.

As conceived by Gandhi and his followers, the long-range goal of basic education was no less than a social and spiritual reconstruction of society. Gandhi, while concerned with the material poverty about him, was most disturbed by what he considered to be a prevailing spiritual poverty. Western culture and education, to the degree that they had divorced Indians from their own cultural heritage, were, he felt, a major contributor to this latter problem. The introduction of crafts into the schools was seen as one way of developing a respect for labor which, in turn, might soften class barriers. Finally, it was hoped that the rural and vocational bias of instruction would retard the migration of young people from village to urban areas.

Although basic education is still very much on the scene in India – indeed, the policy at both state and national levels is to turn all primary and lower secondary schools into basic schools – its degree of success remains a controversial issue. There has been a lingering confusion about its precise purpose and content. Many schools which bear the prefix "basic" offer little work in handicrafts and, in effect, equate activity methods of instruction with basic education. Such conditions lend credence to the view of some social scientists and educators that basic education is hardly more than a romantic experiment which can make few serious contributions toward meeting the country's real social and economic needs.

Further, not all of the rural classes have supported programs in basic education or more general campaigns for community development. Certain landowners, for example, "see the Community Development programs as part of what they call the 'new order' and this order has meant to them more than just new agricultural methods and hymn-singing: it has meant the attempted abolition of landlordism together with the spread of anti-caste and anti-privilege ideology which thereatens further inroads in their dominant position."[51]

Finally, developmental goals of enterpreneurship and industrialization and the increased centralization of the Indian economy have eroded much of the justification for the antimaterial focus of the basic education movement, as well as much of the economic argument for decentralization.

In summary, new structures and new functions are being acquired by the educational system, in keeping with the changing nature of the system inputs. In the past, learning and cultural activity were the exclusive province of a small elite. During the nineteenth century, while popular education made rapid gains in Western nations and in Japan, there was little extension of the educational franchise among the Indian masses. In democratic and socialist India, however, popular education is seen both as a human right and as a necessity for economic survival. Within the classroom, techniques of memorization originating from religious instruction in the dim past persist in contemporary schools; however, dogmatic instruction and an uncritical student response to subject matter are being replaced in a few schools by a more dynamic view of the learning process. Unfortunately, the teaching input, which tends to place a qualitative limit on schooling, has been neglected. Whereas the teachers for the elite schools of the past were recruited from upper-caste Brahmans, teachers for today's mass education tend to come from the lower classes – a condition which undermines confidence in status-conscious India.

EDUCATIONAL OUTPUT

We have already engaged in some discussion of the nature of the societal inputs into the Indian educational system. Brief attention has also been given to the structure and workings of the system itself – the ways in which the inputs are "processed." The question now posed is: To what extent does the educational output represent a fit between the educational system and the other systems it has been called upon to support? Again the coverage is selective and attention will be limited largely to relationships between education and the manpower (or occupational) system and between education and the system of social structure.

First, looking at the output in gross terms, one finds over recent years a sharp increase in output at all three major educational levels. This holds true whether output is defined as graduates or as "unfinished products," e.g., dropouts. At the primary level, although the national target of free, compulsory education through the age of 14 has not been reached, the number of pupils reading grade eight has grown from 448,000 (1946) to 2,900,000 (1965). As percentages of the corresponding age groups, enrollments in the upper primary grades have grown from 13.0 (1950) to 36.5 (1965); at the lower secondary level, from 6.5 (1950) to 19.1 (1965); and at the upper secondary level, 1.9 (1950) to 7.0 (1965). In higher education, enrollment in arts, commerce, and science grew from 191,000 in 1950 to 759,000 in 1965; postgraduate enrollment increased from 18,000 to 86,000; and professional enrollments grew from 54,000 to 249,000. The overall increase as a percentage of the age group (18 to 23) was from 0.7 to 2.1.

Education, Manpower, and the Economy

Clearly, the output of the educational system has not been in keeping with the national economic and social needs. First, among the educational outputs, there have been surpluses of certain kinds of skills and shortages of others.[52] Second, evidence is not conclusive that education has contributed significantly toward such goals as increased social mobility and increased interchange of ideas and information among the various social groups.

No extensive and reliable data exist on either manpower shortages or surpluses; however, the general problem areas are easily identified. The unemployed graduates (or, for that matter, dropouts) from the upper secondary schools tend to have been enrolled in the general course. At the university level there has been a distinct overproduction in arts and commerce, and unemployment rates among the graduates in these fields is on the increase. On the other hand, however, there is, as yet, little unemployment in most of the professional fields, particularly in agriculture, engineering, and medicine. Further, a general shortage tends to persist at the postgraduate and research stages in all fields.[53]

Table 11 indicates the relatively small numbers of graduates in medicine and engineering who have been registered as unemployed between 1953 and 1961. In comparison, the large and growing number of unemployed matriculates (those who have completed 11 years of schooling) and intermediates (those with some undergraduate university level study) should be noted. Further, the 50,000 unemployed graduates ("Others") in 1961 may be assumed to include a large percentage of arts and commerce graduates. One study estimated that over half the educated unemployed were seeking clerical work, which for a number of years has been the most overcrowded area of employment in India.

Other data further substantiate the lack of fit between the educational and occupational systems. Table 12 shows the employment distribution of India's educational manpower. This table suggests several important characteristics of educational output in India. First, the nearly 10 lakhs of educated employment seekers is dangerously large when compared to the total of educated employed. The figure representing employment seekers becomes more meaningful when seen as a proportion of yearly educational output. The total number of secondary-educated employment seekers is just about twice the number of secondary-educated manpower cohorts in the previous year, while the total number of higher-educated employment seekers is somewhat less than the total number of higher-educated manpower cohorts in the previous year.[54]

It is possible to express the ratio of educated employment seekers to educated manpower cohorts as an interval or "average waiting period" between leaving school or college and becoming employed. For the secondary school leavers, this "average waiting period" was 104 weeks in 1960-1961. For a student entering employment after completing higher education it was 45 weeks. Clearly the figure of 104 weeks is an exceedingly lengthy waiting period and represents a serious misfit between

TABLE 11   India: Educated Unemployed on Live Registers of Employment Exchanges at the End of the Year, 1953 to 1961 (Thousands of Persons)

Year	Matriculates	Intermediates	Graduates				Total
			Engineering	Medical	Others	Total	
1953	125	17	1.1	0.2	19	21	163
1954	145	22	0.9	0.2	21	22	189
1955	164	26	0.6	0.2	25	26	216
1956	187	31	0.5	0.2	26	27	244
1957	237	39	0.5	0.2	32	32	308
1958	283	45	0.5	0.2	36	37	364
1959	344	49	0.6	0.2	39	40	433
1960	400	61	1.2	0.3	45	47	507
1961 (June)	447	70	0.9	0.2	50	51	568

Source: National Council of Educational Research and Training, *Review of Education in India, 1947-61*. New Delhi: Ministry of Education, 1961, p. 93.

TABLE 12 Employment Pattern of Educationally Classified Manpower, 1960-1961

Employment category	Higher edu-cated man-power	Secondary educated manpower	Educationally classified manpower
Industrial and service industries[1]	1.91	5.91	7.82
Employment services[2]	10.04	28.09	38.13
Total	11.95	34.00	45.95
Farm-home employment[3]	1.42	10.36	11.78
Employment seekers[4]	0.95	8.60	9.55
Manpower total	14.32	52.96	68.2

Source: India, Ministry of Education, *Report of the Education Commission (1964-66), Education and National Development.* Delhi: Manager of Publications. 1966, p. 534. All figures are in lakhs (1 lakh = 100,000).

1. This category includes extraction of minerals, production of manufactured products, generation and distribution of electricity, employment in transportation and communication services, etc.

2. Any employment other than those included under "Industrial and service industries" and "Farm-home employment." This category includes employment in the various social, cultural, and personnel services of the Government.

3. Employment in farming, household industry, and housewifery.

4. This category includes all persons, excluding students and persons over 65 years of age, not included in any of the above three categories.

secondary schooling and employment. Estimates based on trend data suggest that the average waiting period by 1975 will be 137 weeks.

A second major conclusion to be drawn from Table 12 is the relatively minor employment role being played by industrial and service industries. This situation suggests the narrow industrial base from which contemporary India must build. However, economic growth projections call for a very rapid expansion of manpower needs in industrial employment, and it is in this area that the most severe shortages of educated manpower are anticipated.

How serious is the problem of the "educated unemployed" and of the attendant waiting period preceding employment? In 1967 the "educated unemployed" (matriculates and beyond) constituted between six and seven percent of the total stock of labor. In other words, in that year one out of every 15 matriculates and graduates was looking for work. If these data indicate a serious condition, as most Indian educators appear to assume, further attention must be given to the underlying causes and to rectifying policies.

One common explanation of the rapid expansion of secondary and higher education suggests that the prestige of a diploma or a degree is sufficient incentive for Indian students to stay in school regardless of career prospects. A second explanation already alluded to is that Indians simply demand the wrong kind of education. The first explanation assumes that advanced education in India is not a good investment (in monetary rate of return) for an individual, while the second assumes that students prefer the already glutted occupations. Sparse but pertinent data relating to both of these assumptions are available.

Some data on the returns from educational investment are available. For example, a sample of less than 6000 persons in Hyderabad suggests that the returns to the employed individuals may be considerable and most favorable in those pursuits requiring postgraduate or higher professional study (see Table 13).

More conclusive data are presented by Blaug, Layard, and Woodhall to demonstrate that, in spite of the prospects of a lengthy waiting period for graduates, education is a good investment. This study concludes that ". . . all levels of education in India are profitable investments for private individuals at 8 percent (the typical interest rate in a commercial bank), indeed, they remain profitable even at cut-off rates as high as 10 percent."[55] Thus, despite the fact of "educated unemployment," the decision to continue one's education is rational when viewed in terms of financial returns.

The second explanation, which relates "educated unemployment" to the academic (and hence vocational) choices of Indians, appears to have considerable merit. Although, as mentioned earlier, it is not possible to explain "educated unemployment" simply as a preference for clerical work, the fact remains that the majority of those seeking employment are doing so in clerical and commercial pursuits. Yet this fact may say less about their preference than it does about the nature of their schooling. Matriculates and graduates restricted by academic or financial reasons from obtaining technical or scientific training are forced to seek employment in occupations which require few specific skills.

TABLE 13 Distribution of Monthly Male Earnings by Schooling, Hyderabad

Earnings (rupees)	Illiterate	Primary	Secondary	Lower professional and technical
–25	658	264	220	14
26–	912	541	308	15
51–	376	407	510	44
101–	68	190	417	66
201–	6	15	158	55
501–		3	21	18
1001–			8	3
2501–			3	1
5000+			1	2
Total	2020	1420	1646	218

Earnings (rupees)	Under-graduate	Graduate-postgraduate	Higher professional and technical	Total
–25	4	2	2	1164
26–	18	1	4	1799
51–	59	22	25	1443
101–	51	56	42	890
201–	49	117	54	454
501–	8	36	9	95
1001–	4	5	11	31
2501–		2		6
5000+				3
Total	193	241	147	5885

Source: C. A. Anderson and M. J. Bowman (eds.), *Education and Economic Development*. Chicago: Aldine Press, 1965, p. 18. Original source: Indian Institute of Economics, *A Socio-Economic Survey of Hyderabad*. Hyderabad Government Press, 1957. The data refer to males having "some" primary, "some" secondary education, etc.

Even this cursory examination of the fit between educational output and the economy suggests that Indian leaders have some hard, immediate decisions to make regarding enrollments in secondary and higher education. Drastic adjustments will have to be made to avoid a continuing inflation among some educated manpower groups and to eliminate educational scarcity among others. In spite of the long-announced intention to do so, India thus far has been unable to effect the serious adjustments necessary to bring the educational system into line with even the most broadly conceived manpower objectives. As a minimum, action is needed, on the one hand, to produce more primary school leavers and, on the other hand, to halt the open-door policy which allows uncontrolled growth in enrollments in the general education course of the upper secondary schools and in the arts and commerce courses at the higher education level. Second, special and intensive efforts must be made to vocationalize upper secondary education and to develop further professional education at the university stage. Finally, within or outside educational agencies, organizational arrangements must be established at both the national and state levels which will effectively relate estimates of manpower needs to educational inputs.

Related to this latter point is the need for an improved system of vocational guidance. In the mid-1960's most matriculates and graduates were obtaining jobs through direct application or with the assistance of family or friends. Teachers and employment offices played a relatively minor role. At the higher education level, the creation of the University Information and Guidance Bureaux may prove to be a valuable means of identifying for students the nature of current manpower demand.

Education and Societal Integration

Attention needs to be given to the output of the educational system in other than occupational terms. Some discussion has already been undertaken concerning the manner and extent of the impingement of social attributes on educational imputs. One of the major educational aims of independent India has been the amelioration of existing deep social cleavages. Consequently, as a second perspective on educational output, the focus may be turned to the social characteristics of those who have participated to varying degrees in the educational system.

As has been indicated, there is considerable evidence pointing to a close relationship between the occupational and educational positions of various caste groups. Other evidence suggests that educational expansion tends to benefit the upper castes most. This is most dramatically the case at the university level, but true nontheless at lower levels.[56]

Unfortunately, fewer studies appear to be available which identify the precise extent to which education has served directly to promote interclass and intercaste mobility. Earlier in this chapter it was noted, however, that every caste does contain some members with advanced education.

Therefore, it is important to examine the characteristics of this educated group. From scattered field studies and the observations of a number of social scientists, there are indications that the more educated Indians are rethinking the prescribed interaction allowed between castes. For example, some confusion in caste relationships has been observed in an anthropological study of a village in Kerala:

Particularly in the matter of addressing each other, members of the different castes having nearly equal economic and educational status experience embarrassment. Linguistic indices of traditional status differences have gone out of vogue among educated people, in public offices and courts (though not fully in the latter).[57]

More evidence as to the effects of education on social interaction has been provided by Cormack, who concludes from her study of Indian students: ". . . it is obvious that most of the students believe in social interaction with different castes, classes, and sex. . ."[58]

In a study of a village in Kerala, Aiyappan comments that, "Educational institututions in which boys and girls of all castes mixed freely did a great deal to reduce social distance. Even the parents feel inclined to treat the class fellows and friends of their children on terms of less caste rigidity. Education served as one of the best social bridges."[59]

Moreover, not only schooling but even the promise of education has helped to promote communication between classes and castes:

Quite apart from its formal educational functions, the school system has played a significant role in social solidarity. The public-spirited efforts made by many people to establish schools in the four-village and still larger units have helped to knit the different villages together. It is noteworthy that membership on committees for this purpose cuts across caste, village, and faction lines; this is a hopeful indication for the future.[60]

In viewing the output of the educational system in terms of new attitudes and values which are supportive of India's democratic and socialist principles, at least three reservations must be considered. First, much of the evidence regarding education's role in softening social cleavages and in promoting social integration is impressionistic, or, at best, based on a small student or population sample. Second, in order for the educational system to function more effectively in this role, a viable policy effecting equality of educational opportunity among the various social, ethnic, and linguistic groupings would have to be established. Finally, it must be borne in mind that advanced education may itself create new postures, new prejudices, and a new alienation for its recipients. While a realignment of class lines based on level of education may well be more desirable than the traditional ascriptive bases for social demarcations, even a meritocratic class structure could frustrate goals of cultural and national integration.[61] Unfortunately, perhaps, there is a distinct tendency for those with advanced education, regardless of social background, to associate themselves with the views and prejudices of the upper class; fortunately, however, the values and attitudes of the upper class are in a state of transition.

SUMMARY

Many signs of modernization in India may be seen. A structural shift in the economy has fostered a movement away from the agricultural sector; since independence, per capita income has increased somewhat; and from 1950 to the early 1960's, industrial output more than doubled. However, an exceedingly high rate of population growth has eaten sharply into the per capita benefits of increased productivity. Furthermore, the effects of economic development have left the great masses of the population unaffected. The rural areas particularly have been relatively untouched by the benefits of growth in national production and expansion of social services.

Educational expansion at all levels has been significant in independent India, yet educational enrollments have been more susceptible to social demand than to the rationality of planning. Especially at the higher levels, demand has far outstripped supply. Educational progress, moreover, has been burdened not only by a demographic structure in which a high proportion of the population is below the age of fifteen, but also by long-standing social and linguistic cleavages. For example, school attendance and school achievement have been strongly linked to level of urbanization, sex, and socioeconomic status. At the higher education level, the decline in the use of English has threatened to lower the standards of even the most distinguished institutions. Furthermore, the national leaders and educated elites have been at times ambivalent in their commitment to a secular, socially integrated society. The frustration with the new and the alienation from the old have been well reflected in the Indian universities, which have been described as institutions where the "demoralized" teach the "digruntled."

On the brighter side is the increasing national commitment to development of human resources in the broadest sense. Modernization, many Indian leaders recognize, will mean nothing short of a pervasive social transformation, ". . . a wrenching reorientation of values concerning time, status, money, work."[6][2] In this process, educators and planners are hammering into educational policy the idea, novel to India, that an educational system should be explicity related to productivity targets and other national ends. If educated manpower represents a fundamental resource for modernization, then it follows that any program of educational development must be balanced in terms of scientific and general, vocational and liberal, education. From these and more profound insights may emerge successful educational planning.

NOTES

1. Edward Shils, *The Intellectual Between Tradition and Modernity: The Indian Situation.* The Hague: Mouton and Co., 1961.

2. I. N. Thut and Don Adams, *Educational Patterns in Contemporary Societies.* New York: McGraw-Hill, 1964, p. 388.

3. T. Walter Wallbank, *A Short History of India and Pakistan.* New York: New American Library, 1958, p. 26.

4. Oscar L. Chavarria-Aquilar (ed.), *Traditional India.* New York: Prentice-Hall, 1964, p. 91. For other comments on the disappearance of Indian Buddhism, see pp. 106-108.

5. Buddhism, too, left an educational legacy, but this was far less significant in India than in several other Asian nations. Some Buddhist monasteries grew into substantial institutions of learning and education. The "university" of Nalanda is said to have had several thousand monk-teachers and many more students. Both the student and teaching bodies are reported to have been of high quality. However, although such centers of excellence arose, and although Buddhism was more supportive of popular, or even secular, education than was Hinduism in India, few of the Buddhist educational traditions survived the revival of Brahmanism.

6. Gunnar Myrdal, *Asian Drama,* Vol. III. New York: Pantheon, 1968, pp. 1627-1628.

7. *Ibid.,* p. 1631.

8. Eric Ashby, *Universities: British, Indian, African – A Study in the Ecology of Higher Education.* Cambridge: Harvard University Press, 1966, p. 48.

9. It has been pointed out that the state of Kerala, which holds the record for literacy in contemporary India, achieved this status partly because of the cooperation of its rulers with the missionaries in educational efforts.

10. Myrdal, *op. cit.,* p. 1637.

11. Quoted in S. N. Mukerji, *History of Education in India,* Baroda: Acharya Book Depot, 1951, p. 32.

12. Ashby, *op. cit.,* p. 52.

13. G. Ramanathan, *Educational Planning and National Integration.* London: Asia Publishing House, 1965, p. 21.

14. Eric Ashby, *African Universities and Western Tradition.* Cambridge: Harvard University Press, 1964, p. 2.

15. Myron Weiner, "The Politics of South Asia," in Gabriel A. Almond and James S. Coleman (eds.), *The Politics of the Developing Areas,* Princeton, N. J.: Princeton University Press, 1960, pp. 165-167.

16. *Ibid.,* p. 167.

17. J. P. Naik, *Educational Planning in India.* Bombay: Allied Publishers, 1965, p. 67.

18. Quoted in Naik, *op. cit.,* p. 69.

19. One Indian scholar identified nine "great principles or programmes" which should guide the development of Indian education: (1) democracy, (2) secularism, (3) economic development, (4) adoption of science and technology, (5) cultural renaissance, (6) national integration, (7) equality of educational opportunity, (8) socialism, and (9) pursuit of excellence. For a discussion of these, see Naik, *op. cit.,* pp. 73-115.

20. George Rosen, *Democracy and Economic Change in India* Berkeley: University of California Press, 1966, p. 212.

21. *Ibid.,* p. 213.

22. For a more detailed examination of national planning efforts in India, see John A. Laska, *Planning and Educational Development in India,* New York: Teachers College Press, 1968.

23. Naik's explanation of the disproportionate expansion of secondary and higher education is worth quoting at length: "Expansion was inevitable for several reasons. . . . The expansion of elementary education created pressures from below which gradually mounted up to the secondary and university sectors also. The old 'job' values which went with elementary education practically disappeared, and hence the job-seekers came to look upon secondary as the 'minimum' and 'university' as the optimum education they need have. This created further pressures in secondary and higher education which were increased still further by the policy to provide very liberal free studentships and scholarships and to open new institutions without adequate (or even any) regard to the essential facilities needed for a minimum standard of education. The growing unemployment among secondary school leavers induced parents to send their boys to colleges 'just to keep them busy' and the rising age of marriage brought many a girl to secondary schools and colleges in an attempt to utilise pleasantly the period of waiting to be married. Consequently, expansion at the secondary and university stages has been even greater than at the elementary stage and has now gathered a momentum which would be extremely difficult to control in the future. 'Planning' in this regard has, therefore, meant not so much a measure of control of forced growth, but merely a drift with an existing current. The only exception, of course, is technical, vocational and professional education where

planning has been effective in every sense. But this streak of silver lining forms an exception and proves, rather than controverts, the thesis put forward above." Naik. *op. cit.,* pp. 18-19.

24. M. Blaug, P. R. G. Layard, and W. Woodhall, *The Causes of Educated Unemployed in India* (forthcoming).

25. India, Ministry of Education, *Report of the Education Commission (1964-66), Education and National Development.* New Delhi: Manager of Publications, 1966, p. 464. The latter figure is an estimate. Expenditures were calculated in current (rather than constant) prices. In 1968 the exchange rate was approximately eight rupees to the dollar.

26. *Ibid.,* p. 465. Again, the last figure is an estimate.

27. C. Mamoria, *Social Problems and Social Disorganization in India.* Allahabad: Kitab Mahal Private, Ltd., 1965, p. 103.

28. Shils, *op. cit.,* p. 70.

29. J. H. Hutton, *Caste in India.* London: Oxford University Press, 1946.

30. Kingsley Davis, *The Population of India and Pakistan.* Princeton, N. J.: Princeton University Press, 1951, p. 168. Cited in Edwin D. Driver, "Caste and Occupational Structure in Central India," *Social Forces,* Vol. XLI (1962), No. 1, pp. 26-31.

31. Driver, *ibid.*

32. *Ibid.*, p. 30.

33. Myrdal, *op. cit.,* p. 1722.

34. *Ibid.*, p. 1718.

35. *United Nations Demographic Yearbook,* 1964, p. 130.

36. Yet it is not only within the school system that pressures will be felt. Basically because of the youthful population structure, the cost of increased enrollments will place a heavy burden on the working-age population. In India the ratio of the working-age population to the school-age population is much lower than that of Western nations, making the cost of education per worker exceedingly high – another example of the fact that progress frequently requires more effort in the less developed nations.

37. Naik, *op. cit.,* p. 77.

38. *Ibid.,* pp. 116-128.

39. UNESCO, *World Survey of Education. II: Primary Education.* London: UNESCO and Evans Brothers, 1958, p. 537. While government expenditure on education has increased nearly five times between 1950 and 1965, there has been a decided shift in the proportionate share of educational costs borne by the national government and the states. Although the percentage of the total cost of education met by the "Center" was approximately 45 percent in 1946-1947, by 1965 it was reduced to 7.3 percent. Likewise, by 1965 the states were contributing over 65 percent of the total expenditure. The remainder of the educational expenditure was largely derived from fees and endowments.

40. India, Ministry of Education, *op. cit.,* p. 277.

41. Eric Ashby, "Adaptation of Universities in India and West Africa," *The Bulletin of the International Association of Universities,* November 1962, p. 253.

42. Nine other institutions were also accepted as universities under the University Grants Commission Act. These included scientific and research institutes, institutes of technology, etc.

43. Indians argued, for example, that the humanities, in particular, should incorporate in some meaningful way the ancient culture of Asia. Many Indian scholars would probably agree with the views of the principal of Ripon College, R. S. Trivedi, that "Western Education has given us much, we have been great gainers; but there has been a cost − a cost as regards culture, a cost as regards respect for self and reverence for others, a cost as regards the nobility and dignity of life." Quoted in Ashby, *Universities: British, Indian, African,* p. 116.

44. T. V. Sathyamurthy, "Relationship Between Teacher and Pupil in Ancient India: An Upanishadic View." *Educational Theory,* Vol. XV (January 1965), pp. 26-34.

45. *Ibid.,* p. 29.

46. M. Venkatarangarija, "The Plight of the Indian Teacher," *Atlas,* Vol. III (1962), pp. 277-280.

47. Naik, *op. cit.,* pp. 37, 24.

48. Myrdal, *op. cit.,* p. 1736.

49. Quoted in Hamayan Kabir, *Education in New India.* London: G. Allen, 1956, p. 23.

50. Quoted in A. H. Hanson, *The Process of Planning*: *A Study of India's Five-Year Plans 1950-1964,* New York: Oxford University Press, 1966, p. 43.

51. J. T. Hitchcock, "Centrally Planned Rural Development in India: Some Problems," March 1961. Quoted in John W. Hanson and Cole S. Brembeck (eds.), *Education and the Development of Nations,* New York: Holt, Rinehart and Winston, 1966, p. 436.

52. Education may, of course, be supportive of production and economic growth through more general qualitative changes in a nation's human resources. In India, there are at least fragmentary empirical data to suggest that level of education is directly related to innovation, rationality, punctuality − those characteristics considered vital to a work force in a modernizing society. See, for example, M.N. Srinivas, "Changing Institutions and Values in Modern India," in T.K.N. Unnithan, Indra Deva, and Yogendra Singh (eds.), *Toward a Sociology of Culture in India,* New Delhi: Prentice-Hall of India (Private) Ltd., 1965, pp. 427-438. Furthermore, schooling may also affect the size and rate of growth of the population, and thus have a significant but indirect effect on the economy. Unfortunately, few data appear to be available in India, or any Asian nation, explicitly linking educational output to desired family size, propensity to control fertility, etc. The general function of knowledge and literacy in successful family planning appears well recognized, however. Instruction regarding the use of contraceptives, birth control pills, intra-uterine devices, etc., has been noticeably less abundant than in those areas with higher educational levels.

53. The phenomenon of the "educated unemployed" has been visible in India since the last quarter of the nineteenth century. By the 1880's unemployment was described as "chronic" among the educated class. In one government report in the 1920's it was estimated that only 20 percent of the educated classes had "employment in keeping with the standard of their educational qualifications" and 10 to 15 percent had no employment at all. See Walter Kotschnig, *Unemployment in*

the Learned Professions: An International Study of Occupational and Educational Planning, London: Oxford University Press, 1937.

54. India, Ministry of Education, *op. cit.,* p. 535.

55. Blaug, Layard, and Woodhall, *op. cit.*

56. Social climbing in Indian society frequently depends on elevation of the family or status groupings which the individual inherits. Mandelbaum suggests that in order to rise, a jati must have economic power and use his wealth "to engage in purer and more prestigious group rituals." In contemporary India new ways of acquiring wealth and power have allowed jatis to circumvent the local stratification structure by appealing directly to higher political authorities. Further, Mandelbaum concludes, "because of the new methods and substance for success, the older *symbols* of high rank have become less attractive. . . . younger people generally are becoming more interested in acquiring the prestige of higher modern education than the badges of [traditional] status." David G. Mandelbaum, *Status-Seeking in Indian Villages,* Berkeley: University of California, Center for South Asia Studies, Reprint No. 270, 1968.

57. A. Aiyappan, *Social Revolution in a Kerala Village: A Study in Culture Change.* Bombay: Asia Publishing House, 1965, p. 86.

58. Margaret Cormack, *She Who Rides a Peacock: Indian Students and Social Change.* New York: Frederick A. Praeger, 1961, p. 63.

59. Aiyappan, *op. cit.,* p. 83.

60. Oscar Lewis, *Village Life in Northern India.* New York: Vintage Books, 1965, p. 45.

61. Shils, for example, finds that Indian intellectuals, while slightly less caste conscious than others, are "fundamentally and humanly insensate to the mass of the population . . . ." Yet the intellectuals are largely drawn from the upper-caste Hindus, and this attitude may be seen more to reflect caste bias than educational snobbishness. Shils, *op. cit.,* p. 70.

62. Robert Heilbroner, *The Great Ascent.* New York: Harper and Row, 1963, p. 66.

SELECTED READINGS

Ashby, Eric, *Universities: British, Indian, African: A Study in the Ecology of Higher Education.* Cambridge: Harvard University Press, 1966.

Cormack, Margaret Lawson, *She Who Rides a Peacock: Indian Students and Social Change.* New York: Praeger, 1961.

Education Commission, *Report of the Education Commission 1964-66: Education and National Development.* New Delhi: Ministry of Education, Government of India, 1st edition, 1966.

Kabir, Hamayan, *Education in New India.* London: G. Allen, 1956.

Laska, John A., *Planning and Educational Development in India.* New York: Teachers College, Columbia University, 1968.

Mukerji, S.N., *History of Education in India.* Baroda: Acharya Book Depot, 1957.

Myrdal, Gunnar, *Asian Drama*, Vol. III. New York: Pantheon, 1968.

Naik, J.P., *Educational Planning in India*. Bombay: Allied Publishers, 1965.

Shils, Edward, *The Intellectual Between Tradition and Modernity: The Indian Situation*. The Hague: Mouton and Co., 1961.

chapter four
china

In the past, many social and intellectual traditions emanated from China and exerted influence over other parts of Asia. It was to Golden China that Asian scholars for centuries came to study, observe, and imitate; for in China, learning and culture were the marks of the well-bred and prerequisites for admittance to government positions. Until the twentieth century, Chinese scholars were tutors and advisers in Japanese and other Asian courts. Quite understandably, the Chinese scholars abroad and the foreigners studying in China utilized the Chinese language, curriculum, and instructional methods in the pursuit of knowledge, thus extending the influence of the early pattern of Chinese education.

Contemporary China, with its vast land mass and huge population, although perhaps no longer the fount of learning and culture that it was in the past, still occupies a pivotal position in Asia. A dynamic Communist government is seeking to induce such changes as are conceived to be necessary for the rapid creation of a modern industrial state. Education through the formal school system and through every organized social group is designed to prepare the people psychologically and through knowledge and skills to build the new society.

SOCIAL AND RELIGIOUS TRADITIONS

The social philosophy which most influenced China until the advent of Communism may be described by the somewhat amorphous term, Confucianism. Confucius, the most famous of Chinese sages, lived and taught in the sixth and fifth centuries B.C. His teachings, reexamined and elaborated on by his disciples and other scholars, became the official curriculum for Chinese scholarship and strongly influenced all formal schooling in China until the twentieth century.

Confucianism was concerned with the identification of precepts that could guide social relationships in the formation of an ideal state. The goal was to define precise ways of behaving and mutual obligations between family members, men and women, youth and elders, and strangers of different rank. The practice of proper conduct was expected to begin in the home, and the concept of filial piety was a key to its understanding. Ideally, the state was merely the family writ large, with the head of state serving as the father of the national family.

The avoidance of the spiritual and the theoretical, and the focus on the problems of social relationships have given rise to the use by Western scholars of the terms utilitarianism, rationalism, and even humanism, when describing Confucianism. These Western concepts are not entirely applicable, for Confucius saw as the key to societal improvement the development of virtuous men. And virtue consisted ultimately of establishing the proper middle path between excess and denial — "the doctrine of the mean." Not all could expect to discover the Way (Tao), for there were hereditary variations in the nature of men. But those favorably endowed and properly educated, the "superior men," could (and were obliged to) find and pursue the Way, illuminating the path so that others might follow.[1]

Through the centuries the worldly doctrines of Confucianism were challenged by Buddhism, Taoism, Legalism, Christianity, and a number of smaller religious and ideological movements. Taoism as a religion, and even more as a philosophy, supplemented mundane Confucianism with visions of transcendentalism:

Confucianism has represented the mind of the Chinese scholar-gentleman in his office or study, being a good family man, a conscientious bureaucrat, and a sober, responsible citizen; Taoism has represented the same gentleman in his private chamber or mountain retreat, seeking surcease from the cares of official life, perhaps a little drunk but more likely intoxicated by the beauties of nature or of the world of the spirit.[2]

The father of Taoism was Lao Tzu, a contemporary of Confucius, who rejected the Confucian emphasis on finding wisdom in the written word.[3] Rather, "introspection" and "reflection" were the proper methods of acquiring important knowledge and the means for understanding nature's way. According to the paradoxical words of Lao Tzu: "He who seeks learning may daily increase. He who seeks the way will daily diminish. He will diminish and keep on diminishing until he does nothing. When he does nothing, then he will accomplish all things."[4]

But neither Taoism, which disparaged society as artificial and corrupting, nor Buddhism, which taught the rejection of this life through meditation, made the impact that Confucianism did on basic Chinese institutions. As Reischauer and Fairbank have noted, "Chinese society was firmly knit together by Confucianism. This great ethical institution, which in a sense occupied in China much of the place filled by both law and religion in the West, produced strong social cohesion and extraordinary equilibrium."[5]

But a few paragraphs on social and religious thought scarcely give an adequate picture of the functioning of traditional Chinese society. The nature of the economy, the language patterns, the geography, and the social structure are also important considerations. While comments will be made regarding a number of these areas when we consider the societal context of contemporary Chinese education, it seems particularly appropriate here to give some attention to the pattern of traditional social structure which was so effective in shaping Chinese institutions over the centuries.

First, it should be noted that, in China, historically it was the family rather than the individual, state, or church, which was the most significant unit of society. Of the five traditional social relationships, ruler-subject, father-son, husband-wife, elder brother-younger brother, and friend-friend, three were determined by kinship. It was in the family that the individual found security, and to a large extent the family was the source of his education and economic status. Through the tradition of "ancestor worship" the family even became the source of religious succor. The subordination of the individual to the family was further symbolized by the arrangement of marriage for sons and daughters.

While the respect shown to elders is common to family norms in most traditional societies, filial piety in China was the most admired of virtues. Although Confucian ethics stressed mutual obligations in intra- and extra-family relationships, in reality there existed a rigid hierarchy of power within the family. The two most important factors in determining respect and authority were age and sex.

The national family, whose paternal head was the Emperor, was further divided into a hierarchy of four classes extending downward in the following order: scholar-official, farmer, artisan, and merchant. In practice the merchant in China, as in Japan, was frequently able, through the accumulation of wealth, to wield considerable power. The prestige of the scholar-official, however, was never challenged.

Family patterns and class structure clearly promoted security and conformity. Equally clearly, the social structure resisted change and innovation. Recognizing this to be the case in the twentieth century, first the Republican government in minor ways, and later the Communist government by more drastic means, attempted to modify family and social class relationships.

TRADITION OF ORTHODOX SCHOLARSHIP

In the pre-Confucian period a body of learning developed in China which came to be known as the "Classics." These included descriptions of divination, historical documents, poems and songs, and texts on ethics and government. In the form in which these have been handed down, Confucius, at minimum, played the role of commentator. In time, the book of Mencius,[6] together with the *Analects* (or *Conversations*) in which the followers of Confucius tried to distill his more important thought, became the core of a new body of classics. During the Sung period the great scholar Chu Hsi (A.D. 1130-1200) combined these two texts with the earlier essays *The Great Learning* and *The Doctrine of the Mean* to form the Four Books.

In 124 B. C. the Imperial College was founded to teach the Classics to students chosen from the various provinces. The Academy, along with a number of private academies, some of which came into prominence as early as the Later Han period (A. D. 25-220), continued in existence into the twentieth century. During this time the Classics and the Four Books remained, in effect, the basic curriculum for study and research.

In keeping with the second stage of educational differentiation, there was considerable ritual surrounding education in early China. Learning to read and write had a sacral quality, for the child was obliged to (1) petition a teacher to guide him in his lessons, (2) receive a new identity, a "book name," if admitted, and (3) give regular obeisance to the tablet of Confucius. Moreover, the contents and style of learning were closely associated with age sets.

Instruction during the Sung (A. D. 960-1279), Ming (A. D. 1368-1644), or Ching (A. D. 1644-1912) periods, at least for the sons of the more wealthy families, began approximately at the age of seven. From the thirteenth century the first primer given to the child was the famous *Three-Character Classic* which in jingle form gave a summary of basic knowledge and precepts regarding human nature and social relationships. The next readers for the child were likely to be the *Thousand-Character Classic* and the *Three-Thousand-Character Classic,* which contained many of the ideas found in the Four Books.

The earliest instruction was offered in a village reading and writing school or through the services of a private tutor. As mentioned above, the source for more advanced education was the private academies which were centers for scholarly study, discussion, and bibliographic work. Academies offered tuition and maintenance to scholars and students and maintained small libraries; they were usually under the patronage of high officials or rich merchants. Some 300 academies were to be found throughout the country in the Ming period.

However, it is inaccurate to suggest that China prior to the nineteenth century had a well-articulated and differentiated educational system. Rather, educational advancement came through a system of examinations controlled by the state. These civil service examinations (so called because they led to appointment as a state official) are said to have had their beginnings as early as the Hsia (2205-1766 B. C.) and Shang (1766-1122 B. C.) periods. At the least, these examinations were functioning for the two millennia prior to the Republic.

During their long history, the civil service examinations were given varying emphases and included different content, thus reflecting the prevailing social thought and ideological preferences of the times. When Confucianism was in disrepute, their role in the selection of officials was reduced, but they were always an important supplement to existing educational institutions. During the T'ang period (A. D. 618-907) the examination system assisted in shattering the domination of political power by the aristocracy. And during the Sung period (A. D. 960-1127) the tradition that the examinations should test knowledge of the Four Books and Five Classics became firmly entrenched.

While it is difficult because of changes in different historical periods to describe either the operation of the system or the content of the examinations, the following steps indicate roughly the route followed by the successful Chinese scholar during the sixteenth to the twentieth centuries:

1. Matriculation examination at the local level.

2. Examination for the first degree, Hsiu T'sai (glowing talent), held in the chief city of the district. The Hsiu T'sai is sometimes referred to by Western students of China as the baccalaureate degree. This admitted the successful to the honored class of literati.

3. Examination for the second degree, Chu Jen, held at the provincial capital. One out of every 100 to 200 candidates was likely to achieve the distinction of passing this examination.

4. National examination for the degree of Chin Shih, held at the capital.

5. Examination by the emperor.[7]

The examination system clearly provided a route for social mobility. Reischauer and Fairbank note: "The examination system . . . gave China the world's first educated bureaucracy, chosen fundamentally on the basis of merit . . . "[8] An examination of historical changes in stratification patterns reveals that the social composition of the high-level Chinese official class became increasingly diversified from the Sung period onward. In addition to being a mechanism for the selection of an elite on the basis of achievement rather than ascriptive criteria, the examination system contributed to the intellectual unification of the country.

The ruling class thus came to have a uniform education, actually not unlike the classical education that produced a successful ruling class for the British Empire in modern times. Since Confucian ideology lay at the basis of this education the ruling class was thoroughly imbued with ethical principles, concepts of loyalty to existing authority, and a strong sense of the values of proper rituals and decorum.[9]

However, there were also significant weaknesses in the examination system. The orthodoxy of academic learning which enshrined the ideas of a few authors lapsed into literary scholasticism. Scholarship, narrowly defined, became a vocation in itself. Mencius had said, "Those who labor with their minds govern others; those who labor with their strength are governed by others." Science, at least applied science, and technology might involve the use of hands and were thus to be avoided by cultured men. Moreover, the pattern and prestige of scholarship to some extent substituted for earlier aristocratic tendencies by helping to perpetuate a division in Chinese society between the privileged few and the masses. Finally, scholastic antiquarian scholars rarely proved themselves to be efficient managers or effective political leaders.

The traditional Chinese educational pattern was different, then, in many respects from that found in Japan or India. Neither of the latter nations had had a long heritage of civil service examinations completely circumscribing the curriculum. Unlike the experience of these nations, the mainstream of education in China was never linked tightly to a particular social or religious group. Thus "education according to one's station" has never been an officially condoned policy in China.

Chinese education was, in one sense, secularized at an earlier period than was Japanese or Indian education, but in its limited function and rigid certification procedures it was supportive of an entrenched social pattern antithetical to modernization, and this social pattern was probably stronger than traditional value patterns found in earlier Japan or India. In terms of educational differentiation, it might be argued that China entered the third stage earlier than its neighbors and indeed acquired, in the form of achievement norms, certain characteristics usually associated with the fourth stage. However, in subordinating educational policy to a small group of scholar-administrators, China proved the most effective in walling out changes which might lead to higher levels of educational differentiation.

CULTURAL AND EDUCATIONAL CONTACT WITH THE WEST

China's first extensive contact with the cultural and educational ideas of the West came as a result of the work of the European Catholic and Protestant missionaries. Jesuits arriving in the sixteenth century had by the following century become well known to the Chinese court through their impressive knowledge of mathematics, mechanics, astronomy, and architecture. For their part, the Jesuits were ardent, and often profound, students of Chinese language, philosophy, and art and, therefore, the foremost interpreters of China to Europe.

As a result of actions on the part of the Catholic Church and counteractions from the Chinese Court, the eighteenth century saw a wane in missionary activities. The Church ruling in 1704 which forbade Catholics to take part in Confucian or ancestral rites was counteracted by the Emperor's ban, never fully enforced, on the proselytizing activities of Catholics. The abolition of the Society of Jesus in 1773 threatened for a time to eliminate Catholicism in China. Catholicism did survive, but by the nineteenth century it had far fewer Chinese converts than it had two centuries earlier.

Protestant missionaries, first English and later American, began arriving early in the nineteenth century. The conclusion of two successful wars (1839-1844 and 1856-1860) waged on China by European powers brought great expansion in mission activities. The Protestants, unlike the Catholics and only after considerable controversy within their ranks, gave attention to the development of schools as a means of winning converts and introducing Western culture. In this regard, an early educational society founded by the combined efforts of American and English Protestants proposed to " . . . establish and support schools in China in which native youth shall be taught and in connection with their own, to read and write the English language; and through this medium, to bring within their reach all the varied learnings of the Western world. The Bible and books on Christianity shall be read in the Schools."[10]

Educational institutions at the elementary, secondary, and higher levels were established by the missionaries. While the curricula included both Western and Chinese subjects, no attempt was made to provide the intensive training in the Classics which was necessary for success in the civil service examinations. Indeed, during the Manchu period graduates from mission schools were ineligible to receive government degrees and hence, in effect, were barred from government employment. Thus the foreignness of the mission institutions was even further accentuated and subjected to the scorn of the Chinese intellectuals, who claimed that these schools inadequately met Chinese standards of scholarship.

The quality of the mission institutions could also be challenged in terms of the adequacy of facilities, finances, and the academic credentials of the teachers. Nevertheless, through Western languages and other Western studies, mission schools provided a small number of Chinese students with a window to Western culture. Of even greater, indeed revolutionary, importance was the schooling offered to Chinese women. In Chinese tradition, formal education and other procedures for the certification and evaluation of scholarship were effectively closed to females. It was only in the mission schools (primarily Protestant) that Chinese girls could receive extensive instruction in home arts and occasionally in the regular academic subjects. From these schools came the girls who were to be the leaders in women's education, church work, social welfare, and women's rights movements.[11]

In addition to the introduction of Western education, missionaries made other contributions. Their hospitals and doctors undoubtedly saved many lives and opened the door to modern medicine. Perhaps also the Christian message itself gave something of lasting value to China. For, in spite of the lack of sophistication and even arrogance of many of the missionaries, the new religious ethos offered to the poor the Christian message of hope and to the cultivated classes a spiritual and emotional balance to the austere intellectuality of Confucianism.

But the number of converts was not large, never greater probably than one percent of the national population. Moreover, as Peffer has pointed out, there was "fundamentally something unhealthy and incongruous in the whole missionary idea: . . . to go out to a race of high culture and long tradition, with philosophical, ethical and religious systems antedating Christianity, and to go avowedly to save its people from damnation as dwellers in heathen darkness — in that there was something not only spiritually limited but almost grotesque."[12] Peffer continues: "Essentially the missionary movement rested on power — physical power. It was made possible because the countries from which the proselytizing came were so much stronger than those to which proselytizing was addressed that the missionaries could not be ejected."[13] The Chinese have historically viewed authority as being manifested in two ways; "the way of the prince," which was superior, and "the way of the war-lord," which was inferior. The way of Christianity, unfortunately, was more closely associated with the latter.

The educational effort of the missions was significant not only in the novelty of its content but also in its magnitude. Of the 21 private institutions of higher learning established between 1864 and 1911, twelve were Protestant and three were Catholic. During the Republic the mission effort in higher education continued, and of the 32 nongovernmental universities and colleges established between 1912 and 1936, sixteen were Protestant and three were Catholic. By 1920 there were nearly 20,000 Chinese students enrolled in mission elementary and secondary schools. Including all types and levels of schooling, mission institutions enrolled over 214,000 students as compared to the nearly 4.3 million students in government schools. Thus, approximately five percent of all Chinese students were participating in a Christian education; the percentage was significantly greater at the secondary and higher educational levels.[14]

It was inevitable that the educational efforts of the missions should come into conflict with Chinese policies. Under the Manchu dynasty there appeared to be a certain ambivalence regarding foreign ideas. While certain Western learning was tolerated, the Court did not look with favor on the mission schools, and Confucianism remained the guide to a proper education. By the early twentieth century, after the government of the Republic had become established, mission schools found it increasingly difficult to compete with the new national system of education. Mission schools, short of finances, hamstrung by cumbersome administration, and seduced by the desire to reach large numbers, were, by the end of the first decade of the Republic, surpassed in quality by the national schools.[15] As Gregg notes, "Mission schools and colleges had begun in the nineteenth century and tended to remain in that mold, whereas the government institutions were created by the twentieth-century returned student group from the West who emphasized science and vocational aspects."[16]

In a period of vigorous expression of nationalism, the very foreignness of mission education was an irritant. Although Chinese educators made numerous attempts to influence policy and achieve higher positions within the system, they found little opportunity to do so. Further, the mission schools were not in contact with the Ministry of Education in any formal manner, and were organized as part of a foreign school system to fit the needs of foreign institutions of higher learning. Even negotiations for recognition were carried on through the respective Consuls and thus directly tied to the "foreign Presence."[17]

The question of religious education was also a source of conflict. Since Confucianism had been one of the bases of support for the Manchu and the "old system," the Nationalist Regime was not strongly in favor of organized religion. Funds that had gone to Confucian rites were channeled into government education. Religion presented one of the greatest stumbling blocks to national development and change, and the new government was loath to see it continue in the position of power it had traditionally held. Religious teaching was forbidden in provincial schools by the National Conference of Provincial Educational Associations in 1924, and there was pressure from even Chinese Christians to disallow religious education in the primary schools so that "young minds might not be biased."[18] The forced Bible study and chapel attendance in the mission schools thus ran counter to national policy.

Chinese "student-power" under the Republic became a force for the new order and in 1922 organized an antireligious movement. Primarily anti-Christian, the movement questioned the ability of religion to stand the test of the new scientific way of life, and when discussion of this question was carried on in the press, the majority of the mission community appeared unprepared to defend Christianity in the face of science.[19]

A series of policies by the national government in the 1920's required closer cooperation from the mission schools. In 1927, the pressures for Sinification and against foreigners resulted in all foreign nationals being evacuated to the coastal cities, and the schools were finally Sinified almost completely.

Although much of the literature by Western scholars would seem to imply otherwise, contact with Western education, at least by the middle of the nineteenth century, was not limited to mission schools. As early as 1861, a foreign language institute for the training of official interpreters was opened in Peking. Indeed, between 1862 and 1900, public institutes, academies, and universities were established to offer training, in addition to foreign languages, in mechanics, telegraphy, shipbuilding, engineering, and the military sciences. The introduction of these new schools and courses of study, outside the examination system, were largely in response to military needs. Petitions to the emperor had urged: in order "not to be deceived by them [foreigners], we must know their languages"; "if we can concentrate to exhaust all their essence [Western astronomy and mathematics] therein lies for China the way to attain national power by self-determination"; "unless we can exhaust all the expertness of our enemy, we can never control their destiny."[20]

Yet even attempts to justify Western learning for national defense did not satisfy the majority of the leaders in the Chinese government. To the Imperial Court the superiority of the Chinese culture was absolute and to learn from the West or under Westerners was disgraceful. Not until the Republic was this view vanquished once and for all.

EDUCATIONAL CHANGE UNDER THE REPUBLIC

China, as has been noted, had more difficulty than Japan in accommodating itself to Western learning. Although in 1898 a series of decrees was passed embodying sweeping reforms in education and other sectors, these were quickly erased by a new wave of conservatism two years later. Not until 1903 (more than 30 years later than in Japan) was a plan developed for an articulated, national school system. And not until 1906 was the civil service examination system abolished. The new aims of education proclaimed in a royal decree were reminiscent of those of Meiji Japan, namely, "to develop in the minds of the young generation the following virtues: loyalty to the Emperor, reverence for Confucius, devotion to public welfare, admiration for the martial spirit and respect for industrial pursuits."[21]

After the revolution of 1911 and the creation of the Republic, a new Ministry of Education and a new school system were formed. Indeed the term "new education" came into vogue to distinguish the emerging scientific, coeducational, mass system from the traditional schools. Curricular changes not only included a reduction in attention to the Classics and the allocation of more time to mathematics and science, but also reflected the pragmatic and experimental attitudes popular in the West during the period between the World Wars. Influenced by John Dewey and other progressive thinkers, Chinese educators, such as Hu Shih and other intellectuals who formed the social movement known as the "New Tide," began to argue the merits of such innovations as "individualizing instruction," "relating school to life," and developing "problem-centered experiences" for pupils.

Inevitably, many of the innovations were only subjects for academic discussion and publication in professional journals. With teachers of limited professional background, inadequate facilities, and lingering prejudices among the public – particularly against coeducation and expressions of individualism – classrooms often remained places in which to endure the ordeal of memorization.

If the educational system under the Republic failed in its more revolutionary goals, it did diffuse literacy throughout a significant portion of the population and did give a fairly high-quality, essentially Western education to a small elite. In 1910, for example, the government educational institutions included approximately 86,000 primary schools serving less than three million pupils, less than 400 secondary schools for 52,000 students, and four universities with a few hundred students. Twenty years later there were over 261,000 primary schools with nearly 12 million pupils, roughly 1900 secondary schools with over 400,000 students, and 111 higher education institutions with over 43,000 students.[22]

At the outbreak of the Sino-Japanese war in 1937, however, approximately 80 percent of the Chinese population was still illiterate. In spite of the growth in the number of graduates at all levels, the output of the educational system – measured either in increases in skilled personnel in the labor force or in a higher quality of citizenship – remained disappointing.

It was under the Republic, reflecting the accumulated influence of Western contact and the aspirations of progressive Chinese leaders, that some stabilization began to evolve in the structure and curriculum of the educational system. In terms of structural differentiation, considerable fluctuation was visible in the length of schooling at each level, but the three basic hierarchical stages of elementary, middle, and higher education had become entrenched.

The significant changes in curriculum may be seen by comparing subjects offered and time allocations at the turn of the century with those after the Republic had become well established. In 1903, at the elementary level, the Classics, morals, Chinese language, arithmetic, and physical education together took up approximately 90 percent of the time allotment. With the exception of Chinese language and physical education, the time allotted to each of these had declined by the late 1920's. The Classics were eliminated as a separate subject and the time allocated to morals and physical education was reduced by half. On the other hand, Chinese language, which had occupied approximately 13 percent of class time in 1903, occupied slightly more than 28 percent by 1929.

A substantial increase in the emphasis on science and industrial arts (not offered in 1903) should also be noted. The trend away from the exclusive emphasis on ancient wisdom toward the more standard curriculum (essentially Western in origin) found in contemporary national societies is clear. Two particular qualities of the elementary school curriculum in China should be noted, however. First, the attempt to develop a substantial experience in handwork and in industrial arts represented a desire to attune children to the characteristics of a society bent on industrialization. Such a move has been common to many of the nations in the twentieth century which have sought to shed old educational ways and build a dynamic curriculum which assists the student to relate to "real life" problems.[23] Experiments in "practical," "labor-related" crafts, manual arts, etc., at the elementary school level have had a very checkered history, and unqualified success stories are few. China was no exception, and there is little evidence that the experiences in working with their hands did much to prepare students, either psychologically or practically, for the changes which were taking place in Chinese society.

Yet Western science and vocational subjects did not easily come to dominate the curriculum. Rather, the intellectual climate after the New Cultural Movement of 1919 temporarily tended to favor, particularly in higher education, Western philosophy, literature, and political theory. "Pure" learning and "knowledge for knowledge's sake" were deliberately encouraged and professional and technical pursuits neglected. It has been estimated that at Peking University from 1928 to 1932, 38 percent of the students majored in political science and law, 21.8 percent in literature and the arts, 10.2 percent in engineering, and 8.3 percent in science. The late 1930's saw this trend reversed. By 1938-1942 students majoring in engineering and science accounted for 21.0 percent and 11.3 percent, respectively, of the total college enrollment in the nation. During the same period, majors in law and the arts dropped to 20.2 percent and 11.4 percent, respectively.[24]

The second distinctive characteristic of the curriculum was the place of prominence of the national language, which throughout the period of the Republic occupied between one-quarter and one-third of the total time allotment. The nature of the constraints placed on the curriculum by the distinctive features of the Chinese language needs to be examined. Three such features included: (1) the spoken form and the written form had long been divorced; (2) there were many dialects; and (3) the written language was nonphonetic.[25] Given these characteristics, Chinese educators were faced with a number of questions. Should people write the dialect they spoke? Or should they write the dialect most people spoke? Should a phonetic system be introduced? If so, what would become of the valued literature in the nonphonetic script?

Justified primarily on the basis of the goal of national integration, some attempts were made immediately prior to and during the Republic to standardize the spoken and written languages. In 1903 the Ministry of Education issued a statement which said, in part: "...Mandarin is proposed as the spoken language of the whole Empire. Therefore, from the normal school to the higher primary, the teaching of Mandarin shall be included in the subject Chinese ..." "In the future all school teachers in every province shall teach in the official dialect."[26] In 1930 a Ministerial decree urged that all primary and secondary schools use the national spoken language as the medium of instruction. A set of phonetic symbols was utilized in the schools to facilitate standardized pronunciation. With regard to the written language, equally significant changes were taking place. Between 1920 and 1930 the classical language (a "dead," literary language divorced from the vernacular) was replaced in the lower grades by the vulgate language called Pei-Hua.

The transition to more functional language patterns was linked to literary reform. As a spokesman for the reform, Hu Shih called for elimination of the classical and the obscure and an ushering in of the simple and the common:

1. Down with the decorative and eulogistic literature of aristocracy; up with the simple and expressive literature of the citizens.

2. Down with the decayed and elaborate literature of Classicism; up with the fresh and truthful literature of realism.

3. Down with the obscure and strenuous literature of the woods; up with the clear and popular literature of society.[27]

The change in the form of the Chinese language facilitated as well as reflected a cultural change. Attention to the traditional literature declined rapidly as young people turned their attention to the new writers who were espousing the causes of nationalism, communism, and democracy. This change is documented by a study of the topics of essays written in the middle school from 1916 to 1929. This study showed that Chinese classical and historical subjects accounted for approximately 25.3 percent to 26.2 percent of the total essays from 1916 to 1924, but only 2.4 percent of the total after 1925. Thus, in time, the introduction of the vulgate language and the abolition of the Classics in the primary schools produced changes in the upper schools.[28]

These changes in language, while not fully satisfying the radicals who called for a phonetic written language, were perhaps hardly less revolutionary than the substitution of Italian for Latin in Renaissance Italy. Obtaining a high level of literacy in the national written language, with its thousands of characters, nevertheless remained a difficult hurdle and a major preoccupation of all pupils.

Many of the educational changes during the first three decades of the twentieth century were justified by Chinese leaders largely on the basis of international comparisons. Those who supported mass education, simplification of the language, or modernization of the curriculum frequently did so by pointing out that these reforms had already taken place in foreign countries or that such changes were necessary for China to become a modern state. Indeed, one can find a defense of each subject in the curriculum based on practices in Western education. Curiously enough, even those who wished to keep the Classics in a place of prominence also sought justification through comparisons with the West.[29]

Thus a complete turnabout had taken place since 1900. At the opening of the twentieth century there was both official and popular opposition to the introduction of Western education, with the exception of those elements directly related to military defense. Yet, with the establishment of the Republic, an educational system with a new structure and a new curriculum which drew heavily from the West was haltingly installed. Language changes facilitated new learnings in the school and assisted social communication outside. In keeping with the needs of a nation which was beginning to apply science and technology to its problems, the full gamut of specialized subjects and courses of study appeared at the higher educational levels, and the variety of teacher roles was adjusted accordingly — an advanced stage of educational differentiation had been attained. The Chinese educational system could still not be described as a mass system, and the qualitative shortcomings at each level were readily visible, yet the basic structural and programmatic steps toward a modern system had been taken.

It was clear, however, in the 1930's that the aspirations for widespread literacy and educational opportunity which progressive intellectuals and leaders had articulated in the decade after the establishment of the Republic were going unfulfilled. Educational opportunities were strongly related to family income, social status, and place of residence. In the rural areas even the wealthy families gave little formal education to females.[30]

Outside the educational system, social problems grew rather than lessened in intensity. Ideological divisiveness among the people and corruption among political officials reduced the efficiency of the national government. In the villages of rural China, conditions were particularly ripe for revolution. Fukutake notes:

Where the relations between the landlords and the cultivating peasants were not characterized by the familial paternalism common in Japan, a radical revolution could more easily be carried through; while for peasants of low productivity, living in miserable poverty, the prospect — or at least the possibility — of any improvement in production and income provided adequate motive for supporting the reform. At the same time there were few barriers to revolutionary indoctrination among peasants of low educational levels, little given to self-reliant individualism. These circumstances made possible the radical Communist transformation of the countryside through co-operatives to communes within the space of a decade.[31]

INPUTS TO THE COMMUNIST EDUCATIONAL SYSTEM

In his deterministic theory of economic materialism, Marx took the economic factor as an independent variable and traced associations with religious and other institutional variables. This economic theory of history reveals to the Communist a struggle among social classes produced by man's relentless fight against his environment for food and security for himself and his family. The key to the improvement of man's lot lies in the mastery of the tools of production.

The final social goal, according to Marx, could be achieved only by revolution. "No solution can be found which does not completely unite the man and the citizen, the individual's private and social capacities, and only a revolution by the proletariat, the final class below which no exploited class remains, can achieve this end."[32]

The goal, then, is a new man and a new society. The man is a public man with a public conscience — which demands discipline and industry. Theoretically, there is no conflict between social and individual interests, for societal evolution toward the Communist end is the only measure of progress. Individual behavior which is detrimental to such progress is unacceptable and, as both Soviet and Chinese Communists are fond of saying, "he who doesn't work [i.e., work for the state] doesn't eat."

While the call for a public man with a public conscience might not run counter to Chinese tradition, the concept of class struggle and the apparent goal of obliteration of the significant social role of the family unit do signify revolutionary changes. The conflict of Marxism and Confucianism is apparent and was identified as early as 1927 by Mao Tse-Tung, then a local leader of peasant rebellions in Hunan Province, who perceived a number of evil systems of authority in Chinese society:

1. The system of the state (political authority), ranging from the national, provincial, and county government to the township government.

2. The system of the clan (clan authority), ranging from the central and branch ancestral temples to the head of the household.

3. The system of gods and spirits (theocratic authority), including the system of the nether world ranging from the King of Hell to the city of gods and local deities, and that of supernatural beings ranging from the Emperor of Heaven to all kinds of gods and spirits.[33]

Mao further identified a fourth evil system — the domination of women by the authority of the husband.

To Mao the path was clear. Since the political authority of the landlords was considered to be the foundation of other systems of authority, this group must be eliminated. Even before 1930, steps were taken to transfer certain powers to peasant groups; these steps represent the initial move toward the establishment of a dictatorship of the people. By 1944 the task had been completed and the People's Republic was proclaimed.[34] The Communist Party in China, by fiat and through the many channels of social persuasion, sought to destroy traditional social status arrangements. Explicit steps in bringing about the new social order were numerous, but the major policies may be easily identified. First, by assuming control of the "means of production," the state, under the leadership of the Party, sought to eliminate capitalism and the individual reward system associated with it. Second, new, collectivized productive arrangements were created whereby rewards would be related to the fulfillment of state production targets. Concomitant with these steps, campaigns via all media continued in order to correct "contradictions" in the people's thinking about status.

Modifications in Family Patterns

Policies were also established affecting the kinship system, its status pattern, its solidarity, and its wide-ranging social and economic functions. The contemporary Chinese family, influenced both by the period of modernization under the Republic and by recent Communist changes, more closely resembles the family of the West. The marriage law of 1950, incorporating many of the reforms of an earlier civil code, forbids arranged marriages, childhood betrothals, bigamy, concubinage, and interference with remarriage of widows; furthermore, it gives women equal rights to employment, management of property ownership, and appeal for divorce. The significance of the law (not entirely enforced) is at least twofold. First, it has served to break down the extended family and make the nuclear family the basic structure. This result, coupled with the increased authority and freedom of the woman, has led to a decrease in the size of the family and the elimination of the traditional identification of marriage with the sacred function of perpetuating ancestral lineage. Increased freedom has, quite naturally, also led to marriage resulting from free choice or on a basis of "romantic love" rather than through familial arrangement.

The second result of the increase in economic and social freedom and responsibility for women has been the breakdown of the traditional respect for age. Youth plays a much more important role in Communist China than it did in the previous state; and, conversely, elder members of the family do not wield the authority that they once did. Communist newspapers and other publications are now profusely illustrated with examples of "revolutionary youth" showing "feudal" elders the correct path.

The Communists have viewed entrenched family loyalty as detrimental to the establishment of the socialist state. Older family members, it is feared, are too steeped in bourgeois ideas to successfully give leadership to the socialist revolution. Therefore, it has been necessary to substitute a "friend-to-friend" relationship as a basis for the pattern of human relationships, in place of the formal father-son relationship of former times. The new Communist family, rather than representing a line-and-staff organization, becomes instead a small cooperative in which each member has equal rights and contributes according to his ability.[35]

The change in Chinese family life has undoubtedly undermined the influence which the family now exerts over the children. However, the degree to which influence has been decreased has not been adequately evaluated by Communist or Western writers at this time. Some observers feel that while the family change in Communist China has been great in comparison with the traditional Chinese pattern, the resultant family life is not too dissimilar to that of the West, inasmuch as (1) the number of functions of the family has been reduced, (2) each member of the family has economic independence, and (3) the father, while respected, is not presumed to have supreme authority. Such observers argue that the basic changes which have been wrought are as much the result of industrialization as a planned ideological policy of the Communists. Perhaps the major difference between the new and the old family life, or between the Communist family pattern and that of the West, lies in situations in which the loyalty of the family member to the state is involved. Without exception, in Communist society the individual's prime commitment in loyalty lies with the state, and no conflict between family and state is recognized.

National Production and Economic Targets

To increase national production and to create a viable economy, the Communist government undertook three initial tasks:

1. *to halt inflation and rehabilitate the productive capacity destroyed in the Sino-Japanese War (1937-1945);*
2. *to tighten economic control through the absorption of commercial banks into the government system and to revamp the tax structure;*
3. *to increase the rate of investment with a concentration on the development of heavy industry.*[36]

Some preliminary success at all three tasks can be claimed. From 1950 to 1957 (the end of the First Five Year Plan) the gross national product rose 86 percent (on the basis of 1952 prices).[37] Industrial and agricultural output have both increased substantially and the degree of self-sufficiency in many manufactured items has likewise been improved. Indicating the dimensions of the Communist commitment to industrialization, nonagricultural employment rose steadily at a rate of 2.2 percent and by 1957 had reached 40.9 million.[38] Moreover, during the First Five Year Plan employment in the traditional sector (handicrafts, fishing, peddling, etc.) declined by about four million, while employment in the modern sector (modern factory industry, construction, transport, etc.) increased by eight million. After "the Great Leap Forward" (announced in 1957), industrial employment alone grew from 7.9 to 23.4 million people between 1958 and 1964. This expansion partly reflects the movement to small-scale, labor-intensive industrial efforts – a movement representing explicit Party policy to utilize a large unskilled labor pool in lieu of scarce capital and skills.

While there can be little doubt that the Communists have generated dynamism in the economy, failures have occurred and momentous problems remain. For example, the massive attempt to establish large numbers of small-scale industrial production units has not resulted in the anticipated increase in production. The same could also be said for the commune movement and for agricultural production. Further, the high rate of population growth has offset much of the benefit of economic expansion.

Ideology, Production, and Education

The ideological and economic orientation of the Communist government could be expected to be reflected in new kinds of educational inputs. Indeed, education has been given a vital role to play in modifying old traditions and in shaping the new Communist man and the new Communist society. The importance of education has long been recognized by both Communist theorizers and practical politicians. Marx saw the intervention of education in society as a natural historical phenomenon, and the only difference under Communism was the character of such intervention. Communism sought to "rescue education from the influence of the ruling class."

As a Chinese Communist Party spokesman explained, educational opportunities must first go to the workers and peasants, classes which compose the bulk of the population and upon whose support the Party depends heavily.[39]

Like other state-directed activities, education, then, is conceived as a tool serving the purposes of the Party, which, of course, is the interpreter of the true Communist way. Education must be as pervasive as the total range of the people's social activities, which include "the class struggle, political life, their work in the fields of science and art."[40] The school, the press, the commercial or industrial concern, and the various youth and adult clubs are all educational institutions and therefore all have political objectives. Art, music, and literature receive encouragement and support. However, they tend not to be judged on the basis of what Western critics might term intrinsic artistic merit; rather, the arts receive praise or censure on the basis of the extent to which they operate as educational media in promoting the Communist ideology. And as Mao Tse-Tung has pointed out in a curious metaphor for a Communist, "Not to have a correct political point of view is like having no soul."[41]

That politics should influence educational inputs, then, is central to contemporary Chinese educational policy. This view has been vigorously put forward by the Communist party:

We hold the view that education should serve the politics of the proletariat; the bourgeois class is of the opinion that "education is for education's sake"; this means that education should serve the politics of the bourgeois class . . . we hold the view that education should be directed by the Party, on the line of the masses; the bourgeois class thinks that only expert staff can direct education.[42]

While the political goal is uppermost, the goal of industrializing, modernizing, and scientizing the Chinese society is viewed as being of exceedingly high priority.[43] A second major goal for education, then, is to maximize the productivity of all workers. The means to this end are to make all education scientific and to link all instruction to labor. There can be said to be both a constructive and a destructive purpose for wide dissemination of scientific knowledge among the Communist masses. On the positive side, application of scientific knowledge in the factory and on the farm can lead to increased production. However, Communist theorizers and planners also exhibit great faith in the ability of science to undermine any vestiges of bourgeois religion. In all media of communication, science tends to be represented as the new, the progressive, the "light," while religion is pictured as the old, the reactionary, and the "darkness." In language to which the Chinese Communists would probably subscribe, Khruschev noted: "If you do away with the devil, you don't need the priest." Science has been given the task of eliminating directly the material, and indirectly the spiritual, devil.[44]

Accompanying the emphasis on science has been the objective of uniting education and labor. All Marxist intellectuals since the time of Marx and Engels have urged such a direction as a means of developing proper Communist attitudes toward work and as a means of increasing production. Lenin furthered the idea:

It is impossible to picture the ideal society of the future without the union of study and productive labor for the young generation: neither study and education without productive labor nor productive labor without study and education to parallel it could be established on the high level demanded by the contemporary level of technique and status of scientific knowledge.[45]

In China, where the Communist scriptures appear to be taken quite literally, Party leaders advocate in the strongest, most explicit language possible the marriage of labor and education. Academic endeavors at any educational level unsupported, in principle at least, by physical labor are not tolerated.

Population and Education

In China, as in the other less developed nations of Asia, a large proportion of the population is young and therefore unproductive; about 1960, approximately 40 percent of the total population was under 15 years of age. Moreover, because of the low life expectancy, economic returns from any prolonged educational investment in youth would be less than in the more developed nations.

Precise data on the size, structure, and growth of China's population are not available. The total population has been variously estimated from 700 million to 1 billion. Likewise, the estimated yearly growth rate, while accepted as increasing over the past ten years, varies from source to source, but is generally believed to be in excess of two percent. Life expectancy in China is probably slightly higher than in India but lower than in Japan.[46]

Even the size of the work force is difficult to ascertain. First, with the creation of urban communes and other actions to "liberate women from their households," it is difficult to draw a sharp line between the working and the nonworking population. Second, explicit work campaigns such as the Great Leap Forward nearly doubled the number of workers and employers in one year.

Based on a variety of assumptions regarding fertility and mortality rates, economic development, and food production and distribution, demographers have built various projection models of Chinese population. Under all but the most pessimistic expectations, China's population will exceed one billion by 1985. Table 14 shows the range (applying different models) of population distribution by age for 1965 and 1985.

By 1965 the proportion of the population under the age of 15 was just below or a little above 40 percent. Projections to 1985 suggest that the population will remain comparatively youthful. Both the age structure and the magnitude of the population affect the scale of educational inputs. Population in the primary school age cohort has increased from roughly 75-90 million in 1953 to 110-140 million in 1965. The combined population for primary and secondary school-age children has increased from 145-175 million in 1953 to 200-250 million in 1965.

At least for its first two decades in power, the Communist government has been able to cope with this pressure on its educational system. From 1949 to 1960 primary enrollment increased from 24 million students to over 90 million students, the latter figure representing 87 percent of all children of primary school age. The expansion of enrollments in the general secondary schools during this period showed an even greater proportional increase, from approximately one million to over five million. Because of fluctuations in terminology, it is especially difficult to analyze enrollment changes in higher education under the Communists. There were roughly 200 institutions of higher learning in China when the Communists gained control; in 1957 there were approximately 236 universities and institutes of higher education. From 1958 to 1960, however, the number of universities was said to have trebled. And higher education enrollments grew from 117,000 in 1949 to a reported 820,000 in 1962 (see Table 15). Educational growth, while great in the regular schools, was even more

TABLE 14   Estimated and Projected Distributions of the Population of
Mainland China by Age, Both Sexes, 1965 and 1985

1965

Age	Range, percent
0 to 4 years	14.5 - 15.6
5 to 14 years	24.7 - 26.2
15 to 24 years	17.2 - 18.0
25 to 34 years	13.7 - 14.3
35 to 44 years	10.7 - 11.0
45 to 54 years	7.6 - 7.9
55 to 64 years	5.2 - 5.9
65 to 74 years	2.6 - 3.3
75 years and over	.7 - 1.1

1985

Age	Range, percent
0 to 4 years	12.5 - 17.9
5 to 14 years	21.6 - 23.7
15 to 24 years	16.6 - 19.9
25 to 34 years	15.2 - 17.2
35 to 44 years	10.3 - 11.1
45 to 54 years	7.4 - 8.2
55 to 64 years	4.8 - 5.8
65 to 74 years	2.3 - 3.3
75 years and over	.6 - 1.5

Source: *An Economic Profile of Mainland China.* Studies Prepared for the Joint Economic Committee, Congress of the United States, Vol. I: "General Economic Setting, The Economic Sectors." No. 72-911. Washington, D.C.: U. S. Government Printing Office, 1967, p. 365.

dramatic in vocational schools, "people's schools," "Red and expert universities," and various other work-study arrangements. By way of illustration of the effort in this direction, in 1960 there were over two million youth enrolled in the agricultural half-work, half-study schools.

In order to meet the teaching needs for the expanded enrollments, the size of the teaching force was increased by 3.5 times between 1949 and 1964. This growth represented, at the primary level, an increase from 832 thousand to over 2.5 million; at the secondary level, an increase from 82 thousand to 590 thousand; and in higher education, an increase from 16 thousand to 145 thousand.[47]

142

142

TABLE 15 Enrollments of Full-time Students in Institutions of Higher Learning in Communist China, 1949-1950 to 1962-1963

Academic year	Enrollment (thousands)	Index number (1949-1950 = 100)
Pre-1949 peak year (1947-1948)	155	132
1949-1950	117	100
1950-1951	137	117
1951-1952	153	131
1952-1953	191	163
1953-1954	212	181
1954-1955	253	216
1955-1956	288	246
1956-1957	403	344
1957-1958	441	377
1958-1959	660	564
1959-1960	810	692
1960-1961	955	816
1961-1962	819	700
1962-1963	820	700

Source: An Economic Profile of Mainland China, p. 529.

Note. Numbers of enrollments reported for 1957-1958 through 1960-1961 are confused and inconsistent. Based on admissions and graduates for each year, the enrollment in 1958-1959 would be 517,000 (441,000 − 72,000 + 148,000), which is 143,000 less than the 660,000 reported by the Chinese Communists. Totals for 1958-1959 and for 1959-1960 have been announced, but have a "Big Leap" flavor. The 1960-1961 enrollment of 955,000 is derived from the announced graduations and admissions based on the 1959-1960 enrollment of 810,000 (810,000 − 135,000 + 280,000). However, a Russian journal gives 900,000 for the 1960-1961 enrollment (*J.P.R.S.*, No. 4493, p. 10). A Chinese official announcement even gave the number as "over a million" for the 1960-1961 enrollment. Discrepancies ranging from 55,000 to 100,000 appear in these three different estimates.

Stratification and Education

It is even more difficult to describe the student or teaching inputs in other than crude quantitative terms. That is, there are few national data concerning the social origins, motivations, or values which affect the "quality" of these inputs. The often reiterated goal of the Communist government has been to bias education in favor of workers and peasants. But to what extent has this been accomplished?

Perhaps a question concerning the nature of social stratification in postrevolutionary China needs to be asked first. With the exception of identifying "enemies of the people" and "bourgeois revisionists," the literature from China presents the official image of social homogeneity. However, although the Party officially recognizes no status differentiation within its ranks or even among supporters of the revolution, Barnett argues that "within a few years after the Communists had assumed power, the bureaucracy had already become highly stratified and notably rank and status-conscious."[48]

One basic status differentiation which has been accorded general recognition is that between cadres (*kan pu*) and the masses (*ch'un chung*). Barnett comments:

All cadres . . . belong to the ruling elite and despite the impressive "mass line" policies promoted by the regime, the gap between the cadres and the non-cadres, i.e. between the elite and the ordinary people, the rulers and the ruled, is very real indeed. As one goes up in the Chinese bureaucracy, the gap between cadres and ordinary people steadily widens, as one might expect, but even at the lowest levels the cadres tend to regard themselves and are clearly regarded by the Chinese masses, as a group apart because of their power and authority.[49]

Salaries have been another important criterion for status and "persons tended to receive deference and respect according to their salary grades, which were generally known by others in their organization." Moreover, these salary and job-level gradations were characterized by "great psychological distance between those at the top and those at the bottom."[50]

In contrast to the ideal portrayed in the slogans and literature, pay scales, level of schooling, and decisionary discretion serve as indicators of social status on a graduated scale which places the masses at the broad base and the highest party officials at the apex. Yet two seemingly anomalous sets of factors appear to complicate the picture: (a) the party-nonparty axis and (b) the intellectual-nonintellectual axis. The latter could also, perhaps, be described as "the proletarian-nonproletarian" axis. A certain degree of parallelism must be recognized between the two pairs, however, for the intelligentsia, with notable exceptions at high bureaucratic levels, are largely nonparty cadres.

Criticism may be found in Communist sources of the privileges of the few, whether these few are in high political positions or are part of the academic intelligentsia: "Under the leadership of the united committees, more than 20,000 proletarian revolutionaries of the Academy of Sciences are fiercely opening fire at the handful of top party persons in authority taking the capitalist road."[51] Also: "The offspring of some unreformed cadres, due to their special living position and environment . . . long ago abandoned thought reform. They have claimed as their own the merit of their fathers. By relying on petty reputations and so-called 'wide and extensive knowledge' they have gained the applause of the masses."[52]

The stratification system is reflected in the functioning of the educational system in a number of ways. First, the Party attempts to reinforce the ideal of classlessness by subordinating school policy to Party policy and involving all school personnel — teachers, students, clerks, custodians — in decision making on less important matters. Furthermore, clerks, caretakers, manual workers, etc., attached to schools belong, on an equal footing with the teachers, to the China Education Workers Trade Union.

Second, since the attitudes, values, and class biases of the teachers impinge on the education of the new generation, the Party Central Committee has given considerable attention to the "right thinking" of teachers and to preventing any resurgence of professionalism. The press, reflecting Party concern, has frequently suggested that teachers are not truly "rectified" and "proletarianized." Blame is laid squarely on the "black line" of certain "top Party members following the capitalist road."[53]

Inquiry into the social origins of teachers in the full-time educational system may indicate the reason for Party fear. Sieh points out the varied backgrounds of the teaching staff and the major groupings into which they are likely to be divided.

Ranks of the profession include "retained personnel" held over from the pre-communist system; educated housewives inducted into the system in large numbers during the early years of the Peking regime; graduates of Communist teacher training colleges; raw recruits arbitrarily assigned to teaching jobs after graduation from junior or senior middle school; and Party, government, factory and commune functionaries engaged in part-time teaching tasks. Writers on education and former teachers interviewed often describe the staffs in dualistic terms suggestive of the principal social groupings within a school. They differentiate between the teachers who are Party members or "progressives" and those who lack Party affiliation, between teachers of worker peasant background and those of bourgeois background, between the young and the old, the experienced and the inexperienced.[54]

A bimodal typing thus emerges, with (a) age, experience, and non-Party affiliation applied to those considered "bourgeois" and (b) youth, inexperience, and Party orientation, if not affiliation, considered as characterizing the new "proletarian" element. These groups are based on two essentially inimical rationales, one in which the "masses" ideally occupy the top status levels, and the other reflecting an intellectual, professionally oriented elite. Here, more than elsewhere in the social system, keeping the ideological pyramid in balance becomes a problem.

A third consideration of the Party has been adjustment of selection and promotion policies in keeping with the social origin of students. Unfortunately, factual material on the social backgrounds of students in the regular school system is rare. A few gleanings from Sieh show, however, that this matter is very much in the minds of teachers and administrators. A teacher is expected to be thoroughly familiar with his students and their family background in order to guide them better along the paths indicated by the Party. Sieh states:

Through conversation with the beginner or by assigning biographical essays in the higher grades, teachers seek . . . to determine the family background of the pupils. "Good families" are judged to be members of the worker-peasant class, with which the "proletarian qualities" of selfless labor, revolutionary enthusiasm and loyalty to the Party are associated. "Bad families," representatives of the bourgeoisie, are supposedly marked by selfish individualism, reactionary spirit, and disloyal tendencies.[55]

Higher education, in particular, has been accused of discriminating against students from the working classes. One of the complaints emerging from the Great Proletarian Cultural Revolution (initiated during the summer of 1966) ·was that privileged classes and bourgeois teachers still existed. Peking University, for example, was strongly accused of serving "capitalistic" politics and playing down production labor. More specifically the accusation was that enrollment, teaching, final semester exams, and work assignments after graduation had been adjusted to restrict the opportunities of descendants of workers and peasants. The rebelling students claimed that although the Anti-Right Movement of 1959 had resulted in high ratios of worker and peasant descendants in the enrollment figures of 1960, after that date the proportion of students from the working classes had declined. The data in Table 16, from the Department of Geophysics, were offered as evidence.

TABLE 16   Social Origin of Students from One Department in Peking University, 1960 to 1963

	1960 class	1961 class	1962 class	1963 class
		Percentages		
Descendants of workers and peasants	61	40	40	
Descendants of poor peasants	41	30	27	18
Descendants of landlords and capitalists	8	12	23	

Source: "Bourgeois Influence and Favoritism in College Enrollment," *J.P.R.S.*, No. 37,712, pp. 1-2. Translation of an article by Yang Kuang-Chi, Tung Shuang-Lin, Tung Shou Xyu, Ch'en Chia-Hui, and Huang K'o-T'ao in Chinese-language newspaper *Chung-kue Ch'ing-nien Pao* [*China Youth Daily*], Peking, August 16, 1966, p. 3.

The following example was cited of "mistaken" enrollment practices:

Student A — poor peasant, member of Communist Youth League, entrance examination score 78.4, good political showing

Student B — capitalist among ordinary masses, entrance examination 80.4, poor political showing

Student B was admitted to Peking University, and Student A was not.

Other fragmentary evidence has been offered that higher academic standards favor the students from a more bourgeois background. As an example, the "revolutionary" students cited the fact that the Department of Mathematics and Dynamics kept back 40 students in 1961, 38 of whom were of peasant-worker origin. In 1962, the same Department disqualified eight of the ten advanced research students who had been admitted the previous year on the strength of their Party membership and Party recommendation. More revealing, President Lu P'ing (of Peking University) was quoted as having made the statement that "refined floral designs simply cannot be applied to coarse china." "Coarse china" in this case referred obviously to students of proletarian background.[56]

In addition to these and other discriminatory practices, the administration of Peking University was also charged with imitating the Soviet Union, emulating the West, and reemploying scholars whose lack of political reliability had earlier caused dismissal.[57]

To a very considerable extent the Great Proletarian Cultural Revolution of 1966, which flooded the urban streets with tens of thousands of youth and sought to erase the final vestiges of bourgeois or Western practices, was directed toward the educated elite. This intelligentsia of professionals and technicians has controlled much of the economy and the educational system. Frequently, they have been in high positions within the Party. Party leaders became alarmed at the pragmatic attitude of many members of this group toward the definition of talent and at their reluctance to accept the priority of ideology in practical matters of economic policy. Such inclinations were all too reminiscent of the revisionist policies of the U.S.S.R.

These dissatisfactions with higher education in China may, of course, be viewed as a branch of the common struggle in developing nations to bring the educational system into line with newer social goals. Yet there are important differences in the Chinese case. First, the goal is not to make education supportive of mobility per se; it is, on the one hand, a means of "intellectualizing" the proletariat and, on the other hand, of proletarianizing the intellectuals. Indeed, the social goal is not one of equalizing educational opportunity among all social groups. On the contrary, although talent and expertise must be given due regard, the peasant-worker class, by virtue of its role in the Revolution, also must receive privileges. Thus the tasks of promoting both "expertness" and "redness" are the only acceptable goals of education. At a given time the emphasis may be on one, while at another time the emphasis may be reversed. The ultimate goal, however, is a marriage of the two.[58]

THE STRUCTURE AND FUNCTION OF THE CONTEMPORARY EDUCATIONAL SYSTEM

According to the Constitution of the People's Republic of China, adopted in 1954, educational power would seem to reside in the state. At the national level is a Ministry of Education which supervises all education. As in all other sectors, the Communist Party, while having no place on the official chain of command, exercises a basic policy-making function. At each level of government there is an educational agency charged with responsibility for supervision (see Table 17): at the provincial level, a department of education; at the municipal level, an educational bureau; at the district level, a cultural and educational section. Since Party units also exist at each governmental level, close control of educational policy is facilitated. Party involvement is reinforced by the assignment of veteran cadres to key positions on the administrative staff of the individual schools.

Primary Education

The contemporary educational system has undergone considerable experimentation under the Communist government, and no attempt will be made to examine in detail the many temporary organizational and programmatic variations. Rather, the focus will be on those structural and functional characteristics of the three basic levels of education which appear to offer insight into the ways in which the system operates to achieve its ideological and production targets.[59]

Primary schools are generally divided into four-year junior primary schools and two-year senior primary schools. The tremendous growth in numbers of primary schools during the last decade is attributable not only to direct government action but also to the establishment of schools by industrial enterprises, cooperatives, communes, and various urban organizations. These schools are called "people-sponsored schools" as distinct from public or state schools.

The basic curricular changes in the primary schools under the Communist government included adding labor to the weekly schedules, rewriting and standardizing textbooks, and incorporating into the curriculum special political instruction. The learning of Chinese characters still occupies a dominant position in the curriculum, taking approximately

TABLE 17 Control of Education under the Communist Government

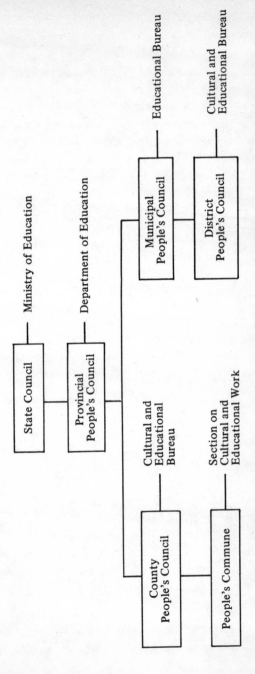

Source: Adapted from Chang-tu Hu, *China: Its People, Its Society, Its Culture,* New Haven, Conn.: Human Relations Area Files Press, 1960, p. 421.

one-half of the time allotment in the first four grades and somewhat less than half in the next two grades.

For the smaller children, engaging in labor has meant spending two or more hours a week in the school garden, in housekeeping chores at home and school, participating in campaigns to eliminate flies or other pests, or assisting in minor ways in making the community more hygienic. The older children may spend several hours a week in regular factory or farm work. Since 1958 extensive attempts have been made to make primary education encompass both study and work, with the result that primary schools are now looked upon as both "centers of production" and "centers of learning." A headmaster at a village primary school explained the new approach to primary education:

The methods we use are different from those of the old days. We have no learning off by heart. We try to stimulate the pupils' own interest in what is being studied. They must want to learn the thing . . . Before, school used to train bookworms who had no understanding of real life. One of my classmates had a father who was a farmer . . . When this father came to visit his son at his school in Lochuan, the boy used to run away and hide, because he was ashamed before the others of having a father who worked with his hands. Now, pupils are brought up to do work with their own hands . . . [60]

Political instruction may take place formally through the standard subjects, or through participation in some Party-sponsored campaign. For example, time is set aside for discussion of current events — those national, international, political, cultural, economic, or military events considered significant by the Party. Frequent topics for discussion over the past decade or so have included "War of Resisting America and Aiding Korea," "Liberation of Taiwan," "The Great Leap Forward," and "Detection and Reporting of Counter-Revolutionary Activities."

Political and labor education forms the core of the teaching of morality, and illustrates to the children the difference between Communist or public morality and bourgeois or individual morality. Stories and poems depict the rewards for honesty, cooperation, and generosity. Again, a village headmaster comments:

We do not want any smooth, slippery personalities. But it is very necessary that they should have the feeling of being ready to work and be collective-minded. Children ought to be group-conscious. We teach the children to help each other. Not to compete with each other . . . Take, for example, the river-crossing down here. After rain it is not easy, and so the older children have to help the younger, and the boys the girls . . . We also train them to be honest. If they find anything on the road, they are to bring it to school.[61]

Explicit adjustments have been made, then, in the teaching methods and the content of primary education under the Communist government. In a study of stories used to teach children how to read, McClelland [62] found the content to reflect a high degree of achievement motivation. This, of course, may suggest little about the level of the children's need achievement, since their behavior was not examined directly. The study does, however, depict something of the nature of the classroom climate — and this is supported by the small number of Western observers privileged to examine the Communist schools at first hand — namely, that the policies advocating diligence and application have, to a large extent, been implemented.

Secondary Education

By 1951, the secondary or middle school had begun to bear the imprint of the full-scale revision of the educational system. Structurally the middle school was divided into two levels: grades 7 through 9 and grades 10 through 12. While both the structure and the function underwent a number of modifications during the alternate emphases by the Party on "red" and "expert," the basic principles regarding political instruction and productive labor persisted.

From an examination of the course of study for middle schools it might be concluded that from one-fourth to one-third of the time allotment was allocated differently under the Communist government than during the Republican period. In addition to approximately four hours a week spent on political education and production work, the curriculum also reflected the faith of the new government in the natural sciences. Explicit political instruction at this level included study of Marxism and Leninism, the policies of the Chinese Communist Party, and the writings of Mao Tse-Tung.[63] However, political education is interlaced with all subject matter, and even the natural sciences are affected by the outlook of dialectical materialism. The application of the principle of labor is not isolated to a few hours on a farm or in a factory, but may also be seen in broader political terms, for students are expected not only to acquire intellectual understanding of their subjects, but, in keeping with the spirit of the revolution of which they are a part, they are also expected to be activists in the broadest sense in the struggle for a modern, Communist state.

While the humanities and traditional social sciences are played down in the general middle schools, they are virtually eliminated from the specialized middle schools. From the time of the First Five Year Plan (1953-1957), educational planning included provision for a variety of specialized, short-time, and part-time middle schools. In addition to the vocational schools and normal schools of an earlier period, new kinds of technical schools and curricula were devised, resulting by the early 1960's in 22 categories of possible specialization at the middle school level.[64]

Since the variety of specialized middle schools was created under different auspices and for different purposes, it is dangerous to lump them together for analysis. For our purposes, however, two characteristics stand out. First, the rapidity with which new, differentiated structures and new, specialized programs emerged was remarkable. Following a pattern found in the Soviet Union, when a particular manpower shortage was identified, an educational program was promptly initiated to meet the need. The narrowness and specificity of such training should be emphasized, for the Chinese — again like the Soviets of an earlier period — rejected the notion that technical training profits either by extensive prior, or by accompanying general, education. The variety of vocational and specialized courses of study had increased by 1960 to 1700, suggesting the high level of structural differentiation attained and reflecting the haste with which China was pursuing the path to industrialization.

A second characteristic of the plethora of specialized and vocationalized middle schools was the overriding utilitarian emphasis. The single criterion of utility was the contribution to productive labor. Traditions could be shattered, standards set aside, endless experiments condoned, if increased production resulted. For example, certain of the part-time institutions, treated in this section as middle schools, were labeled by the Communist government as "universities." Students who had entered one such university had the following educational backgrounds: junior primary, 10.3 percent; senior primary, 58.9 percent; junior middle,

30.4 percent; senior middle, 0.5 percent.[65] Such liberties with standard educational terminology have been interpreted by Barendsen as having a number of purposes: "to satisfy the hunger of the masses for a share in advanced educational opportunities, to delude the masses into believing that somehow, despite the realities of long hours of labor, they are acquiring credentials which will, in accordance with Chinese tradition, eventually raise them above the status of manual workers, and to vitiate the elite attitudes customary among students of the regular full-time institutions of higher education."[66]

Enrollment data further illustrate the rapid adjustments of vocational middle schools to national production targets. While the percentage of students enrolled in such fields as agriculture, forestry, finance, economics, and fine arts declined markedly between 1949 and 1956, enrollment in technical courses expanded more than twofold during the same period.

Higher Education

No educational level received more criticism from the Communists than higher education. The idea of knowledge for knowledge's sake was ridiculed, the practice of students choosing their own majors was considered bourgeois, and the lack of centralized planning to coordinate higher education with national development was viewed as anarchical. In 1950, during the First National Conference on Higher Education, a visiting Russian educator summarized the shortcomings of higher education under the Republic. His comments, as paraphrased by Hsü, were:

Chinese universities and colleges were said to have been developed in the unhealthy atmosphere of semi-colonialism. Western imperialists, seeking to discourage industrialization in China, turned the attention of the educated classes to the humanities and social sciences, with the result that many Chinese professors acquired the colonial habit of lecturing in English rather than in their own native tongue. Many of the libraries had more foreign language volumes than Chinese, and there was no unified translation of foreign technical terms. Chinese higher education exhibited too much dependence on the West. . . . "Chinese universities should turn out not abstract scholars but practical specialists." In the Soviet Union, it was not the university but the technical institute which exercised a decisive influence on national construction.[67]

The slowness with which some of the Chinese universities adapted to the training of "practical specialists" was a continual source of irritation to certain of the Party leaders. Reflecting the criticism, the Rector of the Communist North China University, on his first visit to the distinguished Peking University, raised the question, "Shall we turn Peking University into a cultural salon, or a school for the training of cadres to serve the people?"[68] This question had, in effect, already been officially answered by the succinct statement of the Minister of Education in 1950: "Education must work for economic construction. The emphasis of economic construction is on industry and the emphasis of industrial construction is on heavy industry. This clearly indicates that the primary and foremost task of our higher education should be the cultivation of advanced technicians for industries, mines and transportation."[69]

By 1958 two basic categories of higher education institutions had emerged: universities and technical institutes. There were, at that date, 20 comprehensive universities, all located in cities, which offered the full complement of preparation in the arts, sciences, and professions. At the same date there were also approximately 250 technical and teacher training institutes offering one or more specializations. The function of the institutes was clearly to produce high-level technicians. The universities, however, were in a somewhat ambivalent position, being urged on the one hand also to produce cadres of specialists while at the same time being supported by a number of intellectuals in their traditional function of preparation of theoreticians, research personnel, and university professors.

Beginning in 1958 with the Great Leap Forward, the number of institutions classified as universities and institutes increased nearly fivefold in a period of a few months. By 1962, however, a substantial degree of retrenchment had taken place and the period 1962-1966 was a relatively calm, rational one with heavy emphasis on serious preparation of "experts." In mid-1966 the calm was broken by radical students who led the Great Proletarian Cultural Revolution and demanded that higher education institutions give greater attention to revolutionary (i.e., political) goals.

Although fluctuations might take place between emphasis on "expertness" and "redness," the continued utilitarian thrust of higher education was apparent. During the first two decades under the Communist government, institutional and instructional reforms toward the end of greater efficiency included:

1) elimination of all private institutions;

2) control of enrollments by the state;

3) realignment of colleges and departments in order to create large institutions of similar function;

4) establishment of large numbers of specialized institutes (rather than creation of new universities);

5) creation of "specialties" to replace departments as the academic unit for instruction.

The last reform in particular requires elaboration. Under the Republic a departmental organization of universities had been established. The Communist government, however, claimed that this pattern had led to (a) adjustments of course offerings on the basis of availability of instructors and (b) little attention to the relationship between course content and the needs of society. To eliminate such waste and duplication, a structure determined by the objectives of specialist training was introduced.

Hsü explains in more detail the meaning of specialty:

It is intensive training in a particular subject which prepares a man for a specialized profession. Each specialty has a definite educational program fixed by the state according to the needs of national construction. All courses within a specialty are required; there are no electives. However, capable and healthy students may take additional courses in specialties other than their own. Each specialty may further be divided into two or more "specializations" . . . for greater concentration on the subject matter. [70]

Specialties, then, may be viewed as an organizational adjustment based on a faith that occupational roles can be reduced to highly discrete skills and understandings.

The commitment to specialization as the fastest route to developing the needed technicians and professionals is further demonstrated by the distribution of time within a curriculum. Table 18 provides a comparison of the instructional hours in a number of major curricular categories of the leading Chinese technical institute, a Soviet university, and the California Institute of Technology.

TABLE 18   Allocation of Instructional Hours in Three Technical Universities

Category	Tsing-hau Polytechnical University 1955	Soviet University 1955	California Institute of Technology 1956
Degree	Engineer	Engineer	B.S.
Basic courses[1]	1330	1376	1167
Technical courses[2]	893	1082	921
Specialized courses[3]	1069	1096	367
Average study time per week	31	33	26
Average lecture time per week	17.4	18.7	16

Source: Adapted from I. C. Y. Hsü, *Reorganization of Higher Education in Communist China*, Santa Barbara, Calif.: General Electric Company, 1962, p. 21.

1. Includes mathematics, physics, chemistry, mechanics, and drafting.

2. Includes principles of electrical engineering, thermodynamics, hydraulics, etc.

3. Includes lathe designs, principles of lathe operations, factory organization and management, economics, planning of enterprises, etc.

From the data in Table 18 it would appear that the major quantitative difference represented by the Chinese institution as compared to the American institution lies, as might be expected, in the amount of time spent in specialized instruction. Qualitative differences may also be assumed, for in contemporary China rapid expansion of enrollments, shortages of facilities, lack of trained teachers, inadequate text materials, and a cumbersome language of instruction are bound to have affected the level of student achievement.

Evidence of Privilege in the Contemporary Schools

In the previous section we commented on some of the ways in which social stratification affects educational inputs. Here attention is turned more directly to adjustments in teaching roles and in system structure which have been influenced by stratification patterns. How do the teachers' social background or political consciousness alter their role in the classroom? Within the structural and programmatic variations of the educational system, do the sons and daughters of the rich and powerful find social privileges? Are there some institutions or programs perpetuated for those of "high birth"?

The teacher is obligated by the Party to determine the students' class background and to adapt his teaching accordingly. The teacher's responsibility is great, for through his evaluation reports to the school administration he can affect the whole future of the child. The press and Party spokesmen have often declared that the bourgeois origin of some teachers has resulted in favoritism toward the more privileged children.[71] Sieh, however, insists that what favoritism there is tends to follow the Party bias.[72] The reasons for the alleged discriminatory practices are controversial. The teacher may or may not be "progressive" and prejudiced against the bourgeoisie. Or the many teachers with a middle class background may be primarily interested in protecting their positions against Party criticism and student accusations.

As has already been discussed, several institutional reforms have been made under the Communist government to soften the rigid hierarchical structure of the educational system; for example "universities" which eliminated the usual academic prerequisites for admittance were opened to workers. On the other hand, special schools for the privileged have also had some history under the Communist government. For example, boarding schools were established for children of cadres assigned to isolated posts away from the resources of family and established schooling.[73] Although such schools have outlived their justification (the deployment of cadres having been stabilized), they have continued to proliferate. Ch'un Lei charges: "Cadres' children began to live a comfortable privileged life in a sort of 'Shangri-la' . . . gradually . . . the boarding schools for cadres' children [were led] on the road of British or Soviet style 'aristocratic schools.'"[74]

A second variety of elite schools was subjected to intense criticism during the Great Proletarian Cultural Revolution. These "experimental schools," established for pedagogical experimentation and placed directly under the control of a leading Party theoretician, Liu Shao-Chi, were attacked as bastions of "bourgeois revisionism." Liu was specifically accused of wanting to turn Peking's Experimental Elementary School No. 2 into an "imperial school for the prominent offspring of people of his sort as a means to realize his fond dream of restoring capitalism."[75]

As in the case of the cadre boarding schools, the criteria for admitting students to the experimental schools have been interpreted as antiproletariat and hence antirevolutionary:

Each year several thousand children tried to enter the school, taking the entrance examinations, but very few were accepted. The school used "intelligence" and "intellectual development" as criteria for admission, and devoted a great deal of energy to preventing the children of workers from entering the school. In 1964, for instance, there was only one worker's child among the students, the rest were children of high-level cadres, democratic personalities, high-level intellectuals and cadres in general.[76]

There is, however, very limited factual evidence on the class orientation of either the boarding schools or the experimental schools. From the recent diatribe against them, however, it might be concluded that (1) to some extent these schools have preserved the prerevolutionary ideal of rewarding intellectual effort, and (2) they do not represent efforts to promote "capitalist" solutions to educational problems, but rather represent (a) an attempt to safeguard the survival of the intellectual in an anti-intellectual milieu and (b) a mild rejection of the supremacy of ideology on technical questions.

The recent anti-intellectual clampdown culminating in the Great Proletarian Cultural Revolution would appear to have at least temporarily routed those who sought to maintain "nonproletarian" schools. The apparent victory is for a societal rationale which assumes future development to be in terms of an "intellectualized" (but actually anti-intellectual) proletariat. The image of the future is that of a society pulling itself up by its own bootstraps by means of a homegrown "science" grounded in a mystical faith in the words and inspiration of Chairman Mao. The final "exposure" and "proletarianization" of the elite schools again places the People's Republic of China on the horns of a dilemma — one created by the perennial problems involved in acquiring and then securing for future generations a Utopian classless society, on the one hand, and the raising of the material level of existence to one of respectability *vis à vis* the other powers of the world, on the other.

TABLE 19   Output of Chinese Educational System, 1949-1950 to 1958-1959 and 1959-1960 to 1964-1965

	1949-1950 to 1959-1959	*1959-1960 to 1964-1965*
	Millions	
Primary (6th year) graduates	32.0	53.0
Deduct:		
Increased secondary and higher education enrollment	–12.3	+ 0.4
Increased teaching staff, all levels	– 1.7	– 0.4
Students leaving education system to enter society at 6th and higher grades	18.0	53.0
Approximate composition:		
Primary level	14.7	30.0
Secondary level	3.0	22.0
Higher education	0.3	1.0

Source: *An Economic Profile of Mainland China*, p. 95.

TABLE 20 Graduates from Institutions of Higher Learning in Communist China by Field, 1948-1949 to 1965-1966

Year	Total		Engineering		Natural sciences	
	Number	Per-cent	Number	Per-cent	Number	Per-cent
Total	1,716,000	100	577,840	34	98,387	6
1948-1949	21,000	100	4,752	23	1,584	8
1949-1950	18,000	100	4,711	26	1,468	8
1950-1951	19,000	100	4,416	23	1,488	8
1951-1952	32,000	100	10,213	32	2,215	7
1952-1953	48,000	100	14,565	30	1,753	4
1953-1954	47,000	100	15,596	33	802	2
1954-1955	55,000	100	18,614	34	2,015	4
1955-1956	63,000	100	22,047	35	3,978	6
1956-1957	56,000	100	17,162	31	3,524	6
1957-1958	72,000	100	17,499	24	4,645	6
1958-1959	70,000	100	(23,310)	(33)	(4,410)	(6)
1959-1960	135,000	100	(44,955)	(33)	(8,505)	(6)
1960-1961	162,000	100	54,000	33	10,000	6
1961-1962	178,000	100	59,000	33	11,000	6
1962-1963	200,000	100	77,000	38	10,000	5
1963-1964	200,000	100	(70,000)	(35)	(11,000)	(6)
1964-1965	170,000	100	(60,000)	(35)	(10,000)	(6)
1965-1966	(170,000)	100	(60,000)	(35)	(10,000)	(6)

Source: An Economic Profile of Mainland China, Vol. II, p. 511.

Note. Numbers in parentheses are estimates. Percent detail may not add to totals because of rounding.

EDUCATIONAL OUTPUT

Measured by numbers of graduates, the Chinese educational system substantially increased its output at the primary and postprimary school levels between the 1949-1959 decade and the 1959-1965 six-year period. As shown in Table 19, the magnitude of the overall growth in educational output is outstanding at all levels. The largest increase in graduates is recorded at the secondary level, not only indicating the importance given to the types of skills acquired at this level, but also suggesting the rapid maturing of the educational system in terms of extension of educational opportunity. Also significant is the +0.4 statistic, apparently resulting from a reduction in total enrollment figures at the secondary and higher

Agriculture and forestry		Medicine		Education		Finance and economics		Other	
Number	Per- cent	Number	Per- cent	Number	Per- cent	Number	Per- cent	Number	Per- cent
40,149	8	184,868	11	468,417	27	87,140	5	159,199	9
1,718	8	1,314	6	1,890	9	3,137	15	6,605	32
1,477	8	1,391	8	624	4	3,305	18	5,024	28
1,538	8	2,366	12	1,206	6	3,638	19	4,348	23
2,361	7	2,636	8	3,077	10	7,263	23	4,235	13
2,633	6	2,948	6	9,650	20	10,530	22	5,921	12
3,532	8	4,527	10	10,551	22	6,033	13	5,959	13
2,614	5	6,840	12	12,133	22	4,699	8	8,085	15
3,541	6	5,403	9	17,243	27	4,460	7	6,328	10
3,104	6	6,200	11	15,948	28	3,651	6	6,411	11
3,513	5	5,393	8	31,595	44	2,349	3	7,006	10
6,318	9	9,000	13	(21,000)	(30)	(2,450)	(4)	(3,512)	(5)
10,800)	(8)	(14,850)	(11)	(40,500)	(30)	(4,725)	(4)	(10,665)	(8)
12,000	7	19,000	12	49,000	30	(5,670)	(4)	(12,330)	(8)
20,000	11	17,000	10	56,000	32	(6,230)	(4)	(8,770)	(5)
17,000	8	25,000	12	46,000	23	3,000	2	22,000	11
18,000)	(9)	(23,000)	(11)	(56,000)	(28)	(6,000)	(3)	(16,000)	(8)
15,000)	(9)	(19,000)	(11)	(48,000)	(28)	(5,000)	(3)	(13,000)	(8)
15,000)	(9)	(19,000)	(11)	(48,000)	(28)	(5,000)	(3)	(13,000)	(8)

levels following a policy of retrenchment after the early expansion under the Great Leap Forward.

Some further data add to the picture of quantitative accomplishments of the Communist government. Illiteracy, estimated at 80 percent in 1949 has, according to government sources, been reduced to less than 15 percent. At the other end of the spectrum it has been estimated that by 1967 over 1.7 million persons in mainland China had completed some form of higher education. In technical, scientific, and selected professional fields the effort was even more phenomenal. Between 1949 and 1960, enrollments in engineering increased sixfold, in science nearly four times, in agriculture and forestry over 3.5 times, in health about 3.6 times, and in education over 7.5 times. Table 20 identifies the growth in higher education graduates by field of study.

But such gross data tell a very incomplete story. The value of the output must be measured in terms of the degree of fulfillment of the economic and social goals of the Communist government. Party spokesmen would be the first to admit that increases in literacy or numbers of graduates in themselves are insignificant achievements. Rather, output must be judged against manpower and production needs, against a proletarianized social order and against a securely "red" population.

EDUCATION, MANPOWER, AND NATIONAL PRODUCTION

The three Five Year Plans covering the period 1953 to 1967 identified the educational targets requisite to the meeting of production goals. Yet both national and sectoral planning efforts have been subjected to intermittent campaigns for (or against) particular economic or political postures. Educational planning has been most successful in the expansion of enrollments, the redistribution of students into priority fields, and the development of an educational mystique among the population.

The distribution of graduates by field indicates the extent to which the Communist government has been able to transform an educational system which at the upper level 20 years earlier had been highly oriented toward the study of literature, arts, political science, and law. Between 1948-1949 and 1962-1963 the distribution of graduates from universities and technical institutes was as follows: engineering, 33 percent; education, 27 percent; medicine, 10 percent; agriculture, 8 percent; science, 6 percent; economics, 6 percent; others, 10 percent. Scientific and technical personnel in some engineering pursuits, who numbered only a few thousand in 1940, numbered in the tens of thousands by 1960. In agricultural science, for example, there were by 1958 an estimated 10,800 scientists and advanced technicians, compared to only a few hundred in 1949.[77]

In spite of some rather spectacular successes in the reorientation of educational emphases, the Chinese educational system has failed to achieve its high-level manpower targets. In addition to expressions of political fervor which at times obstructed a more orderly process of planning, those basic statistical data, both internal and external to the educational system, needed for successful planning were unreliable. As late as 1960 an authoritative Communist source characterized educational statistics as "incomplete" and criticized educational planning as "full of defects and without accomplishments."[78]

Educational plans for institutions at all levels included estimates of the number of students to be admitted, the number expected to graduate, the number of teachers needed, extent of facilities, etc. In the institutions of higher education and the vocational middle schools, target quotas for each specific technical field were established. One reported example of ineffective planning involved the performance of senior middle schools during the First Five Year Plan. In order to have an adequate number of entrants to advanced technical and scientific courses of study, expansion of these schools was given a priority second only to that of higher education. It had been estimated that the proper ratio would be two to three senior middle school graduates to one student admitted to higher education. However, partly because of an underestimation of the dropout rate, the number of senior middle school graduates was actually less than the student admittance quotas to institutions of higher education during three of the years under the First Five Year Plan. Thus, in attempting to achieve output targets, universities and technical institutes were required to lower their admission standards.[79]

Other maladjustments within the educational system and between the educational and the production systems can be identified. There appears, for example, to be some danger that China, like many other developing nations, may soon be faced with unemployment among certain categories of its graduates. One estimate suggests that by 1970 there may be 15 million persons with a secondary education in China. To judge from the development experiences of other nations, including the Soviet Union, this figure may well exceed the number of semiprofessional or skilled workers needed in China in 1970. One source suggests that the surplus of secondary school graduates may by 1970 reach several million.[80]

Employment opportunities in the early 1960's also declined for the graduates of institutions of higher education. Not that the graduates of universities of institutes were unemployed; rather, there were indications that a significant number of the recent graduates were underemployed, that is, employed at work which required a lesser skill than that for which they were prepared.

The campaigns to attach factories to schools and schools to factories and farms offer further evidence of shortcomings in educational output. These efforts frequently reflected frenzied, politically inspired activism rather than sober professional planning. As direct attempts to link production and education and thereby add significantly to the quantities of many industrial and consumer items, the half-work, half-study schools met with some success. Through sales of manufactured goods and food crops, the schools were able to reduce the financial burden of the state; indeed, many schools, particularly those in farming areas, claimed complete self-sufficiency. However, the level of skill and planning required in modern industrial processes was clearly misjudged, for shortages of competent teachers, inadequate facilities, and poor intra- and interregional coordination combined to limit the value of the output. Many of the half-work, half-study ventures resulted in nonstandardized products, with inadequate provision for replacement parts, and proved to be exceedingly expensive in terms of man-hours of labor.[81]

The quality of the technical and scientific personnel prepared in the middle schools and institutions of higher education is subject to debate. Communist spokesmen have been ambivalent regarding their interpretation of the quality of education provided under their reforms. On the one hand, it has been argued that all education of importance has been obtained in much less time by eliminating outdated and extraneous curriculum content: " ... the middle and elementary schools have universally raised their standards. The students have improved their basic knowledge, fluency in language, adeptness in mathematics, working habits, and health conditions."[82] On the other hand, the difficulty of maintaining standards has been recognized. Rapid expansion of enrollments, including an influx of Party cadres and discharged servicemen, has put excessive pressure on teachers, equipment, facilities, and finances. Overwork and overspecialization have also been identified as detriments to academic standards. For example, during the brief period (1957) of encouragement of freedom of expression known as the Hundred Flowers Movement, one professor commented: "The People's University is a university in name only, and it resembles a secondary school in the content of its instruction and a primary school in teaching methods."[83]

The abrupt departure of nearly 11,000 Soviet technical and scientific personnel in 1960 had effects on the quality of education as well as the quality of production. China has, however, added to its talent pool by inducing hundreds of young Chinese educated in the United States and Europe to return home. Moreover, since 1960, Chinese students are again being sent to study in Western Europe.

The competence of teachers is usually expected to have some impact on the quality of learning in the schools. Primary teachers in China are prepared in normal schools which are specialized divisions of the middle school system. However, the most promising of the primary school students tend to be channeled into the general middle schools. Moreover, because of the shortage of teachers, normal school programs are frequently shortened or eliminated entirely as a prerequisite to teaching; indeed, most primary teachers have not graduated from normal schools.

Similar severe shortages of teachers exist at the middle school and higher education levels. One response to this problem has been to select as teachers persons proficient in one specialized area, even though their general educational background is weak. At the extreme, this may have meant that an illiterate farmer was called on to teach agriculture or a semiliterate welder to teach machine shop. Such compromises have not only directly affected the quality of instruction, but also have been detrimental to the status, and therefore morale, of the teaching profession.

While it is exceedingly difficult to judge the level of knowledge or skill being acquired by Chinese students through any formal program of instruction, a few of the possible difficulties resulting from the narrowness and specialization of programs of study are readily apparent. When some technical institutes can boast 240 specialties, and mathematics and physics can be divided into 19 or 20 specialties, two types of crucial problems would appear to arise. First, continual and sophisticated planning is necessary in order to get the right "manpower-unit" in the right job. Second, provisions need to be made for rapid educational adjustments in response to the effects of technological changes.

There are indications that planning is a problem which has already been recognized by the Communist government. Reports in the press tell, for example, of engineering graduates sent to a construction company which had not yet been established. Some measure of the degree of dissatisfaction among those graduating from institutions of higher education may be found in the estimate that over five percent of the graduates (1953-1956) asked for reassignment because of the unsuitability of their work.[84]

The difference between producing "well-rounded" technicians and professionals (the ideal in the West) and producing narrow specialists, as in contemporary China, is more than a matter of ideology. Even when all but technical issues are laid aside, the question arises as to whether a student majoring, for example, in railway bridge construction can be a successful engineer without learning something about the railway itself or bridge construction in general. The Communist government answer is a clear "yes," and the "superfluousness" of much of the American engineering curriculum in ridiculed. On the other hand, Western engineers tend to stress the complex problems of achieving proper articulation among individual technical projects; thus bridge construction is linked to questions of markets, to water conservation policies, etc.

The value of a foundation of general education for technical personnel, as typically advocated in the West, has some empirical substantiation. Studies in the United States, Western Europe, and the Soviet Union have tended to indicate that a person with general education as well as technical preparation outproduces the narrowly trained specialist. Moreover, the former is more easily retrainable for new technical tasks. Apparently, however, the Communist government believes that improved planning and management techniques will suffice to maximize the productivity of all workers.

Education, Social Status, and Political Elites

Brief attention has already been given to some of the ways in which social position affects educational inputs and the functioning of the educational system under the Communist government. It was concluded that within the schools in general the Party appears to influence strongly the patterns of association and the deference-dominance modes. That is, the closer one stands to proletarian cultural ideals on the one hand, and Party policies and prerogatives on the other, the higher one's status in the formal organization and in terms of deference shown by one's associates. This principle holds for students as well as teachers and administrators. The especially Party-oriented child of bourgeois background might be "adopted" as a valuable object lesson and model, and find himself the recipient of special privileges and attentions. Otherwise, whatever middle class sympathies teachers and students might harbor tend to be hidden out of respect for present-day realities.

Graduates achieve status in the same manner, that is, by being distinguished in "expertness" or "redness." Barnett reported in his study of Ministry M[85] that within the bureaucracy the technical specialists were in a sense a group apart. His data suggest that these experts received better salaries than the Party cadres and that for them there was less emphasis on politics. Education as a requisite for status was reported to be probably more important for non-Party cadres, some of whom were well educated and looked down on less educated Party cadres.

Those who did not achieve expertise through the educational system succeeded in achieving occupational status to the extent that they displayed enthusiasm and involvement in Party activities. Yet, at least to date, it appears that "redness" without advanced education is rarely enough to ensure high status. In a study of top leaders in the political elite, the Central Committee of the Chinese Communist Party, it was found that over 60 percent of all members, full and alternate, had college-level training.[86] Further down the Party hierarchy, new personnel in the Ministry-level cadre also tend to be drawn from a well-educated population:

One of the most important sources of new younger cadres, both Party and non-Party, consisted of recent graduates from institutions of higher learning. Every year the regime assigned a sizeable number of new graduates to the ministries, and many of these had at least some specialized training relevant to their assignments. This steady flow of young people was a major channel for the infusion of new talent into the central bureaucracy. Assignments to work in the central ministries not only were rated as important by the regime, but also were viewed as desirable by most graduates, and some of the ablest young people in the country were drawn into the ministries – although ability was judged on the basis of one's political activism as well as intellectual accomplishments. Frequently, these young people were sent for a preliminary period of training in the ministry's cadre school before being assigned to regular posts in the ministry itself. The percentage of educated young cadres, roughly from twenty-five to thirty-five years of age, steadily rose over the years, therefore, and they filled a sizeable proportion of rank-and-file ministry jobs.[87]

The contrast between the idealized model of the Communist social structure, which posits that the highest positions are occupied by workers and peasants with the cadres and intellectuals in lesser supportive positions, and the real situation, in which status is reversed, creates a dilemma for the educational system. Schools in China as elsewhere are expected to perform the dual functions of (a) inculcating the ideals and norms underlying the society and (b) providing the skills necessary to maintain a viable unit. The sensitivity of the position of the educational system in China is thus heightened by the fact that it exists within a tightly organized bureaucracy which denies the existence of graded distinctions in status. Can the schools teach the norms of classlessness on the one hand, and the intellectual skills for achieving status on the other?

SUMMARY

In noting the changes in higher education in China, one author notes: "What was once the land of philosophers and artists has been transformed into a huge, throbbing plant of bustling technocrats. Eager engineers, active scientists, and busy industrial workers become the mark of New China, while dreamy classical scholars in flowing robes have long since passed into the oblivion of history."[88]

In a movement beginning with the Republic and culminating under the Communist government, China has rejected much of her educational and cultural heritage as inimical to modernization. The dangers of tension are obvious in a society which attempts to eradicate the past abruptly, for the older and hence more powerful groups may struggle to retain their cherished ways. In Communist China the competing sources of social power were assumed to lie among the intellectuals and government officials; therefore, the recalcitrant among these groups were the early targets of opprobrium. In substitution for the traditional culture, the Communist Party has offered one all-inclusive alternative. Achievement of success has been assumed to lie largely in the Party's ability to create a high level of ideological commitment among the younger generation.

The framework for guiding the development of new institutions and new social roles has been drawn not from the lessons of Chinese history nor from cultural contact with the West, but from the writings of Marx, Lenin, and Mao. The goal of an industrialized, socialist state has consistently been viewed as possible only through intensive and pervasive educational efforts. These efforts, with respect to the formal educational system, have meant essentially (1) a rapid structural and programmatic differentiation in order to prepare large numbers of specialists and (2) proletarianization of the teaching and student bodies.

Measures of the output of the contemporary educational system suggest partial success in these tasks. In gross terms the increases in quantitative output have been remarkable and rarely, if ever, duplicated in the educational history of other Asian nations. Further, the percentage of students in middle schools and higher education from working classes has steadily increased in the postrevolutionary period. Yet at least two major assumptions of Communist educational policy remain to be tested: namely, (1) that the fastest, most efficient route to modernization lies in highly specialized vocational and technological education; and (2) that a rigid, bureaucratic Communism provides sufficient scope and reward for the exercise of human talent.

NOTES

1. I. N. Thut and Don Adams, *Educational Patterns in Contemporary Societies.* New York: McGraw-Hill, 1964, p. 251.

2. William Theodore de Bary (ed.), *Sources of Chinese Tradition.* New York: Columbia University Press, 1960, p. 50.

3. Little is known about Lao Tzu. The major work attributed to him, *Tao Te Ching,* has been called "one of the most mysterious documents in the history of religion." For comments on the possible meanings of *Tao Te Ching,* see Kenneth Rexroth, "Tao Te Ching," *Saturday Review,* July 20, 1968, p. 17. Also see a translation of the work by Arthur Waley, *The Way and Its Power,* New York: Barnes and Noble, 1956.

4. Howard S. Galt, *A History of Chinese Educational Institutions.* London: Arthur Probsthain, 1951, p. 181.

5. Edwin O. Reischauer and John K. Fairbank, *East Asia: The Great Tradition.* Boston: Houghton Mifflin, 1958, p. 30.

6. Mencius is referred to by the Chinese as their second sage.

7. S. Wells Williams, *The Middle Kingdom,* Vol. I. New York: Scribners, 1904, pp. 546-560.

8. Reischauer and Fairbank, *op. cit.,* p. 166.

9. *Ibid.,* p. 166.

10. George H. Danton, *The Culture Contacts of the United States and China.* New York: Columbia University Press, 1931, pp. 52-53.

11. The mission schools, in a somewhat indirect way, may also have contributed to the development of the emerging merchant class. Some Chinese with entrepreneurial ambitions found it advantageous to be in direct contact with the West and with Western ways. Attending a mission school and accepting Christianity could well be the means to profitable business ends.

12. Nathaniel Peffer, *The Far East.* Ann Arbor: University of Michigan Press, 1958, p. 118.

13. *Ibid.*, pp. 118-119.

14. The kinds of institutions under mission control included kindergarten, lower primary, higher primary, middle school, normal, college, Bible schools, theological, law, medical, nurses' training, schools for the blind, and schools for the deaf. See *Christian Education in China,* New York: Committee of Reference and Council of the Foreign Missions Conference of North America, 1922, Appendix I.

15. Several distinguished educators, including Paul Monroe, had recommended that mission education should cut back, reorganize, and stress quality. This advice, offered in the early 1920's, went unheeded.

16. Alice H. Gregg, *China and Educational Autonomy.* Syracuse, N.Y.: Syracuse University Press, 1946, p. 115.

17. *Ibid.*, pp. 52-53.

18. H. C. Tsao, "The Present Situation of Christian Education in China," *Educational Review,* October 1928, p. 375. Quoted in Gregg, *op. cit.,* p. 116.

19. Gregg, *op. cit.,* pp. 110-111.

20. Excerpts from petitions quoted in Chiu-Sam Tsang, *Nationalism in School Education in China,* Hong Kong: Progressive Education Publishers, 1967, pp. 33-35.

21. Quoted in Chai-Husan, *Tendencies Toward a Democratic System of Education in China,* Shanghai: Commercial Press Ltd., 1922, p. 24.

22. L'and Leang-Li (ed.), *Reconstruction in China.* China Today Series. Shanghai: China United Press, 1935, pp. 69-72.

23. Examples include the folk schools of Scandinavia, experiments in Communist nations combining schooling and labor, the community schools in the United States and more recently in several nations in Asia, and the "basic school" originated by Ghandi.

24. Leo A. Orleans, *Professional Manpower and Education in Communist China.* Washington, D. C.: National Science Foundation, U. S. Government Printing Office, 1961, p. 71.

25. As will be noted later, certain modifications were made in the language under Communism.

26. Quoted in Chiu-Sam Tsang, *op. cit.,* p. 66.

27. Quoted in Chiu-Sam Tsang, *op. cit.,* p. 69.

28. Reported in Chiu-Sam Tsang, *op. cit.,* p. 70.

29. "Education in every country respects and preserves its native language, literature, history, customs and traditions and its native religion. . . . The religion of Confucius is magnificent and all-embracing; he is not only worshipped by the eternal generations of China but also by all peoples of the five continents as their common sage. . . . In recent years the acquisition of knowledge and skills of their [Japan's] citizens can compete with those of the Europeans and Americans, but they still train their pupils daily in the teachings and philosophy of the sages and saints of our country. . . . Therefore, we shall put the Classics as a required subject in all schools whether they be of university or primary level." Quoted in Chiu-Sam Tsang, *op. cit.,* p. 63.

30. See, for example, Sidney D. Gamble, *Ting Hsien, A North China Rural Community,* New York: Institute of Pacific Relations, 1954, pp. 187-188.

31. Tadashi Fukutake, *Asian Rural Society: China, India, Japan.* Seattle: University of Washington Press, 1967, p. 7.

32. Karl Marx and Friedrich Engels, "The Communist Manifesto," in Arthur P. Mendel (ed.), *Essential Works of Marxism,* New York: Bantam Books, 1961, p. 29.

33. de Bary, *op. cit.,* p. 872.

34. Mao Tse-Tung described the classes in Chinese society in 1926: "(1) the landlords and compradors (managers or senior employees in a foreign company) – the reactionary segment of the intelligentsia is found here; (2) petty bourgeoisie – including owner-peasants, master handicraftsmen, lower level intellectuals such as students, primary and secondary teachers, lower government functionaries, office clerks, small lawyers, small traders; (3) semi-proletariat – including semi-owner peasants, poor peasants, small handicraftsmen, shop assistants, pedlars; and (4) the proletariat – including industrial workers (leading force in revolution), dockers, rickshawmen, sewage carters, street cleaners, farm laborers, peasants who lost their land, handicraftsmen without work." Mao Tse-Tung, "Analysis of the Classes in Chinese Society," March 1926, in *Selected Works of Mao Tse-Tung,* Vol. I. Peking: Foreign Languages Press, 1965.

35. In addition to direct attempts at establishing the concept of a "new family," other Communist policies also had their effects on the family. For example, the formation of a variety of collective arrangements to perform irrigation and farming functions, by removing responsibility from the clan, further reduced parental control over the young and removed the family from its position as core of the village social structure.

36. Chang-tu Hu *et. al., China: Its People, Its Society, Its Culture.* New Haven, Conn.: Human Relations Area Files Press, 1960, pp. 280-281.

37. *Ibid.,* p. 282.

38. John Philip Emerson, "Manpower Absorption in the Non-Agricultural Branches of the Economy of Communist China, 1953-58," *China Quarterly,* No. 7 (July-September 1961), p. 73.

39. Chi Tung-wai, *Education for the Proletariat in Communist China.* Communist China Problem Research Series. Kowloon, Hong Kong: The Union Research Institute, 1956, p. 2.

40. N. S. Khrushchev, quoted in N. M. Malkov, "Education in Atheism in History Lessons," *Soviet Education,* Vol. III (September 1961), p. 8.

41. Mao Tse-Tung, *On the Correct Handling of Contradictions Among the People.* Peking: Foreign Languages Press, 1960, p. 42.

42. *Peking Review,* May 10, 1960. The term "class" is used frequently in Communist literature, but in a somewhat different way than in non-Communist societies. As in the West, social class in China is understood to involve such measures as income, educational level, and style of living. However, the word as it is used in Communist publications carries a heavy evaluative component. In addition, "class" carries Marxist-derived meanings which relate to a somewhat modified Marxist model in which the peasant and the worker comprise the proletariat and stand in opposition to the bourgeoisie, i.e., the nonproductive element of society.

43. Indeed, although the two goals may be viewed as analytically distinct, operationally they are quite inseparable, since economic modernization is always a political goal in Communist societies.

44. The term science as used in Communist writings must be treated with care, however, since all orthodox learning is "scientific" to the Marxist. In this sense the humanities or fine arts are as much a part of science as chemistry or physics. For this reason, numbers of "science workers" or "scientists" reported by Communist nations

may be misleading. It is thus, in the final analysis, a people's science which is under consideration. The object is to have every citizen think scientifically, that is, apply objective and technical knowledge to his way of living. This view is one of the "five loves" being taught to all: love of the fatherland, love of the people, love of labor, love of science, and care of public property.

45. V. I. Lenin, *Gems of Norodniks, "Hair Brain Schemes."* Quoted in I. A. Kairov, "Basic Questions Related to School Re-organization," *Soviet Education,* Vol. I (January 1959), p. 5. This stand should not be surprising in light of Marx's general theory of economic materialism. Marx argued, like several of the "classical" economists of his day, that the amount of time a worker needed to produce an item determined its "exchange value." However, Marx not only believed that workers under capitalism would never receive wages equal to the value of goods produced, but also that the capitalists, through the accumulation of surplus wealth, had the power to increase productive means and hence lower wages. Indeed, such action, he argued, was necessary in order to operate a competitive capitalistic system. During the advanced phases of Communism, by contrast, labor brings not only higher absolute rewards but eventually ceases to be merely a means of livelihood and becomes an accepted duty to the sacred cause.

46. Since the most serious overpopulation problems existed in the big cities and certain thickly settled farming areas, the steps taken by the Communist government have largely involved moving people to less densely settled farming areas. Actions have also been taken to stem the flow of villagers to the urban areas. However, the government, after some ambivalence, has in more recent years condemned birth control as a method of containing population pressures.

47. *An Economic Profile of Mainland China.* Studies Prepared for the Joint Economic Committee, Congress of the United States, Vol. I: "General Economic Setting, The Economic Sectors." No. 72-911. Washington, D. C.: U. S. Government Printing Office, 1967, p. 451.

48. A. Doak Barnett, *Cadres, Bureaucracy and Political Power in Communist China.* New York: Columbia University Press, 1967, p. 38.

49. *Ibid.,* p. 39.

50. *Ibid.,* pp. 42, 43.

51. *Jenmin Jih-Pao,* July 14, 1967 (*J.P.R.S.,* No. 42,503, p. 90).

52. *Chung-Hsueh Feng-Pao,* Peking, May 27, 1967; *Joint Publication Research Service* (*J.P.R.S.*), No. 42,260, p. 35. This absorption of the father's status and position by the sons was a notable feature of the traditional family system in China, and one which is often credited with leading to family (even including dynastic) downfall as the result of idleness and unearned luxury. See F. L. K. Hsü, *Under the Ancestor's Shadow.* New York: Columbia University Press, 1948.

53. *J.P.R.S.,* No. 42,269, p. 68; *J.P.R.S.,* No. 42,070, p. 22; *J.P.R.S.,* No. 41,889, p. 59.

54. Marie Sieh, "The School Teacher: A Link to China's Future," *Current Scene* (Hong Kong), Vol. III (1965), No. 18, pp. 5-7.

55. *Ibid.,* pp. 9-10.

56. C. T. Hu, "The Chinese University: Target of the Cultural Revolution," *Saturday Review,* August 19, 1967, p. 54.

57. *Ibid.,* p. 68.

58. Again, however, the ambivalence and the conflict between "redness" and "expertness" is apparent, for the intellectuals, even in the anti-expert campaign

described above, did not entirely bear the brunt of the fury of the youthful Red Guards: "As regards scientists, technicians and ordinary members of working staffs, as long as they are patriotic, work energetically, are not against the Party and socialism, and maintain no illicit relations with any foreign country, we should in the present movement continue to apply the policy of 'unity, criticism, unity.' Special care should be taken of those scientific and technical personnel who have made contributions." Quoted in Hugo Portisch, "China: Behind the Upheaval," *Saturday Review,* December 10, 1966, pp. 29, 100.

59. The first formal schooling for children is in nursery schools and kindergartens, which in China form an integral part of the educational system. Not only are these institutions typically included in the educational policy of Communist nations, but they were given a particular impetus in China by the communalization of rural area and by productive efforts using intensive labor techniques – efforts which utilized large numbers of female workers.

60. Jan Myrdal, "Education in a Chinese Village," in Robert Havighurst (ed.), *Comparative Perspectives on Education,* Boston: Little, Brown and Co., 1958, p. 130.

61. *Ibid.,* p. 131. As in other Communist societies, in China the Young Pioneers play a leading role in molding behavior patterns in and out of schools. Pioneer officers, for example, acted as inspectors in the "Four Pests" campaign of 1959. The following episode recounted in the *Peking Review* illustrates model Pioneer behavior. "A man, while strolling along the street, suddenly spat. He was immediately approached by a little girl who politely asked him if he had spat. The man admitted he had and was about to walk away when the girl stopped him and gave him a discourse on the evil of spitting. She smiled when she had finished, handed him a slip of paper, apologised for having taken up his time, and wished him good-day. The man looked at the slip of paper. The girl was a member of a Young Pioneers' Health Inspection Team which was doing its part in the campaign against spitting." Quoted in Theodore H. E. Chan, "Elementary Education in Communist China," *China Quarterly,* No. 10 (April-June 1962), p. 113.

62. David McClelland, "Motivational Patterns in Southeast Asia with Special Reference to the Chinese Case." *Journal of Social Issues,* Vol. XIX (1963), No. 1, pp. 6-19.

63. The following description of the middle school textbooks was offered: "Wherever context allows, the text books glorify manual labor and production, vilify the West, inculcate the impossibility of existence with capitalism and exalt revolutionary activities and leaders. They are one of the most powerful instruments of indoctrination. They are a device for co-ordinating education with the Party line. Their authors do not flinch from interpreting or even altering facts to support Party propaganda. A Chinese historian, Chen Hua-Hsin, writing in a Peking newspaper in December 1961, stated that there was proof that the Chinese discovered America well over 1,000 years before Christopher Columbus. As suggested by H. G. Greel 'it is by no means impossible that the idol of old China [Confucius] may come to be hailed as a forerunner on the revolutionary tradition of Marx, Lenin, Stalin and Mao Tse-Tung, a hero of the new China.' " Evelyn L. Harner, *Middle School Education as a Tool of Power in Communist China.* Santa Barbara, Calif.: General Electric Company, 1962, p. 29.

64. Harner, *op. cit.,* p. 16.

65. Quoted in Robert Barendsen, *Half-Work, Half-Study Schools in Communist China: Recent Experiments with Self-Supporting Educational Institutions,* OE 14100, Washington, D. C.: U. S. Government Printing Office, 1964. p. 45.

174

66. Robert Barendsen, *Labor Universities.* Paper presented at meeting of Cooperative Education Society, Washington, 1962. Mimeo.

67. I. C. Y. Hsü, *Reorganization of Higher Education in Communist China.* Santa Barbara, Calif.: General Electric Company, 1962, p. 13.

68. Quoted in Hsü, *op. cit.,* p. 11.

69. Quoted in Hsü, *op. cit.,* p. 14.

70. *Ibid.,* p. 16.

71. Sieh quotes the Canton *Southern Daily*: "It cannot be denied that many of our teachers welcome students from among workers and peasants with open arms. But an incorrect attitude, influenced by bourgeois thinking, is evident on the part of many teachers. In essence, it is cold and discriminatory treatment for children of workers and peasants. They think that the worker-peasant students coming from families untouched by culture for generations are a most retarded and unresponsive group." Sieh, *op. cit.,* p. 11.

72. *Ibid.,* p. 11.

73. Ch'un Lei, "On Exclusive Boarding Schools for Cadres' Children," *Peking Review,* April 13, 1967 (*J.P.R.S.* No. 42,015, p. 163).

74. *Ibid.* (*J.P.R.S.,* No. 42,015, p. 163). It should be noted that these *exposés* were published at the height of the Great Proletarian Cultural Revolution.

75. *J.P.R.S.,* No. 42,070, p. 3.

76. *Ibid.,* p. 4.

77. *An Economic Profile of Mainland China,* p. 533.

78. Quoted in *An Economic Profile of Mainland China,* p. 423.

79. *Ibid.,* p. 423.

80. Harner, *op. cit.,* p. 48.

81. Naiveté is reflected in many aspects of the national drive for industrialization. The inadequacy of research in applications of technology to agriculture and water utilization has resulted in heavy crop losses and flooding. Moreover, the mass approach to productivity has frequently resulted in gross inefficiency. The heralded "backyard furnace" drive (for iron and steel production), which involved over 50 million Chinese, ended in nearly total failure. One author makes this general judgment: "...the Chinese have the technological capability of producing a wide variety of items requiring a knowledge of very recent technologies, such as jet aircraft.... In certain types of mass production, such as textiles (synthetic fabrics excluded) where complicated processes involving long continuous assembly lines and the fitting of precision parts are not involved, it appears that the Chinese can compete with any nation in the areas of cost and quality of product. But...there is much evidence to indicate that the Chinese have not yet mastered the techniques of complicated mass production processes, i.e. the efficient processes required for the production of reliable cars, trucks, tractors, and similar products. The problems here seem to be the same old ones – political interference, poor technical management and a disregard for quality." John A. Berberet, *Science, Technology and Peking's Planning Problems.* Santa Barbara, Calif.: General Electric Company, 1962, pp. 27-28.

82. Yang Hsiu-Feng, "Actively Carry Out the Reform of the School System to Bring about Greater, Faster, Better and More Economical Results in the Development of Education," in Chang-Tu Hu (ed.), *Chinese Education Under Communism,* New York: Teachers College, Columbia University, pp. 100-102.

83. Orleans, *op. cit.,* p. 93.

84. Hsü, *op. cit.,* p. 38.

85. Barnett, *op. cit.,* pp. 46, 55.

86. Donald W. Klein, "The Next Generations of Chinese Communist Leaders," *China Quarterly,* No. 12 (1962), pp. 57-74.

87. Barnett, *op. cit.,* p. 53.

88. Hsü, *op. cit.,* p. 39.

SELECTED READINGS

Barendsen, Robert D., "Education in Mao's China," *American Education,* Vol. II (October 1966), pp. 14-19.

Barendsen, Robert D. *Half-Work, Half-Study Schools in Communist China.* Washington, D. C.: U. S. Department of Health, Education and Welfare, Office of Education, 1964.

Bratton, D. L., "Secondary Literature on Communist Chinese Education." *Sociology of Education,* Vol. XL (Winter 1967), pp. 40-49.

Chen, Theodore Hsi-en, *Teacher Training in Communist China.* Washington, D. C.: U. S. Department of Health, Education and Welfare, Office of Education, Division of International Education, 1960.

Fraser, Stewart (ed.), *Chinese Communist Education: Records of the First Decade.* Nashville, Tenn.: Vanderbilt University Press, 1965.

Hu, Chang-tu (ed.), *Chinese Education under Communism.* New York: Bureau of Publications, Teachers College, Columbia University, 1962.

Orleans, Leo A., *Professional Manpower and Education in Communist China.* Washington, D. C.: National Science Foundation, U. S. Government Printing Office, 1961.

Tsang, Chiu-Sam, *Society, Schools and Progress in China.* Long Island City, N. Y.: Pergamon Press, 1968.

chapter five
regional development and educational planning

Many of the great differences which Asia exhibits in culture, in level of modernization, and in patterns of educational development have been identified through the case studies of Japan, India, and China. Consideration is now given to the region as a whole, its uneven progress, the constraints on more rapid and equitable change, and the efforts through educational planning to hasten the achievement of economic and social goals. A brief summary of demographic, economic, and social conditions provides a rough measure of Asia's level of modernization and at the same time offers a backdrop for the analysis of regional educational change.

1. The annual rate of population growth continues to be higher than in most regions of the world (ranging from 1.4 percent in Nepal to 4.8 percent in Singapore during the decade 1950-1960).

2. Urbanization is growing rapidly; however, the vast majority of Asians still live in villages or rural areas.

3. The demographic structure of the region places great strain on economic growth and educational development.

Over 40 percent of the population in every Asian nation is under 15 years of age – as compared to 31.1 percent in the United States – this creates heavy demands for school facilities and personnel. Because of the population structure, the rate of dependency is high, thus creating a depressing effect on total production.

4. Increasingly since World War II, economic development and, in particular, the social returns from such development have been viewed as the most crucial national issues. Although the 1950's represented a period of economic take-off for several Asian nations, growth in per capita gross national product has been inhibited by rapid population increases and has not met expectations. With the exception of Japan and the Republic of China, growth in gross national product per capita has been less than 40 percent per annum since 1950.

5. Although industrial output nearly trebled between 1950 and 1963, the agricultural sector has generally shown slow growth. Nevertheless, some significant applications of technology to food production and marketing have been made.

6. As measured by conventional economic indicators, regional wealth has risen appreciably; yet added income has not accrued evenly to all social segments. Indeed, as in other regions of the world, modernization and economic growth have generally widened the gap between the privileged and the average.

7. Although difficult to quantify, the levels of societal differentiation and specialization have been raised substantially in all Asian nations. This has meant an increase in the amount of interaction between social groups and between persons, which in turn has required more elaborate systems of cooperation. Because of occupational demands or political pressure, even villagers and farmers have been affected by this phenomenon.

8. On other indices of social progress such as level of nutrition or health, the region ranks low according to standards set by United Nations agencies. For example, the number of inhabitants per physician in 1960 ranged from 100,000 in Laos to 1500 in the Republic of China. In several Asian nations the caloric intake per person is substantially less than the daily requirements suggested by the Food and Agricultural Organization of the United Nations. Nor is the situation necessarily improving. It has been

estimated that in China, for example, the daily diet contained fewer calories in the 1960's than in the 1930's.

EDUCATIONAL PROGRESS

The characteristics of educational systems typically found in other underdeveloped areas are widely found in Asia. A literary and nonempirical tradition which tends to foster a static view of society persists, while experimentation in the physical and social sciences is not yet fully entrenched in the curiculum. These and other characteristics, coupled with a low quality of teaching, have meant that even a large number of those who attend school are not equipped for productive work in a modernizing society, and the alarming rate of unemployment among Asian youth persists.

Moreover, there continue to be a number of educational imbalances. In addition to the very visible disparities between educational opportunities in rural and urban areas, poverty itself acts as an effective barrier to schooling for many. Social taboos, child labor, negative home attitudes, and the like, further restrict educational opportunity, particularly for girls. Of the 300 million illiterates in Asia and Oceania in 1962, more than 61 percent were women.[1]

Another educational problem which plagues all developing nations in Asia is that of high wastage or dropout rates. Although this is but one of many unresearched educational problems, presumably factors both inside and outside the school system act to perpetuate the condition. Much of the literature on education in the developing nations emphasizes "impractical" curricula and poor teaching methods as reasons for a school's low holding power. It is likely, however, that those social constraints which affect enrollments at all levels — poverty, transportation problems, family indifference, and child labor — are even stronger deterrents. In any case, although rates are improving rapidly in the educationally more advanced Asian nations, it is estimated that in the mid-1960's in the region as a whole, out of every 100 children who entered the first grade only 40 reached the fifth grade. Furthermore, wastage continues to be a significant factor even at the postprimary levels. At the second level of schooling, for example, it is estimated that only 50 to 55 percent of those enrolled in the terminal grade actually graduate (see Table 21).[2]

TABLE 21   Progress of a Cohort through Grades, Most Recent Periods[1]

Country	Cohort beginning in:	Grades					
		I	II	III	IV	V	VI
Afghanistan	1955	100	80	69	74	57	50
Burma	1956	100	33	26	19[2]	–	–
Cambodia	1955	100	77	71	67	52	55
Ceylon	1956	100	76	69	64	57	51
China, Republic of	1957	100	95	94	92	92	88
India	1956	100	63	47	37	29[2]	–
Iran[3]	1956	100	96	92	92	74	67
Korea, Republic of	1959	100	95	93	89	88	86
Laos	1956	100	45	49	23	16	13
Malaysia	1957	100	91	84	81	71	70
Singapore	1958	100	94	90	85	79[2]	–
Mongolia	1961	100	96	94	–	–	–
Pakistan	1956	100	46	33	26	25[2]	–
Philippines	1955	100	84	76	69	55	43
Thailand	1959	100	68	61	53[2]	–	–
Viet-Nam, Republic of	1959	100	73	60	45	40	–
Japan	1959	100	100	100	99	99	99

Source: UNESCO, *An Asian Model of Educational Development.* Paris: UNESCO, 1966, p. 88.

Note. Estimation of the extent of wastage should distinguish between dropouts and repeaters. Since data are not available for the two separately, reference to "dropouts" includes the repeaters (the majority of the latter do ultimately drop out).

1. Figures for Indonesia not available.
2. Indicates terminal grade in the first stage.
3. Figures relate to urban schools.

However, even a condition such as wastage must be viewed from several perspectives. To the educator interested in either the goals or the efficiency of the educational system, high wastage rates are intolerable. On the one hand, the waste in human potential may be decried, while, from another view, the cost per student output may be seen as exorbitant. Yet, since the factors external to the educational system are not subject to manipulation from within, control of wastage rates by educators is possible only to a limited degree. Moreover, the social results of an immediate and drastic reduction of wastage would certainly not be entirely beneficial. First, the pressure for entrance to higher levels of education might put excessive strain on existing facilities. Second, the potential political problems created by disenchanted primary or secondary school leavers who unsuccessfully sought advanced education might well be greater than the social problems arising from those who dropped out during early years of schooling.

In quantitative terms, educational expansion among the less developed Asian nations has been impressive. In 1955 nine percent of the total population of certain nations (those treated in a regional planning exercise — see pages 186-192) were receiving an education, while in 1964 this percentage had been raised to 13, a figure corresponding to the world average in 1957.[3] The retarding effect of rapid population growth again becomes clear, however, for even during this period of educational expansion the absolute number of illiterates increased. Moreover, with only 13 percent of the population receiving education and with a high attrition rate within this group, a sizable pool of talent is clearly not being tapped.

Another indication of educational development has been the shift in comparative expansion rates at lower and higher levels. The disparity between Asia and the developed nations of the world in terms of quantity of education available is now primarily in evidence at the secondary and higher levels. And even at these levels a few Asian nations, e.g., Japan, Korea, the Philippines, and Taiwan, are approaching the enrollment ratios of some European nations. Regional enrollment ratios by level are found in Table 22.

The lack of balance in educational development and the failure to link educational policy to changes in the economy have resulted in an abundance of certain skills and a scarcity of others. India has been faced

TABLE 22   Regional[1] Enrollment Ratios[2] by Level

Year	Item	First level	Second level	Third level	Total
1955[3]	Total enrollment (millions)	58.2	6.4	0.8	65.4
	Percentage of total enrollment	89.0	9.8	1.2	100.0
	Enrollment ratio	46	9	1.6	27
1960	Total enrollment (millions)	78.6	10.0	1.3	89.9
	Percentage of total enrollment	87.5	11.1	1.4	100.0
	Enrollment ratio	53	12	2.3	31
1964	Total enrollment (millions)	103.8	14.4	1.9	120.1
	Percentage of total enrollment	86.4	12.0	1.6	100.0
	Enrollment ratio	61	15	3	36

Source: UNESCO, *An Asian Model of Educational Development*, p. 19.

1. Data for those 18 nations participating in the Karachi Plan (see note 8 at end of chapter).

2. Enrollment ratios computed on age groups (6-12, 13-17, and 18-21, respectively).

3. Since the distribution of the population by single years of age and the distribution of enrollment by grades were not available for that year, the 1955 figures were estimated.

with the phenomenon of "educated unemployed" for nearly a century. It has been estimated that in Iran in the mid-1960's at least 50 percent of the diploma holders from the general secondary schools had difficulty in finding employment. In many other Asian nations, most notably perhaps in the Philippines, Korea, and China (Taiwan), graduates from secondary and higher educational institutions were having similar problems. China boasts of no unemployment among any sector of its work force, but like many other Asian nations has graduates working in fields for which they were not trained.

The surpluses of output tend to vary by level and kind of education. There are successively fewer unemployed graduates at each level of education; e.g., unemployment is higher among primary school graduates than among secondary school graduates. Moreover, unemployment rates tend to be higher among those from general or liberal education courses than among those from the applied sciences and commerce. Even in India, where at the inception of the Third Plan there were an estimated one million unemployed high school and university graduates, there has been nearly full employment among graduates from faculties of engineering and medicine.

Another phenomenon affecting the availability of high-level manpower in Asian nations has been the presence of a brain drain, largely in the direction of the United States, Europe, and Africa. Korea, India, the Philippines, and China (Taiwan), particularly, have sent thousands of advanced students to study in the West who have never returned. The outflow of students from China (Taiwan) alone between 1957 and 1963 exceeded the number returning by nearly 7000. Moreover, there is some empirical evidence to suggest that, in general, it is the brighter students who fail to return.

INTRAREGIONAL COMPARISONS OF EDUCATIONAL DIFFERENTIATION

The case studies presented in Chapters Two, Three, and Four made reference to changing levels of educational differentiation. Table 23 presents a scalogram of the structural differentiation of national educational systems for a group of 18 Asian nations. To understand the implications and limitations of this scalogram, some explanation is necessary concerning the data utilized and the technique of analysis employed.

TABLE 23   Scalogram of Educational Structural Differentiation in Asia, 1960[1]

	Ministry of Education[2]	Teacher training institute	Inspectorate	Curriculum agency	Secondary vocational school	Secondary industrial school	University	Pedagog. trng. secondary teachers	Secondary agricultural school	Preprimary school	Special education class	Special education school	Research inst., phys., bio. sciences	Research inst., social sciences	Research inst., agriculture	Univ. faculties, bio., chem., phys.	Research inst., economics	Spec. secondary indust. school	Univ. faculties, soc. or anthrop.
Nepal	X	X	X	X	O	O	X	O	O	O	O	O	O	O	O	O	O	O	O
Laos	X	X	X	X	X	O	O	O	O	X	O	O	O	O	O	O	O	O	O
Cambodia	X	X	X	X	X	X	X	X	X	X	O	O	O	O	O	O	O	X	O
Burma	X	X	X	X	X	X	X	X	X	X	O	O	O	O	X	O	O	X	O
Mongolia	X	X	O	O	X	X	X	X	X	X	O	O	O	O	X	X	X	X	O
Afghanistan	X	X	X	O	X	X	X	X	X	X	O	O	O	O	O	O	O	O	O
Malaya	X	X	X	X	X	X	X	X	O	X	X	X	O	O	O	O	O	O	O
Ceylon	X	X	X	X	X	X	X	X	X	O	X	X	O	O	O	O	O	O	O
Thailand	X	X	X	X	X	X	X	X	X	X	X	X	O	O	O	O	O	O	O
South Korea	X	X	X	X	X	X	X	X	X	X	X	X	X	X	O	O	X	O	O
Philippines	X	X	X	X	X	X	X	X	X	X	X	X	X	X	X	O	O	O	O
Pakistan	X	X	X	X	X	X	X	X	X	O	X	X	X	X	X	X	O	O	O
North Korea	X	X	X	X	X	X	X	X	X	X	X	X	X	X	O	X	X	X	O
Indonesia	X	X	X	X	X	X	X	X	X	X	X	X	X	X	X	O	X	X	O
China (Mainland)	X	X	X	X	X	X	X	X	X	X	X	X	X	X	X	X	X	X	O
China (Taiwan)	X	X	X	X	X	X	X	X	X	X	X	X	X	X	X	X	X	O	X
India	X	X	X	X	X	X	X	X	X	X	X	X	X	X	X	X	X	X	X
Japan	X	X	X	X	X	X	X	X	X	X	X	X	X	X	X	X	X	X	X

Source: Joseph Patrick Farrell, "The Structural Differentiation of Developing Educational Systems: A Large-Scale Cross-National Study," unpublished Ph. D. dissertation, Syracuse University, 1968.

Note. In this study Professor Farrell utilized scalogram analyses to measure educational structural differentiation. Scales were developed for the educational system in Latin America as well as for the underdeveloped nations as a whole. Farrell further used his measures to examine relationships between educational structural differentiation and other variables within the educational system and between educational structural differentiation and variables in other social systems.

1. Coefficient of reproducibility = 0.95.

2. The list of items is clearly neither exhaustive nor random. The choice of items was guided by the nature of the concept of differentiation and the author's general knowledge about the development of educational systems.

Scalogram analysis, originally devised for the measurement of attitudes, has been employed in several empirical studies of differentiation focused on various aspects of society.[4] The data used here represent traits of national educational systems divided into presence-absence categories; X's mark the presence in a nation (as determined through a search of pertinent source materials) of selected structural elements, and 0's mark the absence of such elements.[5] Upon rearrangement, the data provide visual evidence of the pattern shown in Table 23. In this case the pattern has met certain formal requirements set forth in the literature on scalogram analysis. The data do not form a perfect scale, since nations with higher rank do not in every case have all the traits of nations with lower rank. The question of how much imperfection (error) one can permit — and still consider the data as a scale — is usually answered by the result obtained through application of the formula for the coefficient of reproducibility. This coefficient is simply the number of non-error responses as a proportion of the total responses. If the coefficient of reproducibility is above 0.90, then it is generally agreed that a scale is present. For the Asian scale (Table 23), the coefficient of reproducibility was 0.95.[6]

According to Table 23, the educational systems of Japan, China (Taiwan), and India are the most differentiated structurally, while Nepal and Laos exhibit the least differentiated educational systems. Even without a correlational analysis, a visual inspection of the data suggests an association between level of educational differentiation and level of modernization. However, educational differentiation would appear also to be related somewhat to population size — at least, the more highly populated nations have relatively highly differentiated educational systems.[7]

It should not be assumed, however, that proceeding up the ladder of differentiation necessarily means a chronological acquisition of each next "higher" item. Rather, a nation may skip several items and then "backfill." But although a strictly evolutionary view of differentiation is rejected, it may be concluded that unless radically new structural patterns are evolved, modernizing Asian nations will tend to acquire most of those structural elements which now characterize such nations as Japan and India. Again, however, it must be reiterated that differentiation is but one characteristic of a modernizing society or of a modernizing educational system.

PLANNING EDUCATION FOR THE FUTURE

Between 1960 and 1965 at least four regional meetings were convened under the auspices of the United Nations for the purpose of planning education in Asia. The conference which laid a foundation for much of the subsequent regional educational planning efforts was held in Karachi from December 28, 1959 through January 9, 1960 and resulted in the document referred to as the Karachi Plan. Subsequent meetings were held in Tokyo in 1962 and Bangkok in 1965 to appraise progress toward the implementation of the Karachi Plan and to recommend modifications.[8]

Emerging from these conferences were several broad objectives or guidelines which served as a basis for long-range educational planning. Phrased as "needs," these included:

1. The need for balanced development of education at all levels, with the expansion of secondary and higher levels being determined by the ability of pupils, availability of financial resources and manpower requirements of the country.

2. The importance of qualitative considerations for development. The need for achieving higher standards at the second and third levels is imperative. Even at the primary level the maintenance of proper standards in order to prevent wastage and to provide a satisfactory basis for the higher level is essential.

3. The need for diversification of education by enlarging and strengthening vocational and technical education at the second and third levels in line with the developing capacity of the economy to utilize trained skills.

4. Expansion and improvement of science education at all levels.

5. Promotion of programmes of adult and youth and family education as an integral part of overall educational development.

6. Development of education should reflect the principle of equality of educational opportunity and the promotion of international peace and amity.[9]

These objectives generally have been incorporated into the educational plans of the Asian Member States. Yet, with few exceptions, planning for educational development has not been integrated with national economic and social development planning. Studies linking manpower needs to educational development have been carried out in a few nations, e.g., the Republic of China, Pakistan, and the Philippines, but even these efforts have been limited in scope, and both manpower planning and educational planning in relation to general planning may be considered in their infancy. In practice, educational planning tends to be limited to the more traditional approach of extrapolating future educational needs from past educational performance.

Clearly, educational objectives general enough to acquire consensus among several Asian nations lose a certain amount of directive power for policy formulations. The objectives identified above may be criticized for their vagueness and obscurity. What does it mean, for example, to "achieve higher standards," and how do these differ from "proper standards"? What is the *principle* relating to "the promotion of international peace and amity"? Moreover, the possibility of conflict among the various objectives is readily apparent, but is not subjected to careful analysis in Asian regional planning documents. Attempts at achieving the principle of equality of educational opportunity obviously may run counter to the policy of determining educational enrollments by manpower needs. Perhaps, however, the expressed commitment to planning and to a better integration of educational change with national development programs may be assumed, in itself, to be significant.

To assist those Asian nations participating in the Karachi Plan in their long-range educational planning, a systems model was developed under UNESCO guidance which attempted to visualize educational change up to 1980. The "Asian Model" distinguished three groups of nations according to their educational and general development. Group A included Afghanistan, Laos, and Nepal; Group B included Burma, Cambodia, India, Indonesia, Iran, Mongolia, Pakistan, and the Republic of Viet-Nam; Group C included Ceylon, the Republic of China, the Republic of Korea, Malaysia, the Philippines, and Thailand. Nations in Group A are those expected to achieve a minimum of seven years of compulsory education (a recommendation of the Karachi Plan) subsequent to 1980; in Group B, those likely to achieve it around 1980; and in Group C, those expected to achieve it before 1980.

In building this model the authors were careful to point out that "the aim of a long-term plan for educational development is not so much to prepare for specific occupations — the patterns of which will necessarily change with economic growth — as to build into the education system the capacity to meet the needs of training and re-training which short-term plans may identify."[10] In keeping with this aim, the methodology employed in the development of the model was intended to quantify various educational hypotheses rather than to set educational targets:

. . .the Model represents a tool that can simulate the dynamics of future consequences of changes in any quantifiably defined conditions affecting the educational system.[11]

The precise methodology employed and the formulas used consist of statistical projections and programming analyses now common in the educational planning efforts of such international groups as the Organization for European Cooperation and Development (OECD), the International Institute for Educational Planning (IIEP), and UNESCO. For example, the enrollment in the third year of a university science faculty in 1980 is determined by:

(a) the number of children who were born in 1960 and survived to age 6 in 1966 (assuming this to be the school-entering age); (b) the proportion of 6-year-olds entering the first grade in 1966; (c) the proportion continuing through the primary school from grade to grade, which may be affected by such things as compulsory school attendance for a specific duration; (d) the proportion entering second-level education in 1973 (assuming the primary course to be of seven years duration) and the distribution of these among various types of education; (e) the proportion continuing through second level from grade to grade and the distribution among various types of education at various stages; (f) the proportion entering higher education in 1978 (assuming the second level of education to be of five years duration) and the distribution of these among various types of higher education; (g) the proportion in the university science faculty continuing through higher education from year to year until 1980.[12]

To make such projections obviously requires certain assumptions about the relationship of past to future — wastage rates, educational choices, etc. Moreover, many factors which need to be considered in projecting the size and character of an educational system, such as social constraints or technological innovations, do not lend themselves to quantification and are not considered in the Model.

In preparing the Model, 16 formulas were developed to calculate various factors such as enrollment, output, teachers, and costs. By means of these formulas, educational development to 1980 was projected for each group of nations as well as for the region as a whole. A partial summary of the projections for the region includes the following points:

1. The enrollment ratios in the three levels of education will increase from 61:15:3.0 (1964) to 90:33:5.0 (1980).

2. The teaching force (at all levels) will increase by 107 percent.

3. The total cost at all levels will increase from approximately $2.9 billion to $9.4 billion. (The concept *cost* here includes recurring cost, stipends, and capital cost.) If one assumes rates of annual growth in gross national product of either 4 percent, 5 percent, or 6 percent, the cost of education as a percentage of gross national product will increase considerably.

Projected educational output in broad categories of higher-level personnel for each of the three groups of nations is shown in Table 24. The anticipated growth in the technical category in particular should be noted. In terms of the structure of the educational systems, this reflects the growing availability of technical courses at the upper secondary and postsecondary levels. In terms of societal demand as translated into educational planning efforts, this reflects the desire to increase and upgrade middle-level manpower. The decreasing proportion of the total output made up by those in teacher training not only indicates that teacher supply is expected to approach teacher demand at the primary level, but also suggests a structural shift in teacher preparation. In the future, a small but increasing number of primary teachers will be the output of grades XVI and above.

Some international comparisons may shed light on the educational targets identified in the Asian Model. In 1964, the proportion of the labor force of the Member States which had completed grades XII-XV was 1.1 percent. At this date 0.6 percent of the labor force had completed more than Grade XVI. The corresponding 1980 targets were 6.48 percent and 2.18 percent. Compared with other nations, these levels resemble conditions found in Italy in 1951, or the United States in 1910. The achievement of the 1980 targets would still leave the level of education of the labor force below that of Japan in the mid-1960's. Both in terms of such international comparisons and in terms of the growth of demand for

TABLE 24   Trends in Net Cumulative Output, by Type and Grade of School Completed in 1970, 1975, and 1980 (Percentages)

	Grades XII-XV			Grades XVI +		Total of Grades:			Total, Grades XII + ('000)
	General[1]	Technical[2]	Teacher training[3]	Science and other[4]	Arts and other[5]	XII +	XII-XV	XVI +	
Group A:									
Net cumulative output in									
1970 (from 1964-1970)	26	15	39	8	12	100	80	20	39.9
1975 (from 1964-1975)	27	28	29	7	9	100	84	16	121.3
1980 (from 1964-1980)	24	37	22	8	9	100	83	17	297.8
Group B:									
Net cumulative output in									
1970 (from 1964-1970)	27	28	18	13	14	100	73	27	8,876.3
1975 (from 1964-1975)	28	33	14	12	13	100	75	25	19,963.0
1980 (from 1964-1980)	29	37	10	12	12	100	76	24	36,157.4

Group C:								
Net cumulative output in								
1970 (from 1964-1970)	29	34	11	11	16	100	73	27	3,003.2
1975 (from 1964-1975)	31	36	9	11	13	100	76	24	6,126.5
1980 (from 1964-1980)	32	38	7	12	11	100	77	23	10,149.8
The region:								
Net cumulative output in								
1970 (from 1964-1970)	28	29	16	12	15	100	73	27	11,919.4
1975 (from 1964-1975)	29	33	13	12	13	100	75	25	26,210.8
1980 (from 1964-1980)	30	37	9	12	12	100	76	24	46,605.0

Source: UNESCO, *An Asian Model of Educational Development*, p. 79.

1. "General" includes output from the general course of study, Grade XII, and from the arts, humanities, social sciences, etc., Grades XII through XV.

2. "Technical" includes output from technical Grades XII, XIII, and XIV and from science, science-based, and technological Grades XIII, XIV, and XV.

3. "Teacher training" includes output from teacher training, Grade XII, and the continuation course, Grade XIII, and from teacher training, Grades XIII and XIV.

4. "Science and other" includes output from science, science-based, and technological, Grades XVI and over.

5. "Arts and other" includes output from arts, humanities, social sciences, etc., Grades XVI and over.

skilled manpower resulting from anticipated economic progress, the proposed enrollment targets do not seem unrealistic.

To accompany and facilitate educational growth and expansion of the magnitude being anticipated in Asia requires new levels of differentiation and specialization in the educational system. The following list suggests but a few of the needed structural and functional changes:

1. The sheer growth in size of the educational endeavor will necessitate additional subordinate agencies at the subnational level.

2. New machinery will be needed for coordinating the public and private sector in education, coordinating various administration levels, and creating channels to discern public opinion on education.

3. New kinds of supervisory, coordinating, administrative, and other professional personnel will be needed to assist in the operation of larger educational systems with more variegated functions. Educational administration will have to become increasingly specialized and will demand technical and intellectual skills. Moreover, administrators will require a new level of commitment to, and understanding of, achievement and universalistic values as these impinge on student selection and promotion policies.

4. New educational roles will develop as new specialized institutions and research institutes appear and as adjustments in curricula are made (see Table 24).

SUMMARY AND CONCLUSIONS

There are severe fiscal and social constraints on the degree of educational development anticipated in Asian regional planning efforts. One constraint relates to the level of support for educational change which may be found in the attitudes and values of Asian peoples. For example, to what extent are individual and national drives present today comparable to what existed in Japan in the late nineteenth century? Certainly, several empirical case studies have suggested the persistence of attitudinal and value systems which inhibit the modernization of institutions.[13] However, while certain traditions relating to such things as academic prestige differentials and social roles of women may frustrate educational development, generally the social, cultural, and psychological climates appear favorable for explicit development planning in the educational sector. By way of illustration, the caste system in India is increasingly less obstructive to social change, and social mobility through education is increasingly a fact. In Korea, war, the influx of large numbers of foreign soldiers and technicians, and the demands of an expanding economy are rapidly erasing traditional occupational preferences. The advent of Communism in China has virtually enshrined achievement motivation as central to the new national ethos — to learn, to modernize, and to increase productivity is the responsibility of every citizen.

The fiscal constraints on educational development are equally pressing; for, unless efficiency increases considerably, as enrollments expand educational expenditures will grow rapidly, and for most nations it may be assumed that such expenditures will take an increasingly higher proportion of their gross national product. The problem of educational costs will be further intensified by population pressures and by the shift toward raising the rate of enrollment increase at the secondary and higher levels, where per unit expenditures are considerably higher than at the primary level. Because of these and other cost pressures, the educational plans may founder for financial reasons alone. To ensure that financial resources are adequate would involve some combination of (1) a drastic reduction of the planned educational expansion, (2) other sources of financing, or (3) radically new cost-reducing techniques of instruction. While no easy breakthrough may be expected concerning this problem, some relief may be obtained by requiring parents and students to absorb directly more of the educational expenditures, by motivating industrial and commercial concerns to become more deeply involved in skill training, by fuller utilization of educational facilities, and possibly by expanding use of educational media.

Another problem of considerable proportions in many of the Asian nations stems from the variety of linguistic groups which may exist within national boundaries. The choice of a national language has been a divisive issue, for example, in Ceylon, India, and the Philippines. Where the language of the home is different from that of the school, or where regional language options are reflected in school instruction, educational output in terms of academic achievement may be adversely affected. Thus the heritage of colonialism (which typically promoted instruction in a European language for at least the higher levels of education), the postcolonial demands for a national language, and the pressures from linguistic minorities for local language options have influenced the character of national education. While the direction of such linguistic influences is quite understandable, this trend at least temporarily lessens the efficiency of an educational system in terms of the maximization of intellectual output per unit input.

Of a less general nature are large numbers of questions concerning the operation of the schools, the materials of instruction, the utility of media and other products of educational technology, etc. What is needed are guides which are the results of educational research conducted within the particular educational and social context in question. In Asian education, neither the tradition nor the institutional structure for research is well developed. The precise structure which will best facilitate educational research may vary from nation to nation. The role of university faculties of education *vis à vis* national research institutes needs to be worked out within national educational and political traditions. The extent of the utility of multinational research facilities and cooperation needs to be further explored. In any case, the necessary adjustments to promote greater flexibility and adaptability in educational systems will require a high degree of educational expertise which, in turn, must be grounded in experiential or research evidence.

A final limiting condition in the achievement of greater social equity and economic development stems from the present level of ignorance in all parts of the world of what constitutes an educational system and of the nature of its linkages with other social systems. Much about the operation of an educational system in any social context remains a mystery. To what extent, for example, does rapid expansion of enrollments endanger educational "quality"? Indeed, what constitute appropriate measures of "quality"? Or, in another vein, how loose a fit between occupation and education is allowable before serious dysfunction results? What are the most efficacious ways of teaching "functional literacy"? And what "proxy" institutions or agencies exist in the society which might better or more efficiently undertake some of the functions currently performed by the school?

In seeking improved means for examining the processes of education and modernization in this book, the concepts of differentiation and systems analysis have been used. These concepts lend themselves to studies of educational change and provide a framework for cross-national comparisons. As demonstrated, the approach taken here provides some understanding of the adaptability of educational systems to external pressures from the economy, the social structure, etc. Moreover, the concept of differentiation has been shown to be a tool by which the maturity, or degree of development, of an educational system may be directly determined.

To be sure, our use of systems analysis as a way of better understanding educational-societal linkages has resulted in oversimplifications. An educational system cannot be adequately described in terms of a few input, process, and output elements. Further, because of the nature of this work and perhaps also because of limitations inherent in the concept, only intermittent reliance is placed upon educational differentiation as a means of explaining educational phenomena. After all, a few postulates of four truncated stages of educational differentiation provide tools of limited analytic power. Nevertheless, better structural and functional measures of educational differentiation and greater refinement in the use of systems analysis techniques offer continued possibilities for new insights into educational change as part of modernization.

NOTES

1. UNESCO, *An Asian Model of Educational Development.* Paris: UNESCO, 1966, pp. 17-18.

2. *Ibid.,* p. 20.

3. *Ibid.,* p. 18.

4. See, for example, Frank W. Young and Ruth C. Young, "Social Integration and Change in Twenty-Four Mexican Villages," *Economic Development and Cultural Change,* Vol. VIII (1960), Part 1; Robert Winch and Linton Freeman, "Societal Complexity: An Empirical Test of a Typology of Societies," *American Journal of Sociology,* Vol. LXII (March 1957); Phillips Cutright, "National Political Development: Measurement and Analysis," *American Sociological Review,* Vol. XXVIII (1963), No. 2. For further description of the techniques and applications of scalogram analysis, see Allen Edwards, *Techniques of Attitude Scale Construction,* New York: Appleton-Century-Crofts, 1957; and Warren Torgerson, *Theory and Methods of Scaling,* New York: John Wiley and Sons, 1958.

5. These structural elements are defined as: 1. Ministry: ministerial body charged with general responsibility for education. 2. Teacher training institution: any institution at either secondary or higher level which trains teachers for any level of education. 3. Inspectorate: indigenous corps of inspectors for any level of education. 4. Curriculum agency: ministerial agency or group under ministerial supervision charged with responsibility for preparing curricula for any level or type of education.

5. Secondary vocational school: secondary school whose primary purpose is not preparation for university admission. 6. Secondary industrial or crafts-trades school: any secondary school whose purpose is to prepare for occupations in industry or skilled crafts and trades. 7. University: institution of higher learning called "university"; colleges, nonintegrated faculties, or university colleges not included. 8. Special pedagogical training for secondary teachers: any formal program to provide pedagogical training for secondary teachers. 9. Secondary agricultural school: same as (6) for agricultural occupations. 10. Preprimary school: any preprimary school. 11. Special education class: any special provision for education of physically or mentally handicapped students. 12. Special education school: separate school providing education at any level for physically or mentally handicapped students. 13. University research institute in physical-biological sciences: separate institute or department connected with a university whose primary or sole purpose is research in any of the physical-biological sciences, excluding institutes concerned with medical research. 14. University research institute in social science: same as (13) in any social science field. 15. University research institute in agriculture: same as (13) in agriculture. 16. University faculties of biology, chemistry, and physics: separate faculties or departments for all three disciplines. 17. University research institute in education: same as (13) in education. 18. Specialized secondary industrial school: same as (6) for any particular industry (e.g., texitle workers' school or railroad mechanics' school). 19. University faculties of sociology and anthropology: separate faculties of departments of either discipline.

6. Errors, of course, may mean (1) that some educational systems do not in every respect fit the standard pattern or (2) that mistakes are made in coding.

7. Some empirical validation for such conclusions about the association of educational differentiation with indicators of modernization and population size may be found in Joseph Patrick Farrell, "The Structural Differentiation of Developing Educational Systems: A Large-Scale Cross-National Study," unpublished Ph. D. dissertation, Syracuse University, 1968.

8. The Member States participating in the Karachi Plan were Afghanistan, Burma, Cambodia, Ceylon, the Republic of China, India, Indonesia, Iran, the Republic of Korea, Laos, Malaysia, Mongolia, Nepal, Pakistan, the Philippines, Singapore, Thailand, and the Republic of Viet-Nam.

9. UNESCO, *op. cit.,* pp. 21-22.

10. *Ibid.,* p. 25.

11. *Ibid.,* p. 26.

12. *Ibid.,* p. 27.

13. See, for example, Manning Nash, "The Role of Village Schools in the Process of Cultural and Economic Modernization," *Economic Development and Cultural Change,* Vol. XIV (March 1965), pp. 131-143; Lucian Mason Hanks, Jr., "Indifference to Modern Education in a Thai Farming Community," *Human Organization,* Vol. XVII (Summer 1958), pp. 9-14; Chester L. Hunt and Thomas R. McHale, "Education, Attitudinal Change and Philippine Economic Development," *Philippine Sociological Review,* Vol. XIII (July 1965), pp. 127-139; P. C. Joshi and M. R. Rao, "Social and Economic Factors in Literacy and Education in Rural India," *Economic Weekly* (Bombay), January 4th, 1964, pp. 21-27.

bibliography

bibliography

Abegglan, J. C., and Hiroshi Mannari, "Leaders of Modern Japan: Social Origins and Mobility," *Economic Development and Cultural Change,* Vol. IX (October 1960), No. 1, pp. 109-134.

Adams, Donald K., and Robert Bjork, "Modernization as Affected by Governmental and International Educational Influences: Japan," Chapter 16 in Stewart Fraser (ed.), *Governmental Policy and International Education.* New York: John Wiley and Sons, 1965.

Anderson, Ronald S., *Japan: Three Epochs of Modern Education.* Washington, D.C.: U. S. Office of Education, 1959.

Ayal, Eliezer B., "Value Systems and Economic Development in Japan and Thailand," *Journal of Social Issues,* Vol. XIX (1963), No. 1, pp. 35-51.

Barnett, A. Doak, *Cadres, Bureaucracy and Political Power in Communist China.* New York: Columbia University Press, 1967.

Bellah, Robert N., "Values of Social Change in Modern Japan," *Asian Cultural Studies,* Vol. III (October 1962), pp. 13-56.

Berberet, John A., *Science, Technology and Peking's Planning Problems.* Santa Barbara, Calif.: General Electric Company, 1962.

Chi, Tung-wai, *Education for the Proletariat in Communist China.* Communist China Problem Research Series. Kowloon, Hong Kong: The Union Research Institute, 1956.

Comparative Education Review, Vol. XIII, (February 1969), No. 1. Special issue on Chinese education.

Cormack, Margaret L., *She Who Rides a Peacock: Indian Students and Social Change.* New York: Frederick A. Praeger, 1961.

Curle, Adam, *Planning for Education in Pakistan.* Cambridge: Harvard University Press, 1966.

Danton, George H., *The Culture Contacts of the United States and China.* New York: Columbia University Press, 1931.

Dore, R. P., *Education in Tokugawa Japan.* Berkeley: University of California Press, 1965.

An Economic Profile of Mainland China. Studies Prepared for the Joint Economic Committee, Congress of the United States. Vol.I: "General Economic Setting, The Economic Sectors." No. 72-911. Washington, D. C.: U. S. Government Printing Office, February 1967.

Fraser, Stewart E., *Chinese Communist Education: Records of the First Decade.* Nashville, Tenn.: Vanderbilt University Press, 1965.

Fukutake, Tadashi, *Asian Rural Society: China, India, Japan.* Seattle: University of Washington Press, 1967.

Gamble, Sidney D., *Ting Hsien, A North China Rural Community.* New York: Institute of Pacific Relations, 1954.

Gregg, Alice H., *China and Educational Autonomy.* Syracuse, N. Y.: Syracuse University Press, 1946.

Hagen, Everett E., "How Economic Growth Begins: A General Theory Applied to Japan," *Public Opinion Quarterly,* Vol. XXII (Fall 1958), pp. 373-390.

Hall, Robert K., *Education in the New Japan.* New Haven: Yale University Press, 1949.

Harner, Evelyn L., *Middle School Education as a Tool of Power in Communist China.* Santa Barbara, Calif.: General Electric Company, 1962.

Hsü, Immanuel C. Y., *Reorganization of Higher Education in Communist China.* Santa Barbara, Calif.: General Electric Company, 1962.

Hu, Chang-tu, *et al., China: Its People, Its Society, Its Culture.* New Haven, Conn.: Human Relations Area Files Press, 1960.

India, Ministry of Education, *Report of the Education Commission (1964-66): Education and National Development.* New Delhi: Manager of Publications, 1966.

Jansen, Marius B. (ed.), *Changing Japanese Attitudes Toward Modernization.* Princeton, N. J.: Princeton University Press, 1965.

Japan, Ministry of Education, *Japan's Growth and Education.* Tokyo: the Ministry of Education, 1962.

Japanese National Commission for UNESCO (ed.), *The Role of Education in the Social and Economic Development of Japan.* Tokyo: Ministry of Education, 1966, pp. 48-66.

Kabir, Hamayan, *Education in New India.* London: G. Allen, 1956.

Laska, John A., *Planning and Educational Development in India.* New York: Teachers College Press, 1968.

Levy, Marion J., "Some Aspects of Individualism and the Problem of Modernization in China and Japan," *Economic Development and Cultural Change,* Vol. X (April 1962), pp. 226-240.

Lewis, Oscar, *Village Life in Northern India.* New York: Vintage Books, 1965.

Majumdar, D. N., *Social Contours of an Industrial City.* New York: Asia Publishing House, 1960.

Mandelbaum, David G., *Status-Seeking in Indian Villages,* Berkeley: University of California, Center for South Asian Studies, Reprint No. 270, 1968.

Mukerji, S. N., *History of Education in India.* Baroda: Acharya Book Depot, 1951.

Myrdal, Gunnar, *Asian Drama,* Vol. III. New York: Pantheon, 1968.

Myrdal, Jan, *Report from a Chinese Village.* London: Willian Heinemann Ltd., 1965.

Naik, J. P., *Educational Planning in India.* Bombay: Allied Publishers, 1965.

Nash, Manning, "Some Notes on Village Industrialization in South and East Asia," *Economic Development and Cultural Change,* Vol. III (1955), No. 3, pp. 271-277.

Nitobe, Inazo, *Bushido: The Soul of Japan.* Tokyo: Shokwdso, 1901.

Okuma, Count Shigenobu, *Fifty Years of New Japan,* Vol. II. New York: Dutton, 1909.

Orleans, Leo A., *Professional Manpower and Education in Communist China.* Washington, D. C.: National Science Foundation, U. S. Government Printing Office, 1961.

Passin, Herbert, *Society and Education in Japan.* New York: Teachers College, Columbia University, 1965.

Reischauer, Edwin O., and John K. Fairbank, *East Asia: The Great Tradition.* Boston: Houghton Mifflin, 1958.

Report of the United States Education Mission to Japan. Washington, D.C.: United States Government Printing Office, 1946, p. 59.

Ryan, Bryce, "Status, Achievement and Education in Ceylon: An Historical Perspective," *Journal of Asian Studies,* Vol. XX (August 1964), No. 4, pp. 463-475.

Shils, Edward A., "The Intellectuals, Public Opinion, and Economic Development in Southeast Asia," *Far Eastern Economic Review,* Vol.XXIV (May 1958), pp. 614-618.

Silberman, Bernard, *Ministers of Modernization: Elite Mobility in the Meiji Restoration, 1868-1873.* Tucson: University of Arizona Press, 1964.

Singleton, John Calhoun, *Nichu: A Japanese School.* New York: Holt, Rinehart and Winston, 1967.

Taeuber, Irene B., *Population and Manpower in Japan.* New York: Milbank Memorial Fund, 1950.

Taeuber, Irene B., "Urbanization and Population Change in the Development of Japan," *Economic Development and Cultural Change,* Vol. IX (October 1960), pp. 1-28.

Turner, Roy, *India's Urban Future.* Berkeley: University of California Press, 1962.

UNESCO, *An Asian Model of Educational Development.* Paris: UNESCO, 1966.

Wang, Y. C., "Western Impact and Social Mobility in China," *American Sociological Review,* Vol. XXV (1960), No. 6, pp. 843-855.

Ward, Robert E., and Dankwart A. Rustow (eds.), *Political Modernization in Japan and Turkey.* Princeton, N. J.: Princeton University Press, 1964.

index

index

ABCDE79876543210